TO MY WIFE DESPINA
DAUGHTERS ELECTRA AND IRENE and,
MY PARENTS YIANNIS AND MARIA.

I thank them for their love, support and patience

Website address: **www.CyprusWalksEtc.com**

Electronic address: **phivos@CyprusWalksEtc.com**

Tel : **+357 99458366**

ISBN 978-9963-7501-0-8

Table of CONTENTS

1

ABOUT THE AUTHOR

Phivos Ioannides was born in Famagusta in 1966 and before the 1974 war lived in the village of Milia near Famagusta and later in the village of Agios Nikolaos on Keryneia mountain range. Since 1974 he lives in Nicosia. He studied computing at Imperial College, London, UK and business administration (M.B.A.) at UC Berkeley, U.S.A. . He worked as a manager in banking, in an offshore project development and project finance company, as well as in a business incubator. Since 2007 he works professionally on projects related to authentic ecotourism and sustainable governance.

Phivos attended lessons about Cyprus nature as well as about photography (and wine tasting and wine making). He has covered thousands of kilometers exploring Cyprus on foot, on Waterbike, on bicycle and by car. He is one of the founders, and served as the president of Friends of Nature, Cyprus, a bicommunal organisation for the protection of nature. He is a member of Birdlife Cyprus and Friends of the forest. From 2005 he implements a reforestation project on his family private land of seven hectares in a semi mountainous region (**www.Viklareforestationexperiment.org**). Olives and hawthorn were mainly planted and the near future will show whether this venture in the difficult current climatic conditions faced by Cyprus will be successful.

In 2003 he produced the first version of **www.natureofcyprus.org** while in 2008 he upgraded the website adding a large section on nature spots (beaches, walking routes, wetlands, etc – the website has about 1,000 records and many thousands of photos).

Since November 2008 Phivos offers an expanding menu of services related to authentic ecotourism in Cyprus through Cyprus Walks Etc (**www.CyprusWalksEtc.com**).

In 2009 Phivos published an English version and a Greek version of the book 'Guide on Nature of Cyprus'. The present Book enriches and expands the information found in that book.

PREFACE

The natural attractions part of the present Book guide is largely based on the book Guide on Nature of Cyprus published in 2009. The natural attractions section has been significantly enriched and now also includes a section on the north part of Cyprus. Where Guide on Nature of Cyprus had some (yet very limited) elements on the cultural heritage of Cyprus, the present Book introduces nearly 200 cultural attractions of Cyprus, many of which are related to nature (medieval bridges, watermills, etc) and many are very hard to find and unknown to the general public.

The production of www.natureofcyprus.org and the writing of the printed book and the present Book are a result of extensive research and field work. A number of sources were used, including the following books: a) 'Breeding birds of Cyprus' by Louis Kourtellarides, b) 'Birds and Mammals of Cyprus' by George Sfikas, c) 'Birds of Europe' by Lars Jonsson, d) 'Complete Mediterranean Wildlife' by Paul Sterry, e) 'The endemic plants of Cyprus' by Takis Ch. Tsintides, f) 'Wild flowers and other plants of Cyprus land' (in Greek) by the Ministry of Agriculture, g) 'Flora of Cyprus' by Meikle R. D., h) 'Famagusta' by Anna Marangou and Andreas Coutas, 'Agia Triada – Karpasias' (in Greek) by Lefteris Papaleontiou and other books. The archives of Birdlife Cyprus as well as information from the Forestry Department documents, the Water Development Department and the Department of Antiquities were also used. Many visits were carried out to all the natural and cultural attractions and discussions were held with representatives of various municipalities and communities, other officials of the Cyprus Republic, as well as with experts on Cyprus nature and cultural heritage.

I would like to extend my gratitude to all those who assisted me in the production of this Book through the provision of information and especially to those who accompanied me in visits to various attractions especially, to hard to find watermills, medieval bridges and ancient trees all around Cyprus.

I hope that this guide will assist in the exploration of Cyprus nature and cultural heritage, which have so much to offer.

INTRODUCTION

Cyprus, the island of Aphrodite the Greek goddess of love and beauty, is an excellent destination for travellers seeking to explore a sweet land with beautiful nature and rich history. Tucked just south of Asia Minor, Cyprus is found where Asia, Europe and Africa meet. Its strategic position has made it an important trading station, and has been the source of wealth and prosperity, but also of war and destruction. A multitude of empires, civilizations, ethnicities and religions have come to the island saturating Cyprus with influences from near and far places, and enriching its culture tremendously. These influences can easily be observed in historic buildings and constructions as well as in the local cuisine, the spoken language and customs and traditions.

To experience these influences more clearly one needs to withdraw from busy Cyprus urban modern life to the walled cities (in Famagusta and divided Nicosia) and especially to the sleepy countryside. Cyprus, the third largest island in the Mediterranean Sea has a rich natural heritage and biodiverse flora and fauna. Its topography is dominated by two main mountain ranges, the narrow limestone Keryneia (or Pentadactylos) range in the north (which is an extension of the Alps and has max elevation of around 1,000 m – 3,250 f) and the massive (with relation to the island size) Troodos mountain range (regarded as the most complete, intact and studied ophiolite in the world). Troodos is characterised by an inversion of layers, as older rocks are found close to the surface and this makes it valuable for people interested in geology. Troodos has max elevation of almost 2,000 meters - 6,500 f and covers more than 1/4 of the island's surface. Between the two ranges lies the dry, wide Mesaoria plain extending from citrus growing Morphou in the west to the golden beaches of Famagusta in the east.

The few peninsulas on the island (notably Akamas, Karpasia, Kormakitis) are prime areas for exploration on foot (or bicycle) and offer fantastic vistas in a largely undeveloped coastline (that provides first-rate opportunities for coastal sea exploration). Together with Akrotiri wetlands, Larnaka salt lakes and Cape Greko they are very important as stopovers during avian migration in spring and autumn and are thus brilliant locations for birdwatchers. Almost 400 bird species have been recorded on the island, as well as more than 30 mammal, 25 reptile, and about 2,000 plant species, 150 or so of which are endemic (one can find extensive info on the flora and fauna of Cyprus on **www.natureofcyprus.org**).

But visitors should keep in mind that NOT everything is peaceful on Aphrodite's island. There is a conflict in Cyprus (thankfully there has been no killing for fifteen years) and it is good to be aware of people's sensitivities. Cyprus became independent in 1960 after almost a century of British rule. Cooperation between the majority Greek Cypriots (80% of a total population of about 650,000 before 1974) and the minority Turkish Cypriots (20%) in governing the country was not very successful. Problems led eventually to the events of 1974, a coup against Greek Cypriot president Makarios and the military intervention ('invasion' for the Greek Cypriots and 'peace mission' for the Turkish Cypriots) of Turkey. Almost 200,000 Greek Cypriots were displaced from their land which came under the control of Turkey (roughly the third of the island, which is referred to as 'occupied land' by the Greek Cypriots), and the Turkish Cypriots moved from all over Cyprus to the north. Thousands of people were killed and there are still more than 1,000 that are missing (a considerable number from the intercommunal clashes of 1963). A state was declared in the 80s in the north under the name of 'Turkish Republic of Northern Cyprus', still recognised only by Turkey, while the Republic of Cyprus (recognised by all states but Turkey) which has effective control only in the south became a member of the European Union in 2004. Visitors should be aware that many of the monuments in the north have been badly damaged or looted since 1974, that many tens of thousands of people have been brought from Turkey ('settlers' for the Greek Cypriots and 'guest workers' for the Turkish Cypriots) and that there are a few tens of thousands of Turkish soldiers stationed in the north. Explorers should also be aware that unfortunately the Turkish authorities occupying the north part of Cyprus changed the original Greek names of the Greek Cypriot settlements and of many localities (cities, villages etc – which are the vast majority of settlements in the north part of Cyprus) into Turkish. In the present Book we use the official English version of the original Greek names in the north as well as the names adopted by the Turkish occupying forces (in red font - in order to assist explorers in their navigation of the north part of Cyprus) For the south, for Turkish Cypriot villages having a different name than the official English name we also quote the Turkish Cypriot name in red font.

The last years have brought overconstruction on the island, both in the north and in the south part especially near the coastline. Even though this has increased wealth for people in the short run, its long term benefit for the island is debatable. The walks in this book are designed to keep explorers away from these, and take them through many beautiful parts on the island.

5

BIRDS

Cyprus location and climate, as well as the relatively large habitat variety on the island have as a result the presence (as inhabitants or visitors) of hundreds of bird species.

More than 360 species have been recorded. About 30 are inhabitants, 25 constitute mixed populations (inhabitants as well as migratory populations), while about 250 more species visit Cyprus every year for a period of time. Some of the bird species use Cyprus as a stopping station during their seasonal migration between Europe and Africa during spring and/or autumn, others such as flamingos and egrets use it over winter, while others like swallows spend most of the year here except for late autumn and winter. Lastly, more than 50 species are considered occasional visitors as very few sightings have been recorded. The great species variety creates excellent birdwatching opportunities.

Time and location for birdwatching of a specific species depends on many factors such as, a) the weather conditions that affect the arrival and departure of migratory birds, b) the population size for the specific species, c) their habits and diet, d) their size, etc.

Birdwatching is gradually gaining more followers in Cyprus (which lags behind the economically developed world in this area). Slowly but steadily infrastructure is put in place and towers in Athalassa dam as well as next to the Larnaca salt lakes, at the Larnaca Sewage Works (which attract significant numbers of birds and bird species) have already been erected. Better education of Cypriot citizens and visitors will certainly contribute to the development of birdwatching and the protection of birds and also of Cyprus nature in general. Advanced birdwatchers practice this hobby using expensive optic equipment, which magnifies the bird's image tens of times and gives birdwatchers the opportunity to observe clearly from very far without disturbing the birds. But even without expensive equipment (with just very cheap binoculars or even with none) we can observe many impressive bird species, many of them living surprisingly close to us, e.g. in Athalassa dam, in Larnaca salt lakes, in Voroklini lake, in Akrotiri wetlands. With a bit of attention and luck one may observe also in summer around many coasts in Cyprus the exotically beautiful kingfisher, flying just centimeters above the sea surface, scanning for fish while sitting on rocks and then diving with great speed to catch its prey. Around September we may very likely hear in various areas of Cyprus (and see them probably high up the sky, if we are lucky and alert) the equally colourful and speedy bee eaters. In the wetlands there are good prospects of observing among other birds, tall egrets (and sometimes more rare birds such as spoonbills, ibises and storks). In Larnaca and Akrotiri salt lakes one will surely see flamingos (but not in summer as the salt lakes dry out), while in the countryside one will very likely see chukars and hear francolins (they have a distinctive call, but they are a lot more difficult to spot).

Flamingos at Larnaca salt lakes

It is a fact that the population of many species is continuously decreasing and some have either become extinct or are heading that way. There are various reasons, some of which are external. The internal reasons include the deliberate or accidental disruption of the ecosystem (such as habitat loss and hunting). A very sad example of such population decrease relates to the griffon vulture (a very beneficial bird for man) which in older times was abundant in many areas of the island including Pentadactylos mountain range. The vulture stands out for its ability to use hot air masses and be carried high up the sky without exerting significant work. From up there it scans huge areas looking for carrion. Its population fell during 1996 by half when a poisoned carcass, which was intended to kill foxes (very cute mammals, persecuted until recently) ended up in the stomachs of a vulture community in the Paphos area, which was decimated as a result.

The avian world is very beautiful and offers to many people moments of optical and acoustical pleasure. The importance of birds as a group of species in the ecosystem is huge. Unfortunately this world is in danger and our combined efforts are urgently needed to avoid disaster.

A kingfisher in Protaras

7

PLANTS

One can find about two thousand plant species in Cyprus, many of which have been imported from faraway places such as Latin America, China and Australia. Most of these species are found in gardens, plantations and fields, while a few hundred species 'decorate' the other habitats of Cyprus, from the coasts to Olympus peak. The hundred fifty or so endemic plant species (in other words, those that are found only in Cyprus), many of which can be found on the two mountain ranges as well as in the Akamas peninsula, present special botanical interest.

Important examples of native trees of Cyprus include the carob and the olive, both of which constituted in the old days a source of a large part of Cyprus income (the carob was referred to as 'the black gold of Cyprus'). In Cyprus forests the pine dominates (the Calabrian pine and at high altitudes the black pine), while other 'noteworthy' trees include the Cyprus cedar (which we mainly find in Cedar Valley), the golden oak, the strawberry tree, the juniper, the hawthorn, the sumach, the plane tree, the alder, the maple and the storax. Almond trees also have a special place in Cyprus countryside, while we also find oak and cypresses in limited numbers.

Poppy

Examples of bushes include thorny broom, barberry, caper, rock rose, wild rose, sage, myrtle, mastic, terebinth and jujube.

A very distinctive plant of many forested valleys on the island is the bracken, while among climbing plants, the ivy and the honeysuckle stand out.

Just a few examples of wildflowers include the daisy, the poppy, the cyclamen, the Cyprus tulip, the crocus, the lavender, the rock cress, the mandrake and about 50 orchid species.

A special note must be made for vine. Even though it is not a native species, it is nevertheless cultivated in Cyprus for thousands of years, and played and continues to play an important role in the economic life of the island. It covers a large area of many semi mountainous regions of the island, and provides an important source of food for many of the

The climatic conditions on the island and the presence of the specific types of habitat creates very pleasant colour changes in the scenery, depending on the season and the type of habitat. Green dominates almost everywhere in winter, spring is very colourful with yellow having a major presence, in summer there is gold in the fields and green in those valleys with running streams, while in autumn, earthy colours dominate. We can see plants in blossom during every season on the island. Cyprus nature offers excellent opportunities for scenery photography and for the study of the flora on the island, especially of the wild flowers, which offer a vast variety in colours and shapes.

The importance of native plants is increasing in the minds of Cypriots. Various factors contribute to this including, a) better education about the flora of Cyprus, b) the continuous water shortage, as well as c) the strengthening conviction that the importation and cultivation of alien species may have a negative impact and breed dangers for our homeland.

Storax in Paphos Forest

9

REPTILES

Cyprus is inhabited by more than twenty reptile species, which contribute to the biodiversity of the island and represent indispensable constituents of the food chain. Eleven lizard species and ten snake species (including endemics) as well as three turtle species have been identified. Unfortunately in Cyprus society reptiles and snakes in particular, have a very bad name and are being persecuted.

Chameleon

It is not rare to see on local television stations (and in photos in newspapers) people showing off killed snakes, holding them by the tail. But in reality snakes are not our enemies. On the contrary, they contribute to the controlling of pests such as rats. Yes, it is true that one out of (at least) ten snake species found in Cyprus is dangerous for man. But even this will only attack if threatened. Those who happen to encounter a snake do not have to kill it without a second thought. Let's provide it with a way out. Many people find snakes extremely beautiful. Their shape and the way they move are very elegant, while in many species their mating rituals are magical. The king of adaptability amongst Cyprus reptiles is of course the chameleon. Its skin has the possibility to change colour so as to match the background and remain undetected by its prey and predators. Its eyes move in many directions independently and its huge sticky tongue is shot like an arrow catching its prey. The chameleon is a rather rare reptile here, in contrast to the ever-present agama (Greek Cypriots know it as 'kourkoutas') and the gecko (Greek Cypriots know it as 'mishiaros') which are very common in summer at low altitudes.

A special mention should be made of the Cyprus grass snake (Natrix natrix cypriaca). Is it an endemic endangered snake species and without significant urgent action, it will probably become extinct in the foreseeable future.

Laudakia stellio cypriaca – agama – the Greek Cypriots know it as 'Kourkoutas'

MAMMALS

It is only natural that the public doesnot know that Cyprus is inhabited or visited by more than thirty mammal species, as the majority of these either have wings (and are nocturnal) or fins (and are sea mammals). Cyprus is inhabited by sixteen bat species (a recent survey raised their number to over twenty, but the short discussion in the present guide will cover only the confirmed sixteen species) and its sea is inhabited or visited by seven dolphin and whale species (most of them are either rare now or occasional visitors).

Moufflon in Paphos Forest

Bats (which are protected throughout Europe) constitute an important mammal group on the island, as half of the mammal species here are bats. Fifteen out of the sixteen (confirmed) bat species in Cyprus feed on insects while one of them feeds on overripe fruit. Bats are very beneficial animals for man and it is in our interest to protect them (e.g. by blocking the entry for man to caves where bats hibernate, or by installing special bat houses). Unfortunately lately we witness the slaughter of large numbers of bats in Cyprus, which hopefully will stop, otherwise Cyprus will lose a significant degree of its biodiversity. Furthermore, the considerable decrease in the bat population in Cyprus will result in a huge increase in the insect population on the island, with a devastating effect on agricultural production.

Another 'invisible' mammal species is the Mediterranean monk seal (Monachus monachus), which is close to extinction as its total population around the world is only a few hundred animals. Centuries ago, this seal inhabited various coasts of the island (such as coasts around Karpasia peninsula, Cape Greko and Akamas peninsula), but tourism and the overexploitation of our coastline and seas has decimated the population of the species. In other countries (one good example is Greece) serious efforts to save the species are under way. It is time that Cyprus acts too.

Egyptian fruit bat

There are also other, generally unknown mammal species living on the island. These include three endemic species, the Cyprus spiny mouse, the white toothed - shrew (a very small insect-eating mammal species – there is another shrew species on the island) and the Cyprus mouse (Mus cypriacus) which has been recognised as a new species a couple of years ago.

The population of the endemic (subspecies) moufflon after decreasing to just a few dozen of animals in the middle of last century, having been protected has rebounded and now numbers several thousands of animals. Other species such as the Mesopotamian deer or the wild boar have not been so lucky and are extinct from the island.

Finally, the island is inhabited by hares (the wild population is enriched periodically by the Game Fund), foxes (persecuted until recently), hedgehogs (which, like bats, hibernate) and two common rodent species, the rat and the common mouse.

13

NATURAL ATTRACTIONS

INTRODUCTION

Cyprus is the third largest island in surface area in the Mediterranean Sea, and has a relatively high number of habitats, temperate climate and large altitude range (0 – 2,000 meters). It has a rich natural heritage, which we can enjoy (while protecting it) throughout the year, and attractions and locations suitable for a big number of outdoors activities. The Book includes information on more than two hundred and fifty natural attractions, which have been divided in various subcategories as follows:

1) BEACHES AND COASTS

TThe beaches of Cyprus constitute one of the best ingredients of the tourism product of the island. There is a big selection and variety and visitors can find a beach that meets their needs: Cosmopolitan or virtually empty, with white, golden or dark sand, natural or improved, well organised or with no infrastructure at all, in a green or desert-like environment, with calm waters or big waves.

In the south east (Protaras and Agia Napa) the beaches have either golden or white sand, and usually calm waters in summer (though after midday in Agia Napa the sea usually has small waves). Towards the west on the south coast up to Paphos fort, there are many beaches with wave breakers and dark coloured sand and/or pebble. Beaches near resorts and towns in the south part of Cyprus are very organised and popular. In the north, while some of the public beaches are exceptionally beautiful, such as Pachyammos/Golden Beach in Karpasia peninsula, as a rule they have limited infrastructure, no lifeguards and are not cleaned regularly. One seeking peace and quiet needs to go to secluded beaches, like those found east of Polis or in the remote east part of Karpasia peninsula. East of Limassol one can find beaches with a strange combination of dark sand and white rock, while on the west coast (north of Paphos as well as north of Morphou) the sea is wilder. Those seeking complete isolation should visit the coast of Lara (west side of the Akamas peninsula). The beaches of (the south part of) Cyprus are clean and more than 50 have secured the eco-label "Blue Flag" (see more at www.blueflag.org) while 30 even have facilities for persons with mobility difficulties. In the Book readers can find information for almost 90 beaches and coasts all around the island.

It should be noted that in the Book the word 'coast' is used for parts of the coastline with little or no infrastructure (whereas the term 'beaches' refers to stretches on the coastline with more infrastructure).

2) WALKING ROUTES

We have included more than 55 walking routes in the Book. Many of them are official walking trails, while others are routes that I have walked and recommend (some of the routes are on dirt roads and some are on unmarked land). The suggested routes include a large part of the coastline and many walking routes in the forest. The majority of the routes are linear, rather easy, and with a length of less than ten km. There are great opportunities for walking on the island all year round. Walkers are invited to explore and compose their own walking routes.

3) WETLANDS

In the guide there is information on more than 30 important wetlands of Cyprus including the biggest dams. Many of them are very important for birds and great destinations for birdwatching, while most dams (in the south) are open for fresh water fishing (there are of course conditions and a permit is required). The dams were constructed in the last forty five years, and can prove an important constituent of the ecotourism product of Cyprus, and contribute to the economic development of the local rural areas, provided they are managed in a sustainable way.

4) ANCIENT TREES

The Book includes information on more than sixty ancient trees (or groups of trees – the vast majority of these are in the south part of Cyprus and have been declared 'nature monuments'). The selection of each has been carried out using specific criteria; all of them are more than one hundred years old while some are more than one thousand years old. They definitely deserve our admiration and respect. Many of these trees are gigantic. One finds them in rural areas all over Cyprus (yet even in urban areas such as a transplanted olive tree in Nicosia or a sycamore tree in Walled Famagusta).

5) OTHER NATURE ATTRACTIONS

i. Waterfalls

The island has very small waterfalls. We have included four of these in the area around (Pano) Platres village which usually flow all year round, because they are found in idyllic locations and are worth a visit, especially when this is combined with a visit to other attractions in the area.

ii. Sea caves and Other natural attractions

We have also included various (sea) caves in the Book. We do not encourage visitors to enter the caves, but rather to explore the area around them. If you must enter, please make sure that you do not disturb bats, or any other animals who may seek refuge there.

Lastly, there is information on a few quite important areas and on an extremely narrow, river-like small fishing port.

We would like to invite explorers to use services offered by inhabitants of local communities during their exploration. This contributes to better appreciation of the value of nature by the local communities and their better protection.

15

CULTURAL ATTRACTIONS

INTRODUCTION

Cyprus' strategic position, where Asia, Europe and Africa meet, has made it an important trading station, and has been the source of wealth and prosperity, but also of war and destruction. A multitude of empires, civilizations, ethnicities and religions have come to the island (Greeks, Persians, Assyrians, Phoenicians, Egyptians, Romans, Byzantines, Francs, Venetians, Genoans, Ottomans, British, Turks, Armenians, Maronites, Pagans, Christians, Muslims, Arabs, Jews) saturating Cyprus with influences from near and far places, and enriching its culture tremendously. These influences can easily be observed in exquisite buildings and constructions found all around the island.

While a large number of historic buildings and constructions are well protected, there are many (especially in the north) that unfortunately are not. While this Book mainly focuses on nature, it also includes information on about 180 cultural attractions. Many of these, and in particular many watermills and medieval bridges are not well known and hard to find. They enrich our cultural heritage, as well as the tourism value of the island immensely. Selected cultural attractions in Cyprus are shown in the Book on maps and through photographs. The presented cultural attractions have been divided into various subcategories as follows:

1) MEDIEVAL BRIDGES

We have included information on medieval bridges because they are related closely to the rivers/streams/torrents of Cyprus and because they are significant architectural constructions. While a few of the remaining medieval bridges are well known to explorers and tourism professionals, the majority are not. In the Book there is information on 22 medieval bridges and one damaged one. Some are found even in urban areas, others are in or very near villages while others are in the countryside or in the forest, rather far from settlements. While most of the bridges can be easily reached on paved or dirt roads, a few are tougher to get to, either on cleared walking routes or on long abandoned pathways.

2) WATERMILLS

It is indeed surprising to many people when they find out that for centuries and even thousands of years water was the primary source of power used in the production of flour in Cyprus, a country with permanent water shortage. Our ancestors managed a problem, i.e. lack of water, efficiently and utilised nature in a sustainable way, improved their quality of life and increased their wealth. In the past there were hundreds of watermills in Cyprus and many of them operated until the 50s or 60s when diesel engines took over. Even though the technological infrastructure from the watermills is long gone, there is a large number where the structures still stand proud and are well worth a visit. We include information on more than 50 well preserved watermills in Cyprus (one of them in the north part).

3) CASTLES AND WATCHTOWERS

In medieval times (starting from Byzantine rule) many castles and watchtowers were erected around the island (there were castles on the island also in antiquity, e.g. Nitovikla in Karpasia, which is dated to about 1000 BC). Most were built at strategic locations to provide advanced warning of the imminent arrival of enemy ships to the island shores. Fire signals were used to propagate the warning fast to the Cyprus authorities. While many of the constructions are gone (e.g. the castle of Pyrgos village near Limassol – 'pyrgos' is the Greek word for 'tower' - or in Gastria village in Karpasia) many are still in a very good state and excellent destinations for the explorer. In the Book we have information on fourteen castles and medieval watchtowers in Cyprus (including the walls/bastions of walled Nicosia and walled Famagusta).

4) AQUEDUCTS

Aqueducts have been present in Cyprus at least from the time the Romans were here, about two thousand years ago. Aqueducts were built on the island during different historical periods and a few parts of a number of them can still be seen. While many of the aqueducts were a few kilometers short, one stands out having a length of about 50 kilometers transporting water from the springs of Kythrea all the way to Salamis. In the Book we include information on four of the aqueducts (there are a few more, e.g. in modern Strovolos, near Paralimni, in Lefka/Lefke and near Afanteia (or 'Afania' as is widely known to Greek Cypriots)/ Gaziköy).

5) UNESCO WORLD HERITAGE TROODOS PAINTED CHURCHES

These are very beautiful painted churches up to almost 1,000 years old. Some are found inside or near villages (e.g. the small church of Archangelos Michail in Pedoulas) while others are all that's left from past monasteries (e.g. Church of Agios Nikolaos tis Stegis - St. Nicholas of the Roof). The vividness of the colours in many of the frescoes is amazing and one could spend possibly a few days exploring just these churches.

6) OTHER CHAPELS AND MONASTERIES

Saint Paul preached in Cyprus and it is here where he got his roman name 'Paulus'. Cyprus religious heritage is very rich as can be expected by its long history and early adoption of Christianity. There are many hundreds of chapels around the island, a great number of which are at least a few centuries old. In addition to the ten UNESCO World Heritage Troodos painted churches we also include information on fifty of the chapels and monasteries, selected for their beauty, location and religious importance. One should keep in mind that the list is not exhaustive. The reader is in particular invited to explore the tens of historic churches in Walled Nicosia and in Walled Famagusta.

Sadly most of the chapels and monasteries in the north part of Cyprus have been looted and/or abandoned and/or destroyed after the war of 1974 making the people of Cyprus and the world poorer.

7) OTHER CULTURAL ATTRACTIONS

A plethora of ruins scattered around Cyprus are a testament to its long history and the presence of different civilizations and religions from ancient times. Of particular importance are the UNESCO World Heritage sites of Paphos and Choirokoitia. We chose to present nearly twenty of these cultural attractions.

NATURAL AND CULTURAL ATTRACTIONS

This, main section of the Book consists of nine subsections in total (each one having a different colouring scheme); one section per town or resort and one section for the north part of Cyprus. In each subsection there are maps with clearly marked natural and cultural attractions that are nearest to the specific town or resort. There is also description of each natural attraction as well as photos and map information on cultural attractions. At the end of the nine subsections there are tables with all the natural and cultural attractions in the Book.

In the title of each natural attraction page there is the relevant map number. Specifically for beaches, at the end of the description for each one, readers can find symbols related to whatever infrastructure/facilities they have.

LEGEND
FOR MAPS

	Highway
	Secondary road
	Loose surface road
	Walking trail
or	Walking route
	Common part of two or more walking routes
13	Walking route number
	Sovereign Base Area Boundary

	Village/city/resort
Protaras	Village/city/resort name
Girne	Turkish / Turkish Cypriot name of village/town/resort (after the 1974 war the Turkish authorities changed the original Greek names of Greek Cypriot settlements to Turkish)
	Direction
Kamares	Locality / attraction name
	Pointer to Location
	Fishing shelter/port
	Airport
	Limit of area under Turkish occupation since 1974

NATURAL ATTRACTIONS

	River
	Wetland (including manmade)
3	Wetland number
	Beach[1]
	Coast[1]
56	Coast/Beach number

	Mountain peak
	Forest
	Ancient tree
16	Ancient tree number
	Group of ancient trees
47	Group of ancient trees number

Notes: 1 - In this book a 'Beach' is presented as being a coastal place of swimming with relatively more facilities, compared to a 'Coast'

NATURAL ATTRACTIONS - CONTINUED

1	Other natural attractions number (including parks, waterfalls, sea caves, etc)
	Waterfall
	Sea cave/cave

CULTURAL ATTRACTIONS

	UNESCO World Heritage site
	Ruins
	Church/chapel
	Monastery
	Castle/fort/ watchtower
	Walls of Walled city (Nicosia and Famagusta)
	Medieval bridge
	Damaged Medieval bridge
	Watermill
6	Watermill Number
	Aqueduct
	Mosque

NATURE RELATED CONSTRUCTIONS

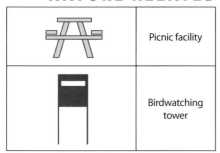

	Picnic facility
	Birdwatching tower
	Environmental education center
	Botanical garden

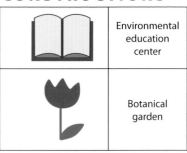

SYMBOLS IN THE TEXT AND THE RELEVANT TABLE ABOUT BEACHES

Blue flag	Umbrellas/beach beds for rent	Toilets	Access to persons with mobility difficulties	Lifeguard

PROTARAS

Protaras is characterised by excellent beaches with golden sand and calm waters. There are attractive walking routes in the northern and the southern end of the coastline. Cape Greko park is just south east of it. There's a wetland (home to the endangered Cyprus grass snake – Natrix natrix cypriaca) between Paralimni, Deryneia and Sotira that usually dries out in summer. The Agioi Saranta chapel in a cave is a lovely surprise. There's a cave-sanctuary close to Agioi Anargyroi church as well as a part of a medieval aqueduct in the buffer zone. There are very old pretty churches in a number of nearby villages (e.g. Agia Anna in Paralimni, Agia Marina and Agios Georgios in Deryneia, Archangel Michail and Agios Andronicos in Frenaros, and many more). Amazing Walled Famagusta is just 30 km away (taking the long route through the checkpoint).

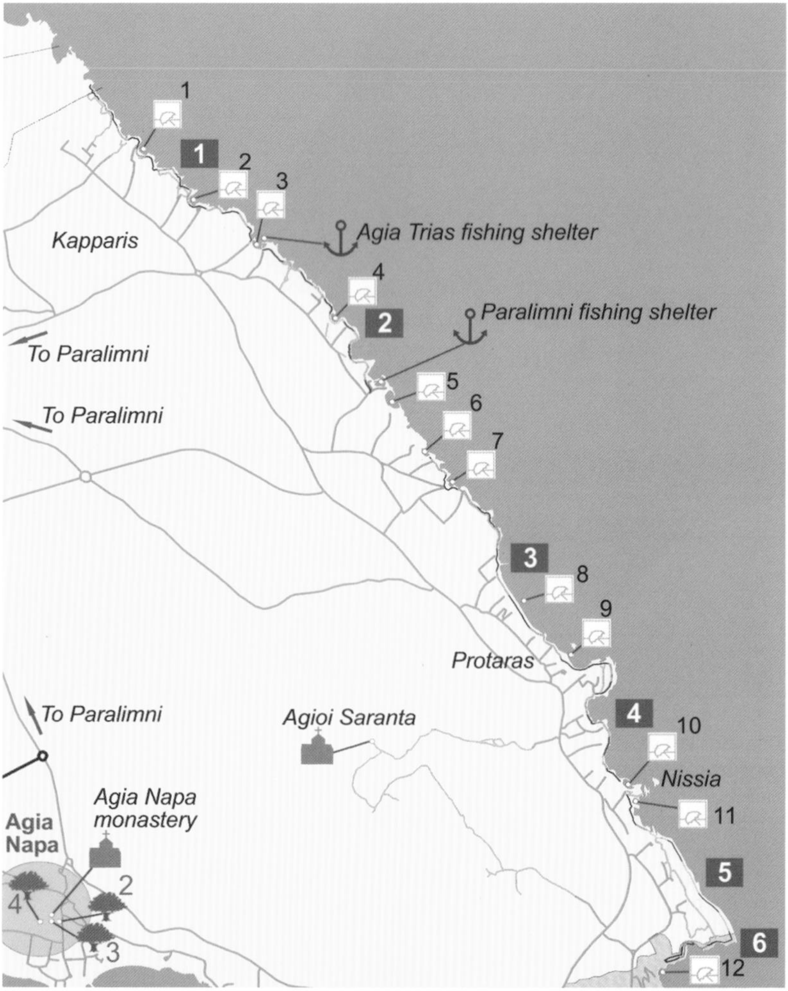

BEACHES/COASTS	
1	Kapparis (MAAD)
2	Malama (Scoutari)
3	Agia Triada
4	Vrisoudia
5	Louma
6	Pernera
7	Potami
8	Vrisi
9	Protaras Bay
10	Loumbardi
11	Nissia
12	Konnos

WALKING ROUTES	
1	Agia Triada Beach – Buffer Zone
2	Agia Triada Beach – Louma Beach
3	Louma Beach – Vrisi Beach
4	Protaras Bay Beach – Loumbardi Beach
5	Loumbardi Beach –Cyclop's Cave
6	Konnos Beach – Cyclop's Cave

OTHER CHAPELS AND MONASTERIES
Agioi Saranta Chapel

KAPPARIS (MAAD) BEACH

(Map 1 – page 21, 1)

This is the last small cove with sandy beach before the Buffer Zone. The beach is just a hundred meters across, at the north part of Protaras (in the area known as Kapparis). It is found some two km north of Agia Triada beach. The beach has been awarded the Blue flag eco-label (www. blueflag.org) and can get congested in summer. The surrounding area is quite scenic with great walking opportunities on the rocks three – seven meters above the sea, unusual rock formations and caves (it is splendid for snorkeling - one may have the luck of spotting sea turtles in summer). I recommend a walk from Agia Triada beach to the Buffer Zone that passes by Malama beach (2.5 - 3 km each way). Though Famagusta is less than ten km away, currently one needs to travel about 30 km through the checkpoint to go there.

Distance (km): Protaras : 6 Agia Napa : 12 Larnaca: 53 Nicosia : 92
Limassol : 119 Platres : 159 Paphos : 187 Polis : 222

Characteristics:  *(Apr-Oct)*

MALAMA (SCOUTARI) BEACH

(Map 1 – page 21, 2)

This is a small cove (nearly 150 meters across) with a sandy beach about one km north of Agia Triada beach. It looks ragged, as it is surrounded by up to ten meters high uncommon rock formations. The beach has few amenities. It can get congested in summer, but the area is quite scenic with caves and great walking opportunities on the rocks (relatively) high above the sea. I recommend a walk from Agia Triada beach to the Buffer Zone in the north, that passes by Kapparis beach (2.5 - 3 km each way). Sea turtles have been spotted many times here. As is the case of all Protaras beaches, the sea tends to be calmer that Agia Napa, which faces south, as (weak) winds blow from the south from late morning.

Distance (km) : Protaras : 5 Agia Napa : 13 Larnaca: 47 Nicosia : 86
Limassol : 113 Platres : 153 Paphos : 181 Polis : 216

Characteristics: 

AGIA TRIADA BEACH

(Map 1 – page 21, 3)

This sandy beach has very good road access. It is found in the north part of Protaras and has a small fishing port right next to it, as well as a modern church by the same name. The surrounding area is rather flat, unlike the (up to ten meters) high rock formations in the coastal area to the north of the beach. Having a fishing port right next to the beach must make it difficult to keep the water of the bay clean. On the other hand the beach has been awarded the Blue flag eco-label (www.blueflag.org). Even though there's been a lot of construction by the beach recently, the area is not excessively developed. There's a sailing club about 200 meters south of the beach. There are good walking possibilities, both to the north and south of the beach. The north route (Agia Triada beach - Buffer Zone) is in an environment that is certainly more ragged and wild. The south route to Louma beach is in a less dramatic setting.

Distance (km) : Protaras : 4 Agia Napa : 10 Larnaca: 46 Nicosia : 85
Limassol : 112 Platres : 152 Paphos : 180 Polis : 215

Characteristics:  *(Apr-Oct)*

VRISOUDIA BEACH

(Map 1 – page 21, 4)

This is a very small cove (about 100 meters across) between the beaches of Agia Triada and Louma. Vrisoudia in Greek Cypriot means "springs", as (according to folklore) spring water enters the bay. Unlike adjacent beaches, this one has some pebble besides sand (while in the north side one may find also soil). The water is sometimes murky because of the currents. Recently Vrisoudia beach became popular with youngsters as there's a club nearby playing loud music. Much of the beach is bordered by the gardens of the nearby hotel. Sirina beach is of a similar size, 300 m south of here, surrounded by lawns and mansions. There is a route connecting Vrisoudia beach with the beaches of Agia Triada to the north and Louma to the south (about 2.5 km in length each way – Vrisoudia is halfway on that route - there's been a lot of construction especially in the stretch between Vrisoudia and Louma in recent years). As the beach is almost encircled by a rocky stretch, one may spot kingfishers flying low, resting, ambushing and fishing.

Distance (km): Protaras : 1 Agia Napa : 10 Larnaca: 48 Nicosia : 87
Limassol : 114 Platres : 154 Paphos : 182 Polis : 217

Characteristics: 

LOUMA BEACH

(Map 1 – page 21, 5)

This is the largest beach in the northern part of Protaras (350 meters long). It has big stretches of sand, which provide good opportunity for sports (e.g. beach volley). It appears that the construction of the adjacent fishing port is such that keeps the water in Louma beach rather clean. There are wave breakers on both ends of the cove (70 m and 40 m long respectively). There are many amenities on the beach and very easy access on paved road. The beach has been awarded the Blue flag eco-label (www.blueflag.org) and has handicap facilities. The beach may be very suitable for families with small children. There are opportunities for a coastal walk to the north as well as to the south side, in both cases next to lawns, mansions and hotels.

Distance (km) : Protaras : 0 Agia Napa : 11 Larnaca: 47 Nicosia : 86
Limassol :113 Platres : 153 Paphos : 183 Polis : 218

Characteristics:  ***(Apr-Oct)***

PERNERA BEACH

(Map 1 – page 21, 6)

Pernera beach is a small naturally protected cove 200 meters across with golden sand, about five hundred meters south of Louma beach, in a very developed, flat and low altitude part of Protaras. There are lawns, hotels and mansions all around it. It has amenities and good road access. The beach has been awarded the Blue flag eco-label (www.blueflag.org) and has handicap facilities. It is very suitable for families with small children. Like in the rest of Protaras, in summer usually the water is very calm. One can do easy walking (including pushing a stroller) on the three km long paved coastal route from here to Protaras bay beach in the south (which is lighted in the evening).

Distance (km) : Protaras : 0 Agia Napa : 9 Larnaca: 47 Nicosia : 86
Limassol : 113 Platres : 153 Paphos : 181 Polis : 216

Characteristics:  *(Apr-Oct)*

POTAMI BEACH

(Map 1 – page 21, 7)

'Potami' means river in Greek, and the beach got this name apparently because a very small stream ends in the cove. Potami beach is a small cove with golden sand, just 70 meters long, 400 hundred meters south of Pernera beach, in a very developed, flat and low altitude part of Protaras. It has amenities and good road access. It is very suitable for families with small children. Like in the rest of Protaras, in summer usually the water is very calm. One can do easy walking (including pushing a stroller) on the three km long paved coastal route from adjacent Pernera beach in the north to Protaras bay beach in the south. The walking route is lighted in the evening and gets quite busy.

Distance (km): Protaras : 0 Agia Napa : 8 Larnaca: 47 Nicosia : 86
Limassol : 113 Platres : 153 Paphos : 181 Polis : 216

Characteristics: 

VRISI BEACH

(Map 1 – page 21, 8)

'Vrisi' means 'small spring' in the Greek Cypriot dialect. Apparently there's a small natural spring bringing fresh water here. Vrisi beach which has golden sand, is the longest beach in Protaras, with a length close to one km, and together with adjacent Protaras bay beach in the south constitute the main beach area of Protaras. It has good road access and many amenities along its stretch. The beach has been awarded the Blue flag eco-label (www.blueflag.org) and has handicap facilities. It is separated from Protaras bay (or Fig tree bay) beach by a small rocky cove, which provides good snorkeling opportunities. There are many four or five star hotels right next to it, and it is probably the most cosmopolitan of the beaches of Protaras, where trendy Cypriots from the capital Nicosia mix with tourists from northern Europe and the UK. One can do easy walking (including pushing a stroller) on the three km long paved coastal route from Pernera beach in the north to nearby Protaras bay beach in the south. The walking route is lighted in the evening and gets quite busy. There's a pier in the north part of the beach. Large boats do excursions to nearby coastal destinations (e.g. Cape Greko).

Distance (km): Protaras : 0 Agia Napa : 8 Larnaca: 47 Nicosia : 86
Limassol : 113 Platres : 153 Paphos : 181 Polis : 216

Characteristics: 

(Apr-Oct)

PROTARAS BAY BEACH

(Map 1 – page 21, 9)

It is also called 'Fig tree bay', after the fig tree(s) found there. On its north side there is a rocky cove beyond which the long Vrisi beach looms, while on the south a four km long rocky stretch leads to Cape Greko (small coves some of them sandy, interrupt the stretch). Protaras bay beach together with Vrisi beach constitute the main beach area of Protaras. The rocky islet (80 m across) in the center of the bay contributes to the calmness of the water. The beach has good road access and many amenities. Inevitably it gets really packed in summer. The beach has been awarded the Blue flag eco-label (www.blueflag.org) and has handicap facilities. There are excellent water sport and snorkeling opportunities in the vicinity. One can do easy walking (including pushing a stroller) on the three km long paved coastal route from here to Pernera beach in the north. The walking route is lighted in the evening and gets quite busy. Alternatively one can follow the route on a dirt road (or even on unmarked rock) to the south (it is about 1.5 km to Loumbardi beach). The extraordinary Agioi Saranta chapel which is merged with a cave can be reached by car mostly on dirt road three km west of Protaras bay beach.

Distance (km): Protaras : 0 Agia Napa : 8 Larnaca: 47 Nicosia : 86
Limassol : 113 Platres : 153 Paphos : 181 Polis : 217

Characteristics:  *(Apr-Oct)*

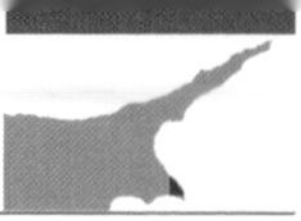

LOUMBARDI BEACH

(Map 1 – page 21, 10)

This is a sandy cove in the extensive four km long rocky stretch that connects the main area of Protaras (Protaras bay beach and Vrisi beach) to Cape Greko park. The beach is almost two km south of Protaras bay beach, it is less than 100 meters wide, and it has good road access and amenities. The beach has been awarded the Blue flag eco-label (www.blueflag.org). There are good snorkeling possibilities in the vicinity. A walk on the rocky stretch is pleasant. The part of the walking route towards the south, beyond the neighbouring Nissia beach can be very difficult and slow, unless explorers walk a bit away from the sea and the sharp rocks. Even though the area is quite developed, especially to the south the buildings are somewhat far from the sea and as a result the area has kept its wild character.

Distance (km): Protaras : 0 Agia Napa : 7 Larnaca: 47 Nicosia : 86
Limassol : 113 Platres : 153 Paphos : 181 Polis : 236

Characteristics: 

(Apr-Oct)

NISSIA BEACH

(Map 1 – page 21, 11)

The beach (also known as 'Green bay') takes its name from the adjacent islands and peninsula ('Nissia' is a version of the Greek word for 'islands') on its north side. It is a 100-meters wide cove with golden sand, and many acacia trees just behind it - in the extensive four km long rocky stretch that connects the main area of Protaras (Protaras bay beach and Vrisi beach) to Cape Greko park. The beach is about two km south of Protaras bay beach, and it has relatively good road access (a short 100 meters stretch of dirt road from the paved road) and umbrellas and beach beds for hire. There are no restaurants by the beach, but they are not that far away. Good snorkeling possibilities exist in the vicinity. A walk on the rocky stretch is enjoyable, yet very difficult and slow (especially to the south), unless explorers walk a bit away from the sea and the sharp rocks.

Distance (km) : Protaras : 0 Agia Napa : 8 Larnaca: 47 Nicosia : 86
Limassol : 113 Platres : 153 Paphos : 181 Polis : 216

Characteristics: 

KONNOS BEACH

(Map 1 – page 21, 12)

Konnos is one of the most scenic beaches on the island. It is not visible from the road that connects Protaras to Cape Greko, as there are steep 50 – m high slopes all around the cove. The vegetation is dominated by pine, juniper and acacia trees and there are views of Cape Greko up to Agioi Anargyroi church from the beach. The beach has golden sand and it's about 150 meters across. The water is fantastic, but sometimes in summer it may get a bit murky because of the currents. The place is packed in summer, and coming here by car can be an ordeal. For beach goes with a bit of stamina, walking down the beach could be the best alternative. The beach has been awarded the Blue flag eco-label (www.blueflag.org). Beachgoers who do not enjoy packed beaches are advised to come to Konnos in summer either early in the morning of late in the afternoon. There are great water sports opportunities, including snorkeling, as well as walking, either towards the north to the nearby Cyclop's Cave or towards the south and Cape Greko. Sea turtles have been spotted many times in the sea near Cyclop's Cave. In summer, many private pleasure boats take refuge in the bay.

Distance (km) : Protaras : 3 Agia Napa : 6 Larnaca: 49 Nicosia : 88
Limassol : 115 Platres : 155 Paphos : 183 Polis : 218

Characteristics:  ***(Apr-Oct)***

AGIA TRIADA BEACH – BUFFER ZONE WALKING ROUTE

(Map 1 – page 21,1)

This is an excellent coastal linear three km long walk from the beach of Agia Triada in the south to the United Nations controlled Buffer Zone in the north. It is possibly as attractive as the coastal routes in Cape Greko park. The area is (still) less developed than most of Protaras in the south, and the scenery is very ragged, with high (up to ten meter tall) rocky pathways, secluded coves, strange rock formations and caves. Caution is needed in some sections as explorers would need to walk on a narrow route very close to the edge. The walk passes by Malama beach and Kapparis beach. Walkers should be careful and follow the signs in the Buffer Zone, as one would not want to get into an area where entry is forbidden. The experience of the Buffer Zone adds another dimension to the walk, as it lands walkers into the harsh realities behind Cyprus political situation. The sea is fantastic for swimming and snorkeling, and those coming here in summer may meet fishermen enjoying their hobby. Walkers will see low vegetation (and some acacia trees) and a few lizards on the walk. People interested in sea turtles may want to bring a mask and snorkel along and watch for sea turtles raising their heads out of the water to breathe (and then take a swim and hopefully have the magical experience of watching a sea turtle 'fly' in the sea). At certain locations on the route one can have eerie views of the ghost city of Famagusta.

Distance (km): Protaras : 4 Agia Napa : 10 Larnaca: 46 Nicosia : 85
Limassol : 112 Platres : 152 Paphos : 180 Polis : 215

AGIA TRIADA BEACH – LOUUMA BEACH WALKING ROUTE

(Map 1 – page 21, 2)

This is a linear two and a half km long coastal walk that starts at Agia Triada beach in the north, passes by Crystal Springs and Sirina beaches and ends at Louma beach in the south (conversely it starts at Louma beach and ends at Agia Triada beach). The area is relatively less developed than the south (main) part of Protaras, but more developed than the north part. Unlike the adjacent route going north to the United Nations controlled Buffer Zone, the walk is overall on flat land with very low elevation. Walkers may see a few fields with crops like potatoes, vegetables and watermelons just inland from the beach, which are however in the last few years being replaced by mansions and tourist houses, at an alarming rate. Walkers pass by a sailing club about 200 meters from Agia Triada beach. The walk is mostly on dirt roads. The last third of the route is next to lawns, mansions and hotels. On a very clear day one could enjoy views also of Karpasia peninsula in the north (maybe even spot where Kantara castle is located), sometimes as far as Apostle Andreas monastery.

Distance (km): Protaras : 2 Agia Napa : 10 Larnaca: 46 Nicosia : 85
Limassol : 112 Platres : 152 Paphos : 180 Polis : 215

PERNERA BEACH – PROTARAS BAY BEACH WALKING ROUTE

(Map 1 – page 21,3)

The walk is on a linear three km long paved coastal walking route that starts at Pernera beach in the north, passes by Potami and Vrisi beaches and ends at Protaras bay beach in the south (or vice versa). It is found in the most developed part of the coast of Protaras, but there are a few places on the route where this is not apparent. It is an easy walk past a few coves, low, relatively flat rocks and small piers. The walk is very suitable for families (including pushing a stroller). No bicycles are allowed on the paved walking route. It is lighted in the evening and gets quite busy. With the hotel and restaurant lights reflection in the sea walkers enjoy a completely different view of the sea in the evening. There are some reed beds and frequently anglers in summer. There are benches to sit on, take a break and enjoy the view, as well as various cafes along the route.

Distance (km): Protaras : 0 Agia Napa : 11 Larnaca: 47 Nicosia : 86 Limassol : 113 Platres : 153 Paphos : 181 Polis : 216

PROTARAS BAY BEACH – LOUMBARDI BEACH WALKING ROUTE

(Map 1 – page 21,4)

This is a linear one and a half km long coastal walk from the excellent, cosmopolitan and usually packed Protaras bay beach (one of the two main beaches in the area of Protaras) in the north, to the small Loumbardi beach in the south. It is pleasant, easy walking on flat rock and on dry soil, past small coves and bays that offer refuge to pleasure boats in summer. Overall, tourist development is some way from the sea, so the place doesnot feel suffocating. On the other hand, the number of mansions in the last years increased a lot and walkers also pass by lawns and gardens. Along the way walkers see the area of Nissia (islands) which is just south east of Loumbardi beach. Nissia have natural small ports and boats take refuge there. They are frequented by diving schools. Cape Greko is a few kilometers further to the south.

Distance (km): Protaras : 0 Agia Napa : 7 Larnaca: 47 Nicosia : 86
Limassol : 113 Platres : 153 Paphos : 181 Polis : 217

LOUMBARDI BEACH – CYCLOP'S CAVE WALKING ROUTE

(Map 1 – page 21,5)

This is a linear two km long coastal walk from Loumbardi beach in the north to Cyclops's cave, which is a small cave by the sea at the north east entrance to the park of Cape Greko. Initially walkers pass by Nissia, a peculiar small peninsula, a small island (the word "Nissia" means islands in Greek) and a secluded adjacent cove (also known as 'Green bay'). The peninsula has very small natural ports and hosts small fishing boats. Because of the natural protection from the sea, diving schools frequent and use the peninsula especially during the early stages of new divers courses. Further south, and if walkers are determined to walk very close to the sea, they have to be very careful. They need to walk slowly and cautiously, as a wrong step could result in their falling on sharp rock edges. In summer one sees thousands of small evaporating pools and salt formations, a good subject for photo shoots. At places, the rock is more like sandstone and in certain points on the stretch it seems that it was cut out and used probably in construction (these seem to be ancient quarries – in antiquity the city of Lefkolla stood in this area). When walkers reach the south end of the route, they can enjoy a view of a big part of the east coast of Cape Greko. The land rises rather steeply from the sea level and the scenery becomes hilly. Cyclop's Cave has two entries, it has the dimensions of a big room and an adult would need to bend down a bit to enter and explore inside.

Distance (km) : Protaras : 0 Agia Napa : 6 Larnaca: 47 Nicosia : 86
Limassol : 113 Platres : 153 Paphos : 181 Polis : 217

CYCLOP'S CAVE – KONNOS BEACH WALKING ROUTE

(Map 1 – page 21,6)

This is an official circular 2.4 km long walking trail. It starts at the very scenic Konnos beach and ascends on the coast (to an elevation of just twenty meters) to the small Cyclop's Cave in the north. The second (return) half of the way is either on the same path or very close to it. The walking trail is close to the edge and walkers (on the return half) enjoy splendid views towards Cape Greko peninsula and Agioi Anargyroi church. On the way walkers can observe some of the local indigenous flora (e.g. juniper) as well as imported plant species (e.g. eucalyptus and acacia). The cave itself is small but explorers can enter it if they walk leaning forward a bit. It has two entrances and plenty of light. In summer sea turtles are spotted frequently in the sea near Cyclop's Cave so those interested in sea turtles may want to bring a mask and snorkel along and explore.

Distance (km): Protaras : 3 Agia Napa : 6 Larnaca: 49 Nicosia : 88
Limassol : 115 Platres : 155 Paphos : 183 Polis : 218

KONNOS BEACH – AGIOI ANARGYROI CHURCH WALKING ROUTE

(Map 2 – page 43,7)

This is an official 1.4 km long linear coastal walking trail from Konnos beach to Agioi Anargyroi church. There are two ways to enter the walking trail, the lower way is from the cafe just above the beach, while the other is higher up, at a parking place. For most of the way the walking trail is on top of a steep slope and near the edge (elevation range between 10 – 25 m) offering walkers excellent view of the light blue sea below and panoramic vistas of the bay. The walk is very easy and the vegetation is dominated by pine, juniper and acacia trees. In summer many pleasure boats take refuge in the bay. Near the end of the trail there's an organised picnic area (and a playground). The end of the trail is at the white, picture-perfect chapel of Agioi Anargyroi. There's a sea cave down the stairs (less than 100 meters away from the chapel - entrance is above sea level) that has a religious status to Greek Orthodox faithful. The sea here is among the calmer around the island and this coast is a popular diving spot.

Distance (km): Protaras : 3 Agia Napa : 6 Larnaca: 48 Nicosia : 87
Limassol : 114 Platres : 154 Paphos : 182 Polis : 217

AGIOI SARANTA CHAPEL (Map 1 – page 21)

AGIOI ANARGYROI CHAPEL (Map 2 – page 43)

AGIA NAPA

Agia Napa has excellent white and golden sand beaches and calm waters. Cape Greko park is very close and the walking route towards the east is very attractive. Other natural attractions include sea caves, ancient trees, the peculiar coastline at Potamos tou Liopetriou port, Achna dam (when there is water) and ragged Xylofagou coast in the west. Agia Napa church (monastery) the tombs in Macronissos, the medieval watchtower on Xylofagou coast and caves – sanctuaries (such as Agia Thekla) are important components of the area's cultural heritage. There's also a restored part of a medieval aqueduct in Agia Napa and medieval churches in nearby villages (e.g. Agios Georgios Chortakion church, Panagia Chortakiotissa church and the ruins of Agios Theodoros Chortakion, all in close proximity near the municipal stadium to the west of the village of Sotira).

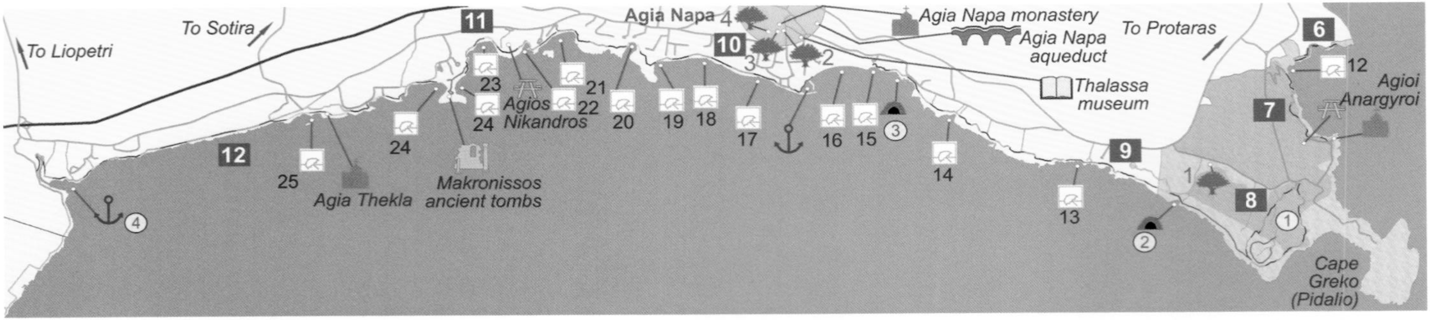

BEACHES/COASTS	
13	Kermia
14	Ammos Tou Kampouri
15	Glyki Nero
16	Pantahou
17	Loukos Tou Mandi
18	Katsarka
19	Pernera
20	Vathia Gonia
21	Nissi
22	Latchi
23	Landa
24	Makronissos
25	Agia Thekla

WALKING ROUTES	
7	Konnos Beach - Agioi Anargyroi Church
8	Aphrodite
9	Agia Napa Sea Caves – Cape Greko Sea Caves
10	Pantahou Beach – Vathia Gonia Beach
11	Vathia Gonia Beach – Makronissos Beach
12	Makronissos Beach – Potamos Tou Liopetriou Port

ANCIENT TREES	
1	Juniper
2, 3, 4	Sycamore trees

OTHER NATURAL ATTRACTIONS	
1	Cape Greko Park
2	Cape Greko Sea Caves
3	Agia Napa Sea Caves
4	Potamos Tou Liopetriou Fishing Port

AQUEDUCTS
Agia Napa Aqueduct

OTHER CHAPELS AND MONASTERIES
Agioi Anargyroi
Agia Napa Monastery
Agia Thekla

OTHER CULTURAL ATTRACTIONS
Macronissos Ancient Tombs

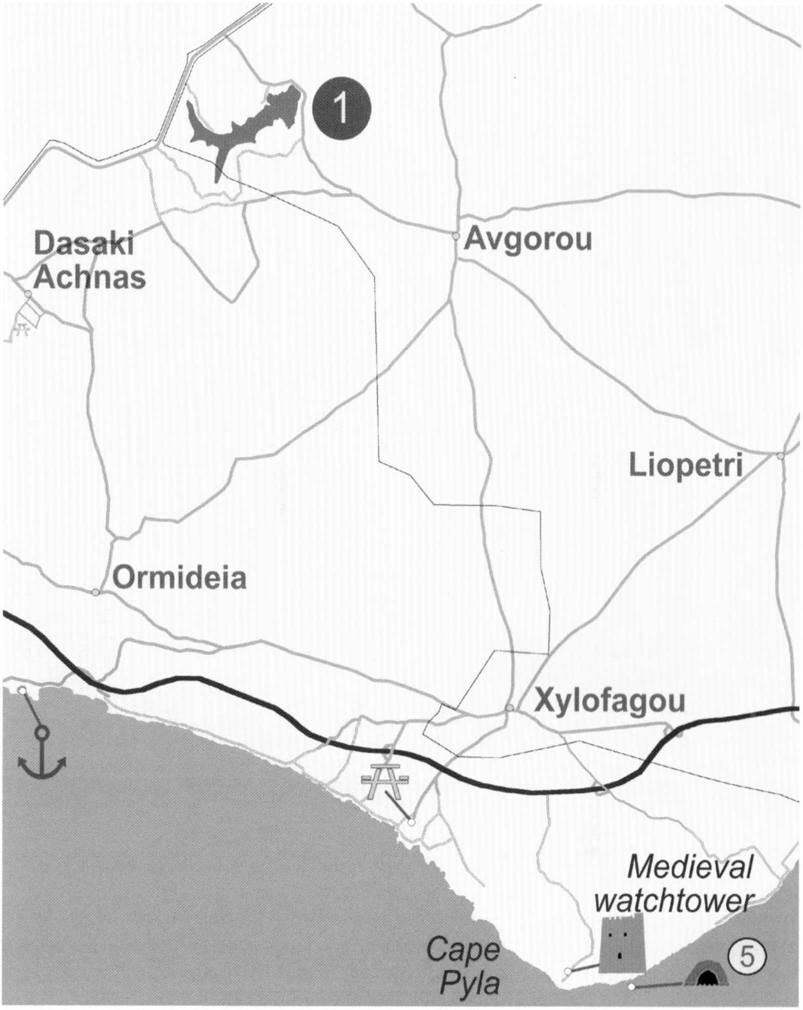

WETLANDS	
1	Achna Dam

OTHER NATURAL ATTRACTIONS	
5	Xylofagou Sea Caves

CASTLES AND WATCHTOWERS
Xylofagou Tower

KERMIA BEACH

(Map 2 – page 43, 13)

This beach (also known as 'Limnara' beach) is in front of a tourist resort (from which it takes its name), in an otherwise relatively undeveloped (for now) area and it is found about three km east of Agia Napa Sea Caves. The beach has been awarded the Blue flag eco-label (www.blueflag.org), it is quite organised and has relatively good road access (maybe the best way to enter if you are not staying at the resort is via a paved road that ends about 300 meters east of the beach; from there one can take the paved walking trail to the beach). Kermia beach is nearly 300 meters long. There is a very small fishing boat refuge to the east side of the beach. It is on the walking route (much of it on a paved trail) between the Agia Napa Sea Caves and the Cape Greko Sea Caves. Though in summer in the afternoon usually it is a bit windy in Agia Napa waters as the wind blows from the south, Kermia is relatively protected. Even though natural rock formations in the sea offer protection against waves, some rocks have been placed in a wave breaker formation.

Distance (km): Agia Napa : 3 Protaras : 6 Larnaca: 44 Nicosia : 83
Limassol : 110 Platres : 150 Paphos : 178 Polis : 223

Characteristics: 

(Apr-Oct)

AMMOS TOU KAMPOURI BEACH

(Map 2 – page 43, 14)

This is a very small beach, just 50 meters long, in a coastal area of Agia Napa with relatively little development (up to now), east of the Agia Napa fishing port. It is found between Agia Napa Sea Caves (one km to the west) and Kermia beach (two km to the east). Ammos tou Kampouri beach has been awarded the Blue flag eco-label (www.blueflag.org). There are amenities at the beach and good (signposted) road access. There's a 150 m dirt road stretch from the coastal paved road. The beach is found on the (largely paved) walking route between the Agia Napa Sea Caves and the Cape Greko Sea Caves. In summer in the afternoon usually there are small waves in Agia Napa waters as the wind blows from the south. The beach is more typical of less developed Greek islands rather than of the average packed Cyprus beach. There's a large taramix tree right on the sand. The beach rarely gets packed (except for a few Sundays in summer). There's a very peculiar minute beach just 30 meters wide around a rocky islet, about 700 m to the east (beach beds and umbrellas may be rented out).

Distance (km) : Agia Napa : 1 Protaras : 7 Nicosia : 81 Limassol : 108
Platres : 145 Paphos : 176 Polis : 211

Characteristics:  *(Apr-Oct)*

GLYKI NERO BEACH

(Map 2 – page 43, 15)

This beach is found in a small cove, right to the west of the Sea Caves of Agia Napa. Its name literal translation is "sweet water" (which means fresh, potable water in Greek; it seems that there's a fresh water spring at the beach). The beach has been awarded the Blue flag eco-label (www.blueflag.org). It is about 100 m across and is found next to the considerably larger (one km long) Pantahou beach, which begins just to the east of the Agia Napa fishing port. In summer in the afternoon usually there are small waves in Agia Napa waters as the wind blows from the south. Even though Glyki Nero is centrally located and welcomes many tourists in summer, it does not get really congested (as the two beaches together are quite long and also because the sand extends inland significantly, on average by thirty meters). The Agia Napa Sea Caves are splendid for sea exploration and photography (sea turtles and rarely a couple of Mediterranean monk seals are spotted here), while the 4.5 km long walking route from the Agia Napa Sea Caves to the Cape Greko Sea Caves, going through the relatively undeveloped east coast of Agia Napa, provides good walking possibilities.

Distance (km): Agia Napa : 0 Protaras : 8 Larnaca: 41 Nicosia : 80
Limassol : 107 Platres : 147 Paphos : 175 Polis : 210

Characteristics:  *(Apr-Oct)*

PANTAHOU BEACH

(Map 2 – page 43, 16)

With a length of more than one km, this is the longest beach in Agia Napa stretching all the way from the fishing port (in its west) to the east of the adjacent Glyki Nero beach. Pantahou beach has been awarded the Blue flag eco-label (www.blueflag.org). It is very centrally located and welcomes thousands of tourists in summer. It has however a very big capacity as it has a lot of depth and hardly feels very congested, unlike smaller beaches. In summer in the afternoon usually there are small waves in Agia Napa waters as the wind blows from the south. As Pantahou is less protected, it gets more waves than other protected beaches. The Sea Caves of Agia Napa are very close for exploration, and for the walkers there are options both to the east as well as to the west. The 2.5 km west walking route to Vathia Gonia beach is quite easy, going through a very developed part of Agia Napa. The 4.5 km long walking route from the Agia Napa Sea Caves to the Cape Greko Sea Caves going through the relatively undeveloped east coast of Agia Napa provides a better environment for those seeking exploration.

Pantachou beach is found one km south of the tall wall-like part of Agia Napa's medieval aqueduct. It was used to transport water to Agia Napa medieval monastery.

Distance (km) : Agia Napa : 0 Protaras : 8 Larnaca: 41 Nicosia : 80
Limassol : 107 Platres : 147 Paphos : 175 Polis : 210

Characteristics: 

(Apr-Oct)

LOUKOS TOU MANDI BEACH

(Map 2 – page 43, 17)

This is a very small beach (just 40 meters across) about 500 m to the west of the fishing port of Agia Napa. There is a bit of sand on the beach and the sea is rocky. In summer in the afternoon usually there are small waves in Agia Napa waters as the wind blows from the south. As Loukos tou Mandi beach is less protected, it gets more waves than other protected beaches. The beach has amenities and relatively good road access (the paved road ends behind a nearby hotel). This minute beach has been awarded the Blue flag eco-label (www.blueflag.org). It is found on the 2.5 km long paved walking route that connects the fishing port of Agia Napa (in the east of Loukos tou Mandi beach) to the beach of Vathia Gonia (in the west).

Loukos tou Mandi beach is found one km south of the beautiful Agia Napa medieval monastery and its ancient trees.

Distance (km) : Agia Napa : 0 Protaras : 8 Larnaca: 41 Nicosia : 80
Limassol : 107 Platres : 147 Paphos : 175 Polis : 210

Characteristics:  ***(Apr-Oct)***

KATSARKA BEACH

(Map 2 – page 43, 18)

This manmade beach 1,200 meters west of the fishing port is less than 100 meters long. The beach and the sea are rocky. There is very little sand on the beach, and it appears that this was brought here from elsewhere. It is very difficult to distinguish most of the beach as it blends with the rocky environment. Katsarka (or 'Katsarga') beach has been awarded the Blue flag ecolabel (www.blueflag.org). In summer in the afternoon usually there are small waves in Agia Napa waters as the wind blows from the south. As Katsarka beach is less protected, it gets more waves than other protected beaches. The beach is found on the 2.5 km long paved walking route that connects the fishing port to the beach of Vathia Gonia. The paved road (and the parking lot) ends about 200 meters north of the beach.

Distance (km): Agia Napa : 0 Protaras : 9 Larnaca: 41 Nicosia : 80
Limassol : 107 Platres : 147 Paphos : 175 Polis : 210

Characteristics: 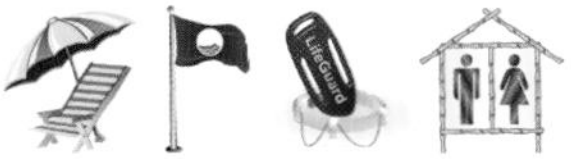

(Apr-Oct)

PERNERA BEACH

(Map 2 – page 43, 19)

Pernera beach is at a small distance (200 m) to the east of Vathia Gonia beach. Some developmenthas taken place at the beach, with rocks moved (some taken inside the water to create wave breakers). There is good road access and amenities at the beach. Pernera beach is about 200 meter wide and has been awarded the Blue flag eco-label (www.blueflag.org). Even though in summer in the afternoon usually there are small waves in Agia Napa waters as the wind blows from the south, Pernera is somewhat protected because of the shape of the coastline immediately to the west of it. The beach is found on the west end of the 2.5 km long walking route that connects the fishing port to the beach of Vathia Gonia. One can also take the four km walk to the west, to Makronissos beach, and visit on the way a few of the picture-perfect, white sand beaches of Agia Napa (like Nissi beach).

Distance (km) : Agia Napa : 0 Protaras : 8 Larnaca: 41 Nicosia : 80
Limassol : 107 Platres : 147 Paphos : 175 Polis : 210

Characteristics:  ***(Apr-Oct)***

VATHIA GONIA BEACH

(Map 2 – page 43, 20)

Vathia Gonia beach is found about 800 m east of Nissi beach. Its Greek name means "deep angle", as per its shape. It is a well protected cove with white sand, and has long rocky stretches on its left and right sides. The beach is about 300 meters wide, it has been awarded the Blue flag eco-label (www.blueflag.org) and has handicap facilities. It is very picturesque and has awesome blue waters, especially before midday. The beach doesnot get usually congested, as it has considerable depth. There are very good snorkeling and walking possibilities in the vicinity. One can either take the 2.5 km long walking route to the east that connects to the fishing port, or the more interesting three km long walk to the west, to Makronissos beach, and visit on the way a few of the other picture-perfect white sand beaches of Agia Napa.

Distance (km) : Agia Napa : 0 Protaras : 9 Larnaca: 41 Nicosia : 80
Limassol : 107 Platres : 147 Paphos : 175 Polis : 210

Characteristics:  *(Apr-Oct)*

NISSI BEACH

(Map 2 – page 43, 21)

Travellers planning to visit just one beach in Agia Napa should come to this beach. Nissi beach is a symbol of Agia Napa, and in many ways one of the best beaches on the island and beyond. It gets its name from the small rocky islet found towards its west side (Nissi means island in Greek). Theoretically, there are two beaches, Nissi beach and Nissi bay, but as they are not very large (together they are about 600 meters in length), so close together and as it is difficult to distinguish their "border", we are treating them as one. It is found about three km west of Agia Napa center. The lagoon-like sea and pure white sand are just amazing. There is a high proportion of young visitors here as well as fine road access and amenities. The beach has been awarded the Blue flag eco-label (www.blueflag.org) and has handicap facilities. There are good snorkeling and water sports possibilities. The rocky islet on the west side of the beach has a surface area of about 7,000 sq.m, rises a few meters above water and is a good place to enjoy panoramic vistas of the area. Youths also use it to dive in the clear blue water from high up. One can walk on the three km long 'Makronissos beach to Vathia Gonia beach' walking route passing through here. The bay is not very exposed to the wind and because of that, in summer after midday when there is usually wind blowing from the south the sea remains relatively calm. The water can at times get murky though. The beach gets really packed in summer, and beachgoers who want to avoid the hordes of visitors should come here early in the morning.

Distance (km) : Agia Napa : 0 Protaras : 12 Larnaca: 41 Nicosia : 80
Limassol : 107 Platres : 147 Paphos : 175 Polis : 210

Characteristics:  ***(Apr-Oct)***

LATCHI BEACH

(Map 2 – page 43, 22)

Latchi is a small sandy beach, less than 100 meters long, very close and to the west of Nissi beach, and about three km from the center of Agia Napa. Some rocks have been placed in the sea as a wave breaker, and some concrete has been poured on the rocks. The beach is protected and usually it doesnot get many waves, when in summer after midday the wind blows from the south. There are amenities and good road access to the beach. There are good snorkeling possibilities in the vicinity. From here one can explore the adjacent rocky islet of Nissi beach, swim in its beautiful lagoon-like waters and walk on the three km long 'Makronissos beach to Vathia Gonia beach' walking route that passes through Latchi beach.

Distance (km): Agia Napa : 0 Protaras : 12 Larnaca: 41 Nicosia : 80
Limassol : 107 Platres : 147 Paphos : 175 Polis : 210

Characteristics:  *(Apr-Oct)*

LANDA BEACH

(Map 2 – page 43, 23)

Landa in the Greek Cypriot dialect means "a small pool of water". Landa beach is a white sand beach, 200 meters wide, found just to the east of the bigger Makronissos beach and some four km west of the center of Agia Napa. It has good road access and amenities. The beach has been awarded the Blue flag eco-label (www.blueflag.org) and has handicap facilities. Landa beach has considerable depth (30-50 meters), so there is a lot of space for visitors. As a result it doesnot get too congested even in the middle of summer. As the beach is protected by rocks on its two sides, usually it doesnot have many waves in summer in the afternoon when the wind blows from the south. There are good water sports and snorkeling possibilities in the vicinity. From here one can walk on the three km long 'Makronissos beach to Vathia Gonia beach' walking route.

Distance (km): Agia Napa : 1 Protaras : 9 Larnaca: 41 Nicosia : 80
Limassol : 107 Platres : 147 Paphos : 175 Polis : 210

Characteristics:  ***(Apr-Oct)***

MAKRONISSOS BEACH

(Map 2 – page 43, 24)

Makronissos in Greek means "long island" and the cluster of three small beaches (combined length about 500 meters) probably takes its name from the peninsula (island like) at its center, where in antiquity there was a Hellenistic and Roman period cemetery. It is found some five km west of Agia Napa center, has good road access and amenities and has been awarded the Blue flag eco-label (www.blueflag.org). The beaches have a lot of depth (30-50 meters) so there is a lot of space for visitors, which include families to a large proportion. As the cluster, because of the peninsula at the end, is not very exposed to the south wind, in summer in the afternoon usually there are not a lot of waves in the bay. There are good snorkeling and water sport possibilities, and one could visit some of the nineteen rock-cut tombs (there was also a temple and a quarry here in ancient times) and/or walk either towards the east on the three km long walking route to Vathia Gonia beach (passing by three other organised beaches) or towards the west and the picturesque fishing port of Potamos tou Liopetriou (six km long passing by the beach of Agia Thekla).

Distance (km): Agia Napa : 2 Protaras : 14 Larnaca: 41 Nicosia : 80
Limassol : 107 Platres : 147 Paphos : 175 Polis : 210

Characteristics:  ***(Apr-Oct)***

AGIA THEKLA BEACH

(Map 2 – page 43, 25)

This is the most remote organised natural beach of Agia Napa towards the west. It is situated six kilometers west of the centre of Agia Napa and has good road access and amenities. The beach has been awarded the Blue flag eco-label (www.blueflag.org). It takes its name from the saint to which the caved sanctuary and the modern chapel are dedicated. The beach is about 250 meters long. It has a small islet in its center (about 100 meters long), which makes the beach very protected from the south winds. Because of the natural protection from waves Agia Thekla can be good for families with small children. On the other hand a good number of visitors may not like the sea here because it is largely rocky instead of the typical white-sand setup of the beaches to the east of Agia Thekla beach. This beach lies on the six km long route between Potamos tou Liopetriou fishing port in the west and Makronissos beach in the east. There are good snorkeling possibilities in the vicinity. Until the last decade, the area had been undeveloped, but the last decade saw the construction of hundreds of tourist villas. There are also a few organized manmade beaches on the coast between Agia Thekla beach and Potamos tou Liopetriou fishing port.

Distance (km) : Agia Napa : 6 Protaras : 16 Larnaca: 39 Nicosia : 78
Limassol : 105 Platres : 145 Paphos : 173 Polis : 208

Characteristics:  ***(Apr-Oct)***

APHRODITE WALKING ROUTE

(Map 2 – page 43,8)

This route is on a circular walking trail in the Cape Greko park (about three km long) that goes round the high rock. I find the (first 2/3s) part around the coast more interesting, so instead of going round, I suggest a return on the same route. The walking route shares the coastal part with the walking route starting at Agioi Anargyroi church (a bit further north east on the coast) and ending at the Sea Caves, a bit further west. Initially it passes through somewhat higher vegetation of juniper bushes, by old shepherds' constructions and cereal fields. The trail then proceeds on the rocky south side (with very low, sparse vegetation) of the big rock of Cape Greko. Walkers enjoy pretty views all around and easy walking (there's a descent of 50 m elevation difference in the first third of the walk). They have the option to visit the Cape Greko Sea Caves (known locally as 'Palathkia' meaning 'palaces') which are just a few hundred meters away. On the return leg, walkers have the option to go around the coast further east (about 500 meters from the start of the walking trail) and visit the natural bridge called "Kamara tou Koraka". Standing/walking on the bridge is not allowed any more as it may be dangerous. During spring and autumn avian migration, walkers have the opportunity to see significantly more bird species and more birds in general.

Distance (km) : Agia Napa : 5 Protaras : 5 Larnaca: 49 Nicosia : 88
Limassol : 115 Platres : 155 Paphos : 183 Polis : 218

AGIA NAPA SEA CAVES – CAPE GREKO SEA CAVES WALKING ROUTE

(Map 2 – page 43,9)

This is a 4.5 km long linear coastal walk in the relatively undeveloped east side of Agia Napa. The walk is on the rocky coast offering continuous views of the sea. The rock at Cape Greko dominates the horizon. The walk, mostly on a paved walking trail, passes by the beaches of Ammos tou Kambouri, Kermia and other coves. At some point east of Kermia beach the paved walking trail ends and it seems like the marked walking trail disappears entirely. Even if walkers don't locate any of the two walking trails, they need not worry. They can keep walking on the coast until they reach Cape Greko Sea Caves which are less than a km to the east. Cape Greko Sea Caves (known locally as 'Palathkia' i.e. 'Palaces') constitute a beautiful site. There is paved road access to Agia Napa Sea Caves and close to the Cape Greko Sea Caves; the last 300 meters are on a difficult at points dirt road. Public buses pass on the paved road near Cape Greko Sea Caves (but the bus stop seems to be 1.5 km away). During spring and autumn avian migration, walkers have the opportunity to see significantly more bird species and more birds in general while they walk. Sea explorers may want to snorkel and explore the area also from the water.

Distance (km): Agia Napa : 0 Protaras : 5 Larnaca: 41 Nicosia : 80
Limassol : 107 Platres : 147 Paphos : 175 Polis : 210

PANTAHOU BEACH – VATHIA GONIA BEACH WALKING ROUTE

(Map 2 – page 43, 10)

This linear walking route is about 2.5 km long, on the coast connecting the two beaches. It is an easy workout by the rocky sea. The area is very developed touristically. Walkers pass by the beaches of Loukos tou Mandi, Katsarka and Pernera. It is a very flat walk as the elevation remains below ten meters all along the route. There is good road access to both ends of the walking route. Certainly not at all as attractive as the east walking route from Agia Napa Sea Caves to Cape Greko Sea Caves. Nevertheless it can be refreshing as it provides an easy workout next to the sea.

Distance (km) : Agia Napa : 0 Protaras : 8 Larnaca: 41 Nicosia : 80 Limassol : 107 Platres : 147 Paphos : 175 Polis : 210

VATHIA GONIA BEACH – MAKRONISSOS BEACH WALKING ROUTE

(Map 2 – page 43, 11)

This is a three km long linear flat (the elevation doesnot rise above ten meters) coastal walking route connecting the beaches of Vathia Gonia and Makronissos. It is easy walking with road access at both ends. The largely paved walking trail passes by many of the picture-perfect white sand beaches of Agia Napa (Vathia Gonia, Nissi, Landa and Macronissos). It also passes by smaller Latchi beach. Walkers can have a picnic just after the middle of their walk at the coastal picnic area of Agios Nikandros.

Distance (km) : Agia Napa : 0 Protaras : 9 Larnaca: 41 Nicosia : 80 Limassol : 107 Platres : 147 Paphos : 175 Polis : 210

MAKRONISSOS BEACH – POTAMOS TOU LIOPETRIOU FISHING PORT WALKING ROUTE

(Map 2 – page 43, 12)

This is a six km long linear easy route connecting the (cluster of) beaches at Makronissos to Potamos tou Liopetriou fishing port in the west. Both ends have road access (and public bus). The route passes by Agia Thekla beach on the way and a couple of other coves. The first part of the route is less developed than the stretch west of Agia Thekla beach, where now there are many tourist villas. The route passes by a good number of villa lawns and now also by a few newly developed manmade beaches. Acacia trees dominate the (higher) vegetation. Potamos tou Liopetriou fishing port is a fitting finish point for the walk as it forms a great photography subject and a place to rest (and possibly eat) after a pleasant coastal walk.

Distance (km) : Agia Napa : 2 Protaras : 14 Larnaca: 37 Nicosia : 76
Limassol : 103 Platres : 143 Paphos : 171 Polis : 206

ACHNA DAM

(Map 3 – page 44, 1)

Achna dam is a birdwatching spot near Avgorou and about 20 Km from Agia Napa. The dam is easily accessible on paved road. It was built in 1987, it has a capacity of 6.8 million cubic meters and covers an area of about 50 hectares. It is frequented by anglers. Fish in the lake include crayfish, carp, mosquito fish, roach and catfish. Water is transported here through pipelines from the west part of Cyprus. The land is flat and one can walk along the perimeter of the manmade lake (covering a distance of about 10 km – this would change depending on the water level in the lake and whether some of the dirt roads/ways are passable). In summer usually it gets almost dry. The lake has good birdwatching opportunities, with many tens of species visiting it. Among the more exotic birds spotted here include egrets and ibises. In the last few years a park has been built in the south side of the dam. It also has birdwatching towers. One could combine a stop here with a visit to some of the medieval churches in the area (e.g. in Frenaros village).

Distance (km) : Agia Napa : 20 Protaras : 25 Larnaca: 30 Nicosia : 60
Limassol : 87 Platres : 127 Paphos : 155 Polis : 190

JUNIPER IN CAPE GREKO

(Map 2 – page 43, 1)

This tree is found in the center of cape Greko park, very close to the road leading to Agia Napa.Coming from Agia Napa on the road to Protaras and after turning towards Cape Greko, one can see the tree on the right, in a field towards the sea. It is a Juniperus phoenicea, 150 years old, five meters high and its trunk has a perimeter of two meters. Lately it seems like young couples use the location for wedding photos. A stop here can be combined with (any of) the exploration activities in the Cape Greko park (especially a visit to the Cape Greko Sea Caves which are less than a km away), walks, nature study, photography, swimming, snorkeling, scuba diving, bird watching and climbing. A public bus line operates very close to the location of the tree.

Distance (km) : Agia Napa : 5 Protaras : 5 Larnaca: 46 Nicosia : 85
Limassol : 112 Platres : 152 Paphos : 180 Polis : 215

SYCAMORE TREES IN AGIA NAPA

(Map 2 – page 43, 2-4)

There are three ancient (Ficus sycomorus) sycamore trees in close proximity to each other, just south of Agia Napa monastery, in the center of Agia Napa village. These are huge trees, especially the two oldest ones. The oldest is 600 years old, has a height of 26 meters and a trunk perimeter of seven meters, the middle one is 350 years old, has a height of 18 meters and a trunk perimeter of 4.5 meters while the youngest one is just 150 years old, has a height of 18 meters and a trunk perimeter of almost 3.5 meters. There's a medieval pool next to the trees and no wonder this has contributed to their growth. Water was transported here via the aqueduct to the north east of Agia Napa, which was constructed to bring water to the medieval monastery (the monastery is a landmark cultural attraction in the area). The sycamore trees are not an indigenous species of Cyprus. Their small fruit is sweet, tasty and edible (it become ripe in summer). There is another huge ancient tree of the same species in Walled Famagusta, in the courtyard of Saint Nicholas cathedral.

Distance (km) : Agia Napa : 0 Protaras : 8 Larnaca: 41 Nicosia : 80
Limassol : 107 Platres : 147 Paphos : 175 Polis : 210

CAPE GREKO PARK

(Map 2 – page 43, ①)

This is a nature reserve in the overdeveloped Agia Napa - Protaras area. It is found about six km east of Agia Napa, about three km south of Protaras and has an area of less than four sq. km. The area's vegetation in terms of trees/bushes is dominated by junipers, acacia, eucalyptus, pines, mastic, olives and hawthorn. Cape Greko is an important area for birds especially during avian migration season in spring and autumn. It is a prime bird spotting destination. The coast all around is rocky and the water is amazing for swimming, snorkeling and diving. In summer, some coves get congested with tourist boats and private yachts. There are very good walking and exploration possibilities, sea caves and high rocks with breathtaking views. Hopefully the park will not be spoilt by tourism. In summer one may be lucky to swim with sea turtles here (loggerhead or green turtles), while a couple of Mediterranean seals (Cyprus waters used to host many in the past) made their appearance again in the last few years.

Distance (km) : Agia Napa : 5 Protaras : 5 Larnaca: 46 Nicosia : 85
Limassol : 112 Platres : 152 Paphos : 180 Polis : 215

CAPE GREKO SEA CAVES

(Map 2 – page 43, ②)

These (ten or so caves) make up a cluster in a small bay (nearly 200 meters long by foot, the radius of the cove is about 50 meters) about five km east from the center of Agia Napa. The Greek Cypriot name for the caves is "Palathkia", which means 'palaces' (it was believed that monk seals lived here). A short 350 m long dirt road (there's a signpost by the paved road) leads to the bay, from the paved road that starts from the main road that connects Agia Napa to Protaras and goes around Cape Greko. In hot summer visitors may see some youngsters (usually) jumping in the water from the (east) top of the rocks. The water is great for snorkelling. There is a small cave with two entrances high on the east side of the cove, that provides excellent view and cool shade. There's difficult access down from the top of the rocks, just to the east of the bay (sometimes with the use of a rope). One can also reach the caves by foot, either on the walking route from the Agia Napa Sea Caves (4.5 km to the west), or from the main area of Cape Greko to the east (the walking route that joins Aphrodite walking trail). The caves here are taller than those of Agia Napa and shallow (it seems usually one cannot swim into any of these). A trip here is a good opportunity for photo shooting. This is a good place to visit on an ecological watercraft (Waterbike, sea kayak, etc).

Distance (km): Agia Napa : 5 Protaras : 5 Larnaca: 46 Nicosia : 85 Limassol : 112
Platres : 152 Paphos : 180 Polis : 215

AGIA NAPA SEA CAVES

(Map 2 – page 43, ③)

The caves are found at the end of Glyki Nero beach, or conversely, at the end of the sandy beaches that start from the Agia Napa fishing port to the east (1 -1.5 km from the fishing port) and they spread over a distance of 500 meters. There is easy paved road access to the caves on the coastal road east of Agia Napa. One can access the caves by land on the 4.5 km long coastal walking route that starts from Glyki Nero beach and goes all the way to the Cape Greko Sea Caves. There is variety in the characteristics of the caves. Some are deep and one can only enter by swimming (or similar). Others are very shallow and one can only walk inside. Some are very narrow and seem to be very difficult for even one person to enter while others are a few meters wide. Some of the caves continue inland for many meters. There's also a cave with two entries (going through on a watercraft needs extreme care) and a natural bridge (near the point where the paved road passes closest to the caves). The bridge is an excellent place for photos and one can descend without getting wet. The caves are a superb destination for exploration, a sea kayaking (or similar) trip, snorkeling, swimming, climbing and photography. The water is calmer in the morning. According to a number of sources monk seals were spotted recently in this area.

Distance (km): Agia Napa : 0 Protaras : 8 Larnaca: 41 Nicosia : 80
Limassol : 107 Platres : 147 Paphos : 175 Polis : 210

POTAMOS TOU LIOPETRIOU FISHING PORT

(Map 2 – page 43, (4))

The Greek name of the port means "river of Liopetri" (village). Indeed, the port is the place where a local stream enters the sea, and probably the stream is responsible for the shape of the coast. It is a peculiar coast not found elsewhere on the island. The fishing boats are picturesque and the area is not very developed or "polished". It looks a lot more wild and primitive than the resort village of Agia Napa (especially near and to the west of the Agia Napa port). To the east lies the area of Agia Thekla, which in the last decade has seen rapid tourist development and the construction of hundreds of villas. On the west 'bank' where the river flows into the sea, the old small chapel of St. George stands. A bit further than one km west of the port there is a fish farm. One could walk on the coast east to Makronissos beach (past Agia Thekla beach and other coves); the distance is about six km of easy walking. For those interested in a move 'primitive' walking experience, it makes sense to walk either on the rocky coast or on the dirt road west towards Xylofagou caves. The port has good paved road access as well as regular public transport from Agia Napa.

Distance (km): Agia Napa : 9 Protaras : 19 Larnaca: 37 Nicosia : 73
Limassol : 100 Platres : 140 Paphos : 168 Polis : 203

XYLOFAGOU SEA CAVES

(Map 3 – page 44, ⑤)

On the south west of Potamos tou Liopetriou fishing port one finds Xylofagou coast, a ten km - long rugged coastline that offers great exploration possibilities to the adventurous walker. For the first 3.5 kilometers the coastline has low elevation and a dirt road (and many makeshift tent-like beach constructions). There's also a fish farm here. This part of the walking route is quite easy. Things get wild and tough when the elevation on the coast rises (to about fifty meters). The coastal road turns inland and the walker needs to mix walking with rock climbing. There are many caves (welcomed news for cavers) some of which are above sea level (some with pygmy hippopotamus fossils or stalactites). British troops use the area for military exercises and tank wreckages scatter the land (offering interesting subjects for photographs). There are no sandy stretches on the coastline (not until one reaches low elevation coastline again, towards Dekeleia), but if walkers manage to come down to sea level there are some fine locations for snorkeling (e.g. at the place known as the 'Red Cliffs'). Acacia is the dominant high vegetation species found on this coast today. On the highest elevation (about 90 m) location near cape Pyla walkers may be able to see Xylofagou watchtower, a medieval Venetian cylindrical/conical watchtower that was part of a chain of towers used to provide advanced warning about incoming military threat. There's no road taking explorers all the way to the tower, but it is not too difficult to reach it on foot (it's just 100 meters from the end of the dirt road). The tower has no door or window; it seems that ropes were used for guards to climb onto the tower.

Distance (km): Agia Napa : 12 Protaras : 22 Larnaca: 40 Nicosia : 76
Limassol : 103 Platres :143 Paphos : 171 Polis : 206

XYLOFAGOU TOWER (Map 3 – page 44)

AGIA NAPA AQUEDUCT (Map 2 – page 43)

AGIA NAPA MONASTERY (Map 2 – page 43)

AGIA THEKLA CHAPEL (Map 2 – page 43)

MAKRONISSOS ANCIENT TOMBS (Map 2 – page 43)

LARNACA

Larnaca has wetlands that are very important for birds and are ideal for birdwatching (especially Larnaca salt lakes). Many of its beaches have wave breakers and dark sand and/or pebble. The wider area has a number of historic churches and monasteries dating back many centuries (1,000 years – Saint Lazarus in Larnaca, Aggeloktisti church in Kiti, Agios Antonios church in Kellia, Stavrovouni monastery) and a wide variety of other cultural attractions (the UNESCO World Heritage site of Choirokoitia Neolithic settlement, the most impressive and best preserved aqueduct in Cyprus, medieval castles and watchtowers, watermills, a medieval bridge, and a good number of picturesque villages, e.g. Lefkara, Kalavasos, Kato Drys).

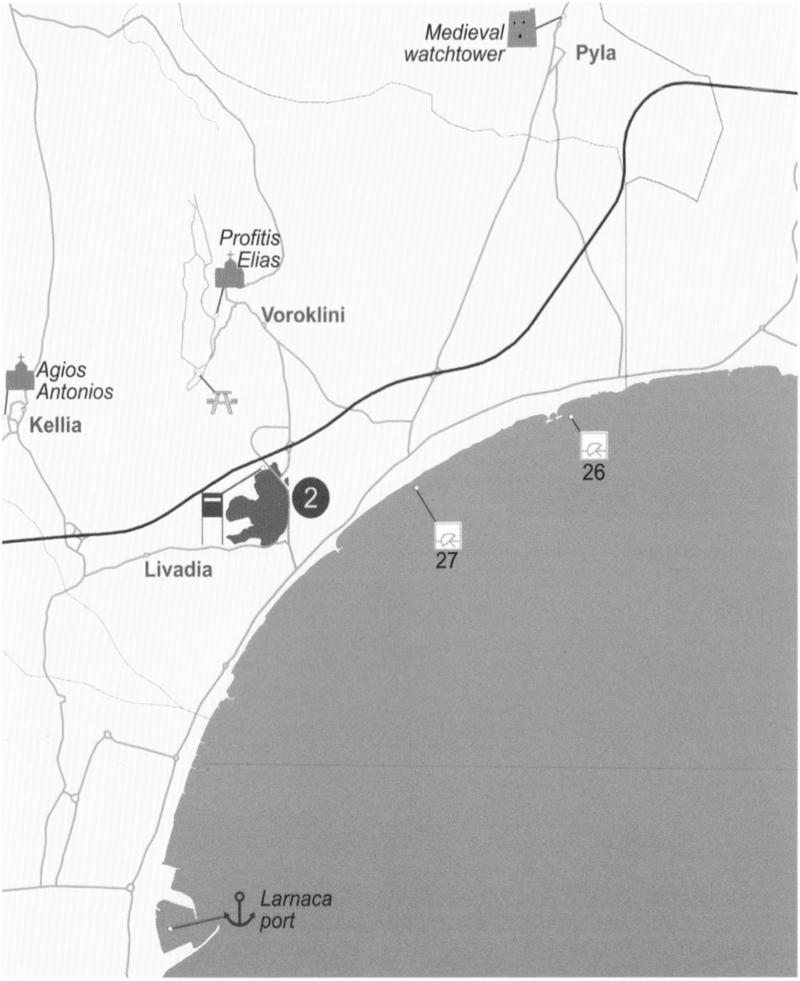

BEACHES/COASTS	
26	Pyla
27	Voroklini (Giannades)

WETLANDS	
2	Voroklini lake

CASTLES AND WATCHTOWERS
Medieval watchtower in Pyla

CHAPELS AND MONASTERIES
Profitis Elias chapel
Agios Antonios

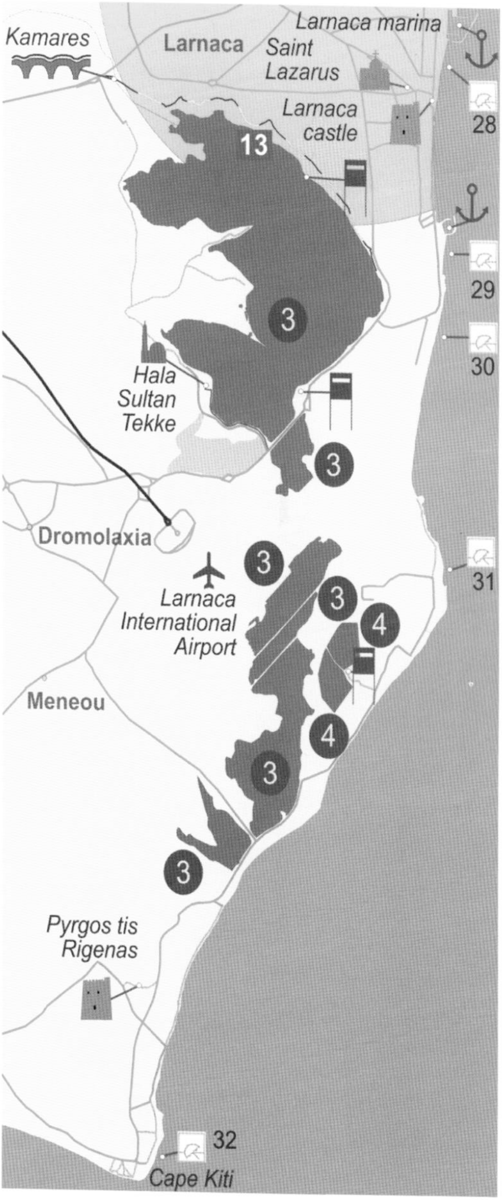

BEACHES/COASTS	
28	Phinikoudes
29	Kastella
30	Mckenzie
31	Spyros beach
32	Faros

WALKING ROUTES	
13	Salt lake – Kamares aqueduct

WETLANDS	
3	Larnaca salt lakes
4	Larnaca sewage works

AQUEDUCTS
Kamares/Bekir Pasha

CASTLES AND WATCHTOWERS
Larnaca castle
Pyrgos tis Rigenas

CHAPELS AND MONASTERIES
Saint Lazarus

OTHER CULTURAL ATTRACTIONS
Hala Sultan Tekke

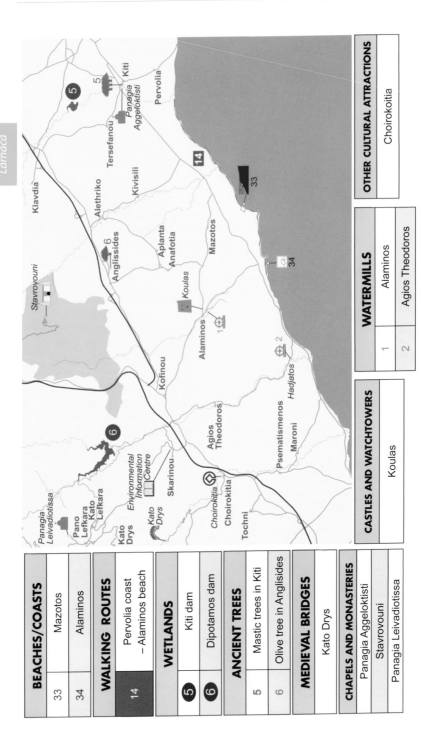

BEACHES/COASTS	
33	Mazotos
34	Alaminos

WALKING ROUTES	
14	Pervolia coast – Alaminos beach

WETLANDS	
5	Kiti dam
6	Dipotamos dam

ANCIENT TREES	
5	Mastic trees in Kiti
6	Olive tree in Anglisides

MEDIEVAL BRIDGES
Kato Drys

CHAPELS AND MONASTERIES
Panagia Aggeloktisti
Stavrovouni
Panagia Leivadiotissa

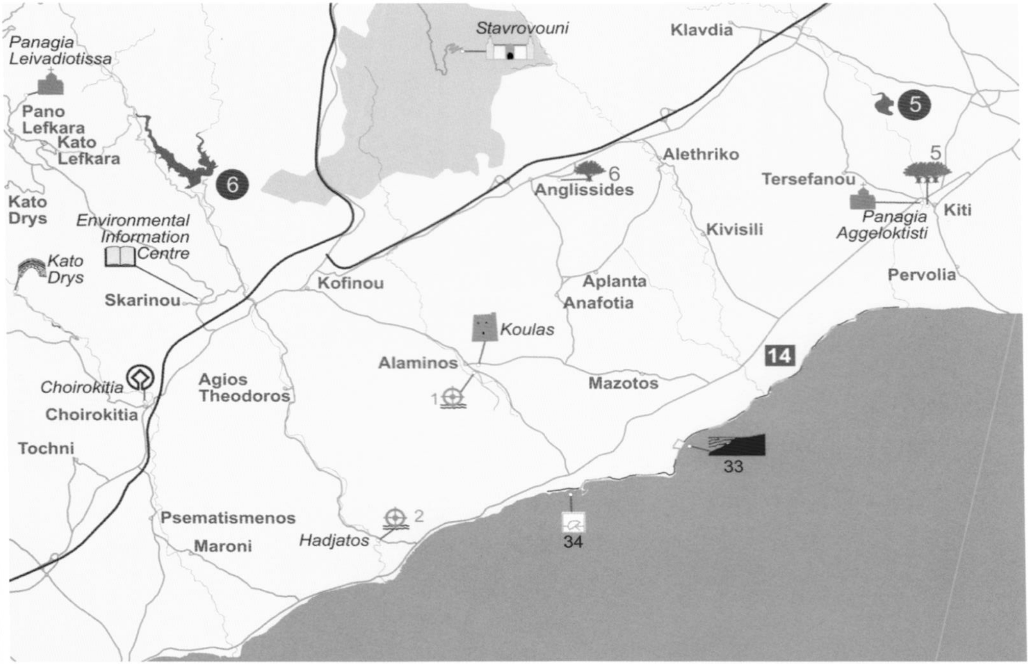

CASTLES AND WATCHTOWERS
Koulas

WATERMILLS	
1	Alaminos
2	Agios Theodoros

OTHER CULTURAL ATTRACTIONS
Choirokoitia

PYLA BEACH

(Map 4 – page 75, 26)

The coast of Dekeleia bay in the area controlled by the Republic of Cyprus is divided into two main parts, Pyla beach and Voroklini beach. There is no clear "border" between the two. Pyla beach is the coastal stretch between the fence that marks the boundary of the British sovereign bases (east end of the beach) and the eucalyptus forest (known as "Dasoudi" i.e. "little forest") in the west. Pyla beach is three km long and its surface is made of a mixture of pebble and sand. There are a number of luxurious hotels behind the beach. The beach is easily accessible as there is a coastal paved road very close to it. There are many wave breakers in the sea in front of the beach. As a result large quantities of sand have been deposited on the beach. The village of Pyla, four km north of the beach is an oddity in Cyprus in that it is a village (one of two – the other one is Potamia) that remains mixed after the 1974 war. It may be worth a visit just because of its bicommunality. It is found within the buffer zone. Pyla is home to a medieval tower (the tower initially belonged to an aristocratic Frankish family – it is in the center of the village and with care one can spot it from the highway going to Agia Napa). The tower is an eight m long by five m wide building (considerably smaller than Kolossi castle) and from the top one can see as far as Larnaca port. It was recently renovated (and nowadays houses many pigeons – it seems that human visitors are not really welcomed here). The medieval church (built around 1500 AD) of Archangel Michail is opposite the tower.

Distance (km): Larnaca: 5 Agia Napa : 36 Protaras : 42 Nicosia : 46 Limassol : 61 Platres : 101 Paphos : 139 Polis : 174

Characteristics: *(Jul-Aug)*

VOROKLINI BEACH (PART OF IT IS CALLED GIANNADES)

(Map 4 – page 75, 27)

The coast of Dekeleia bay in the area controlled by the Republic of Cyprus is divided into two main parts, Pyla beach and Voroklini (or 'Oroklini') beach. There is no clear "border" between the two. Voroklini beach begins at the eucalyptus forest (known as "Dasoudi" i.e. "little forest") in the east and goes up to the first fence of the oil refinery in the west. Voroklini beach is about three km long and can be roughly divided into two parts: the developed (almost two km long) east part which has luxury hotels and many amenities, and the less developed west part. Giannades beach (which is part of Voroklini beach) has been awarded the Blue flag eco-label (www.blueflag.org) and has handicap facilities. The west part has almost entirely pebble on its surface, whereas the east part has many wave breakers and a mixture of pebble and sand. Smallish Voroklini lake, one of seven natural wetlands on the island, where about 200 bird species have been recorded is less than two km inland. On the hills north west of Voroklini village about five km from the beach, one finds the peculiar Profitis Elias chapel and a nearby picnic area with panoramic views of the wetland and the coast.

Distance (km): Larnaca: 2 Agia Napa : 40 Protaras : 46 Nicosia : 46 Limassol : 68 Platres : 108 Paphos : 136 Polis : 171

Characteristics:  *(May-Sep)*

PHINIKOUDES BEACH

(Map 5 – page 76, 28)

Phinikoudes means "small palm trees" in the Greek Cypriot dialect. The beach takes its name from the rows of palm trees (which are really tall now) in the Larnaca promenade. It is a sandy beach that extends from the marina in the east to the Larnaca castle in the west, and has a length of about 600 m. It is quite wide with a capacity for many visitors. Usually in summer after midday the wind is blowing from the south and there are (small) waves in the bay. The beach has been awarded the Blue flag eco-label (www.blueflag.org) and has handicap facilities. The promenade is full of cafes, restaurants and bars.

Larnaca medieval castle has a small relevant museum and hosts various open-air events. Worshippers believe that the body of Saint Lazarus lies in a tomb inside a crypt at nearby Saint.Lazarus church. Saint Lazarus was ordained by St. Paul and St. Barnabas as bishop of ancient Larnaca (Kition). The first Saint Lazarus church is believed to have been built in 900 AD and witnessed additions and changes in the following centuries. The old part of Larnaca has a number of pretty renovated houses as well as an archaeological museum.

Distance (km) : Larnaca: 0 Agia Napa : 41 Nicosia : 44 Protaras : 47
Limassol : 66 Platres : 106 Paphos : 134 Polis : 169

Characteristics:  ***(May-Oct)***

KASTELLA BEACH

(Map 5 – page 76, 29)

The beach has dark sand, it is 400 meters long, 20 – 70 meters wide (on average nearly 40 meters wide), and right on the west of a fishing boat shelter. The beach has been awarded the Blue flag eco-label (www.blueflag.org) and has handicap facilities. There are beach bars and many fish taverns in the vicinity. Usually in summer after midday the wind is blowing from the south and there are (small) waves in the bay. 700 meters south west of the beach one finds the east bank of the biggest of Larnaca salt lakes. One can take the four-km long, linear walking route from there (towards the north west) that leads to the imposing, well preserved Kamares/Bekir Pasha aqueduct.

Distance (km): Larnaca: 0 Agia Napa : 41 Nicosia : 44 Protaras : 47 Limassol : 66
Platres: 106 Paphos : 134 Polis : 169

Characteristics: (Jun-Sep)

MCKENZIE BEACH

(Map 5 – page 76, 30)

This is the western of the organised beaches near the town of Larnaca. It is a 800 meters long, 40 meters wide, dark-sand beach, with many bars, cafes and restaurants behind it. Access to the (south) west of the beach is not allowed (fenced off) as this land is part of Larnaca airport. Like the rest of the beaches on the south coast of Cyprus, usually in summer after midday the wind is blowing from the south, and there are (small) waves in the bay. The beach has been awarded the Blue flag eco-label (www.blueflag.org) and has handicap facilities. Plane spotting may be an interesting activity at least for some of the beachgoers here. Those interested in bird spotting may choose to walk to the nearby salt lake about 800 meters west. About three km further (clockwise) around the lake one finds Hala Sultan Tekke, an 18th century mosque visited by many Turkish Cypriots from around the island.

Distance (km) : Larnaca: 0 Agia Napa : 41 Nicosia : 44 Protaras : 47 Limassol : 66
Platres: 106 Paphos : 134 Polis : 169

Characteristics: 

(May-Oct)

SPYROS BEACH

(Map 5 – page 76, 31)

This is a largely unorganised beach, 600 meters south west of Larnaca airport. Access is through the road coming from the village of Meneou (six km away). The beach is ten km by road from the airport and about 13 km from Larnaca. The name by which it is referred to (Spyros beach) was the name of a tourist establishment in the area that does not exist anymore. It is probably the widest (or deepest in terms of sand) beach in Cyprus, since a part of it with length of more than 300 meters, has an average width of at least 100 meters. The beach is more than one km long and has dark fine sand on its surface. It is quite nice for those seeking to exercise on a sandy beach. In the middle of summer, there is a lifeguard present here during weekends. There are plans to organise the beach in the coming years. It is about one km to the southeast of Larnaca Sewage Works (pools), a great spot for birdwatching. The salt lakes system is also very near. The next organised public beach to the south west is Faros beach (about six km away). One could walk on the coast to Faros beach, but at points it may be difficult (large pebbles on the coast). There are plans to construct a walking route from Faros beach on the coast towards the east. Going towards Faros beach, about one km before the beach and 500 meters inland one comes upon a pretty Venetian medieval watchtower. The six meters by six meters building (also known as 'Pyrgos tis Rigenas' in Greek, translated to 'Queen's tower') has been restored, and it can be easily accessed through the coastal paved road that links the two beaches, but it is still fenced off.

Distance (km) : Larnaca: 13 Agia Napa : 54 Nicosia : 57 Protaras : 60 Limassol : 79
Platres :119 Paphos : 147 Polis : 182

Characteristics: 

(Jul - Aug)

FAROS BEACH

(Map 5 – page 76, 32)

Faros beach is about three km south east of the village of Pervolia, (to the west of Larnaca), seven km south from the village of Meneou (through Meneou passes the fastest way to access the beach from Larnaca), ten km by road from the airport and about 13 km from Larnaca. There are many villas on the coast near the beach. There are supposed to be two (connected) beaches, Faros beach on the west end and the adjacent "Reporters Village" beach, but they really comprise one beach, almost one km long. 'Faros' means lighthouse in Greek, and towards the western end of the beach one can see the lighthouse that was constructed during British rule. It is a well organized beach, with a lifeguard and amenities, frequented by families. It has been awarded the Blue flag eco-label (www.blueflag.org) and has handicap facilities. There is a small 90 m long wave breaker in the sea. The beach is quite wide, at an average width of more than 30 meters. A visit to the nearby medieval Venetian watchtower about one km towards the (north) east is highly recommended. This pretty small six meter by six meters building has been restored, and it can be easily accessed through the coastal road from the east towards Faros beach, but it is still fenced off. There are plans to construct a walking route from Faros beach on the coast towards the east. The next (a bit organised) public beach towards the east is the very wide Spyros beach, some six km away, while towards the west the coast of Mazotos (some 20 km west of Larnaca) can be found. One can combine a trip here with visits to the church of Panagia Aggeloktisti in Kiti and the ancient mastic trees in its yard, and to birdwatching sites (Larnaca salt lakes, Larnaca sewage Works, Kiti dam).

Distance (km): Larnaca: 13 Agia Napa : 54 Protaras : 60 Nicosia : 65 Limassol : 76
Platres :116 Paphos : 144 Polis : 179

Characteristics: ***(Jun-Sep)***

MAZOTOS COAST

(Map 6 – page 77, 33)

Mazotos coast is about twenty km south west of Larnaca. It is more than four km long and has primarily two 'beaches', i.e. Panagia Petounta beach in the west and 'Mazotos beach' towards the east. The beach surface is a mixture of dark sand and pebbles. There are no lifeguards and almost no amenities on the beaches. The area is not very developed (for now) and may appeal to those seeking more peaceful coasts. For those interested in walking, the 13 km route along the undeveloped (mostly to the west of Mazotos coast) coast from Pervolia to Alaminos beach provides a nice exercise. The part of the route west of Mazotos coast is more attractive as the elevation rises somewhat by the coast (up to an elevation of ten meters). Travellers can combine a trip here with visits to Alaminos medieval watchtower, Kiti dam, the church of Panagia Aggeloktisti in Kiti and the ancient mastic trees in its yard, watermills and the olive tree in Anglisides village.

Distance (km) : Larnaca: 20 Limassol : 46 Nicosia : 47 Agia Napa : 83 Protaras : 89 Platres : 92 Paphos : 114 Polis : 149

Characteristics: -

ALAMINOS BEACH

(Map 6 – page 77, 34)

Alaminos beach is about 22 km west of Larnaca. There is a fishing boat refuge here and beaches to its west and east side. The two beaches have a combined length of about one km. There are amenities in front of the hotel in the west side of the beach and lifeguards in summer. As a result of the fishing boat refuge construction and of a number of wave breakers that were erected here, considerable quantities of (dark) sand have been deposited on the beach. There is public transportation passing by the beach. There is a pleasant 13 km long walking route in the east of the beach to Pervolia coast. The first half of the route, along higher elevations (rising to an elevation of just ten meters) and a still undeveloped coast, is the most attractive part of the walk.

Travellers can combine their swimming and/or basking here with visits to peculiar Alaminos watchtower (known as 'Koulas') and the nearby watermill, the watermill near Agios Theodoros coast, Kiti dam (maybe for some birdwatching), the ancient church of Panagia Aggeloktisti in Kiti and the ancient mastic trees in its yard, and the olive tree in Anglisides village.

Distance (km) : Larnaca: 22 Limassol : 45 Nicosia : 46 Agia Napa : 63
Protaras : 69 Platres : 91 Paphos : 113 Polis : 148

Characteristics:   *(Jul - Aug)*

SALT LAKE – KAMARES AQUEDUCT WALKING ROUTE

(Map 5 – page 76, 13)

This walk connects two (or three in its longest version) of Larnaca's prime attractions: the imposing well preserved 17th century Kamares/ Bekir Pasha aqueduct, the main Larnaca salt lake and the 18th century Hala Sultan Tekke mosque. The proximity to Larnaca airport adds the possibility to spot and photograph airplanes during takeoff and landing. In its shortest version this is a four km long linear walk going from Kamares aqueduct clockwise around the salt lake. Higher vegetation is primarily made up of acacia trees and reeds and initially the route passes by a stream. For some distance there is a park to the east of the walking route. There are stretches where the walking route has trees on both sides and other where it offers unobstructed views towards the lake. The view towards the lake changes dramatically as the seasons change. The Tekke mosque behind the lake offers an Arabian oasis-like view in late autumn, winter and spring, with thousands of flamingos and other water birds living (or passing by) here. During most of summer the lake is nearly completely dry, alien and hostile. There are two birdwatching towers near the walking route.

The walk can be composed as a circular 13 km long route, with stretches on the pavement of a paved main road between Larnaca and the airport, as well as on the dirt road from the Tekke to the Aqueduct. There is another small park to the west of the lake as well as extensive fields (many walkers may find the north west stretch unattractive) towards the north. It is rather easy to lose the route, in which case one would need to backtrack, maybe a couple of kilometers. One could do part of the circular walking route (e.g. from Kamares aqueduct to Tekke mosque) and choose to use public transportation to return to the start of the walking route.

Distance (km) : Larnaca: 0 Agia Napa : 41 Nicosia : 44 Protaras : 47 Limassol : 66
Platres : 106 Paphos :134 Polis : 169

PERVOLIA COAST – ALAMINOS BEACH WALKING ROUTE

(Map 6 – page 77, 14)

This is a 13 km long easy route from the outskirts of Pervolia village on the coast, up to Alaminos beach towards the west (the beach is about 22 km from Larnaca). The first half of the walk is on flat, low elevation land, very close to sea level. This part of the coast is lately getting (more) developed. The route passes through Mazotos coast (the two main Mazotos 'beaches' and other coves along the coast). To the west of the beaches the route is more appealing, along higher elevation (up to ten meters high) on the coast, and a more dramatic, ragged and less developed coastline. There are fields along the whole way.

The wider area has good cultural attractions including two watermills (near the Agios Theodoros coast and in Alaminos village), the peculiar Koulas medieval watchtower in Alaminos and Pyrgos tis Rigenas watchtower on the Pervolia coast, and Panagia Aggeloktisti church in Kiti. The UNESCO World heritage Neolithic site of Choirokoitia is quite near as well. The hard to find Kato Drys medieval bridge is in a remote valley close to Choirokoitia and suitable for more adventurous explorers.

Distance (km) : Larnaca: 12 Limassol : 45 Nicosia : 46 Agia Napa : 53 Protaras :58 Platres : 91 Paphos : 113 Polis : 148

VOROKLINI LAKE

(Map 4 – page 75, 2)

This is a marsh about five km to the east of the town of Larnaca, between the village of Voroklini (also called 'Oroklini') and the tourist area of Dekeleia bay. Voroklini lake is very important for a number of bird species on the island and a great birdwatching place. A total of about 200 bird species have been recorded at the lake. Until recently it was degrading because of human intervention. Fortunately from 2012 significant efforts are carried out to reverse the situation and manage the lake sustainably. Usually an area of about three hectares has water (during most years even this dries out in summer) but sometimes the lake has water in an area of about 30 hectares. The Blue Flag Voroklini beach is less than two km south east of the lake. The peculiar Profitis Elias chapel on the hills north west of Voroklini village and a nearby picnic area with panoramic views of the wetland and the coast are about three km from the lake. Agios Antonios church in Kellia village dating back to the 9th century AD is about six km to the north west of the lake.

Distance (km): Larnaca: 5 Agia Napa : 38 Protaras : 44 Nicosia : 46
Limassol : 71 Platres : 111 Paphos : 140 Polis : 175

LARNACA SALT LAKES

(Map 5 – page 76, 3)

They constitute a system of wetlands adjacent to the town of Larnaca and its airport. Together they have a surface area of about five square km. Until the early 80s, every summer, when the main lake was completely dry, salt was collected and carried on donkeys for processing. The lake is inhabited by a different krill than the one in Akrotiri salt lake. It has different salinity as it hardly receives water from rivers. The salt lakes are great birdwatching spots. Thousands of flamingos and a plethora of other bird species visit it (the system) to escape the cold and spend the winter here. The birdwatchers' tower at the nearby sewage works pools offers excellent year round (less so in summer) birdwatching possibilities. As in the case of the Akrotiri salt lake, it is one of the wetlands under the Ramsar Convention (www.ramsar.org). There is a picnic area in the adjacent forest and the presence of the nearby Hala Sultan Tekke Mosque gives the lake an Arabic, oasis-like aura. There are a couple of birdwatching towers around the main lake. It is possible to walk all around it (the 'Salt lake – Kamares aqueduct' walking route). A visit to the Mosque and the Aqueduct is recommended.

Distance (km) : Larnaca: 1 Agia Napa : 42 Nicosia : 45 Protaras : 48 Limassol : 67 Platres : 107 Paphos : 135 Polis : 170

LARNACA SEWAGE WORKS

(Map 5 – page 76, 4)

They are situated only a few hundred meters south east of the Larnaca airport and about twelve km from Larnaca. Access to the complex is from a not so good, short dirt road. It is no more than 250 meters to the coastal paved road. The complex is made of two pools and constitutes a very important birdwatching spot for the area. Access is not allowed inside the fenced pools, but one can use the birdwatchers' tower next to the pools. There is high density of birds and of bird species (not so much in summer though).

There are many natural and cultural attractions in the area. A trip here can be combined with a swim in the beach nearby or a visit to the Larnaca salt lakes (also to Hala Sultan Tekke Mosque and maybe to the imposing Kamares aqueduct), to Pyrgos tis Rigenas medieval watchtower on Pervolia coast, to Panagia Aggeloktisti church in Kiti village and the ancient Mastic trees in its yard.

Distance (km) : Larnaca: 12 Agia Napa : 53 Nicosia : 56 Protaras : 59
Limassol : 78 Platres : 118 Paphos : 146 Polis : 171

KITI DAM

(Map 6 – page 77, 5)

The dam is about three km north of Kiti village and eight km from Larnaca. It was constructed in 1964 on the river Tremithos, (the smaller Lympia dam was constructed upstream in 1977) has a capacity of 1.6 million cubic meters and covers an area of about twelve hectares. It is a birdwatching spot (- provided there is water in the lake - though not as interesting as the nearby salt lakes). About 200 m south of the dam one finds (frescoed) Agios Georgios Arperas chapel, built in the 18th century. The dam is actually closer to Tersefanou village (two km) and the chapel is under the jurisdiction of the Tersefanou clergy. It is possible (or likely) that the lake virtually dries out from late spring until late autumn.

Distance (km) : Larnaca: 8 Nicosia : 48 Agia Napa : 49 Protaras : 55 Limassol : 70 Platres : 110 Paphos : 138 Polis : 173

DIPOTAMOS DAM

(Map 6 – page 77, ❻)

The dam can be accessed either through Skarinou village or through the village of Kato Lefkara. It is about 30 km west of Larnaca. It was built in 1985 on the river Pentaschoinos at an altitude of about 200 meters and has a capacity of 15.5 million cubic meters. The fork shaped manmade lake has a surface area of about 50 hectares. Fish in the lake include carp, mosquito fish, roach, tench, pikeperch, bass and catfish.

There are many natural and cultural attractions near Dipotamos dam. These include many picturesque villages like Kato Lefkara, Pano Lefkara and Kato Drys and very old churches (in Pano Lefkara there are at least two, including Leivadiotissa, which is found in the company of many ancient olive trees). There is an Environmental information Center of the wider area in Skarinou. UNESCO World Heritage Choirokoitia Neolithic site is found a few km away. Lefkara dam is also very near, as well as the monasteries of Stavrovouni near Kornos and Agios Minas near Vavla and the medieval bridge near Kato Drys.

Distance (km) : Larnaca: 30 Nicosia : 43 Limassol : 44 Agia Napa : 71
Protaras : 77 Platres : 85 Paphos : 112 Polis : 147

MASTIC TREES IN KITI

(Map 6 – page 77, 5)

These are four huge mastic trees that "fill" the yard of ancient eleventh century Panagia Aggeloktisti church in the center of Kiti village. The sheer size of these trees is amazing. The church is a major religious and cultural attraction near Larnaca (an ancient mosaic inside the church depicting standing Virgin Mary holding young Christ is of particular importance). There was a bridge in medieval times in Kiti but now only ruins of it remain.

Other significant attractions in the area besides the ancient church include the (frescoed) Agios Georgios Arperas chapel and Kiti dam, Pyrgos tis Rigenas medieval watchtower on Pervolia coast, Larnaca salt lakes, the Hala Sultan Tekke Mosque and the 700 years old olive tree in Anglisides village.

Distance (km) : Larnaca: 5 Nicosia : 46 Agia Napa : 46 Protaras : 52 Limassol : 67 Platres : 107 Paphos : 155 Polis : 190

OLIVE TREE IN ANGLISIDES

(Map 6 – page 77, 6)

The tree is found on the south side of the old Limassol – Larnaca road. It can be accessed on a secondary paved road just before Anglisides village (coming from Larnaca). Look for the sign for the tree and ask the locals if you have trouble finding it. This olive tree (Olea europea) is 700 years old, has a height of six meters and a trunk perimeter of almost 10.5 meters.

For those who want to explore the area, Alaminos (with its peculiar medieval watchtower called 'Koulas' and a nearby watermill) is less than ten km away and Kiti (with 11th century Panagia Aggeloktisti church, the mastic trees and Kiti dam, and nearby Pyrgos tis Rigenas medieval watchtower by Pervolia coast) is about 15 km away.

Distance (km) : Larnaca: 16 Limassol : 50 Agia Napa : 55 Nicosia : 58
Protaras : 61 Platres : 90 Paphos : 118 Polis : 153

KATO DRYS MEDIEVAL BRIDGE (Map 6 – page 77)

WATERMILL NEAR ALAMINOS (Map 6 – page 77)

WATERMILL NEAR AGIOS THEODOROS (Map 6 – page 77)

PYLA TOWER (Map 4 – page 7

LARNACA CASTLE

(Map 5 – page 76)

PYRGOS TIS RIGENAS WATCHTOWER

(Map 5 – page 76)

KOULAS WATCHTOWER (Map 6 – page 77)

KAMARES AQUEDUCT (Map 5 – page 76)

PROFITIS ELIAS CHAPEL (Map 4 – page 75)

AGIOS ANTONIOS CHURCH (Map 4 – page 75)

SAINT LAZARUS CHURCH (Map 5 – page 76)

PANAGIA AGGELOKTISTI CHURCH (Map 6 – page 77)

STAVROVOUNI MONASTERY (Map 6 – page 77)

PANAGIA LEIVADIOTISSA CHAPEL (Map 6 – page 77)

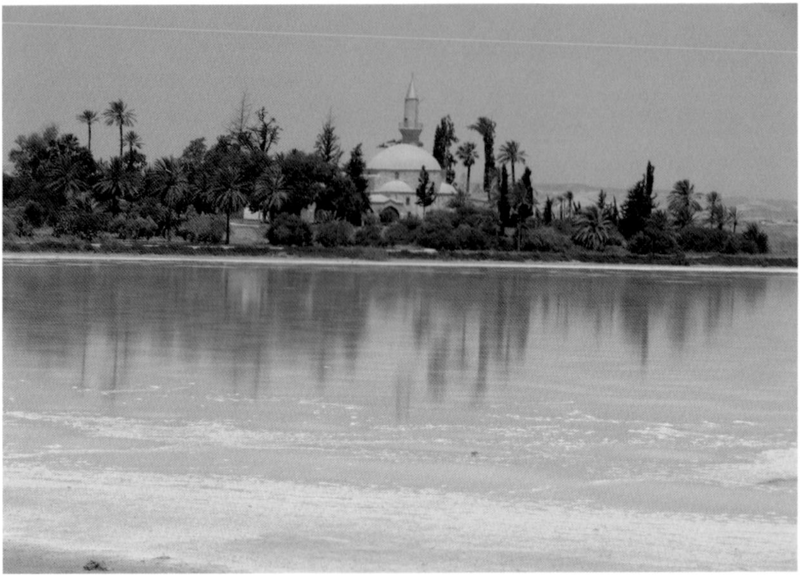

HALA SULTAN TEKKE (Map 5 – page 76)

CHOIROKITIA NEOLITHIC SETTLEMENT (Map 6 – page 77)

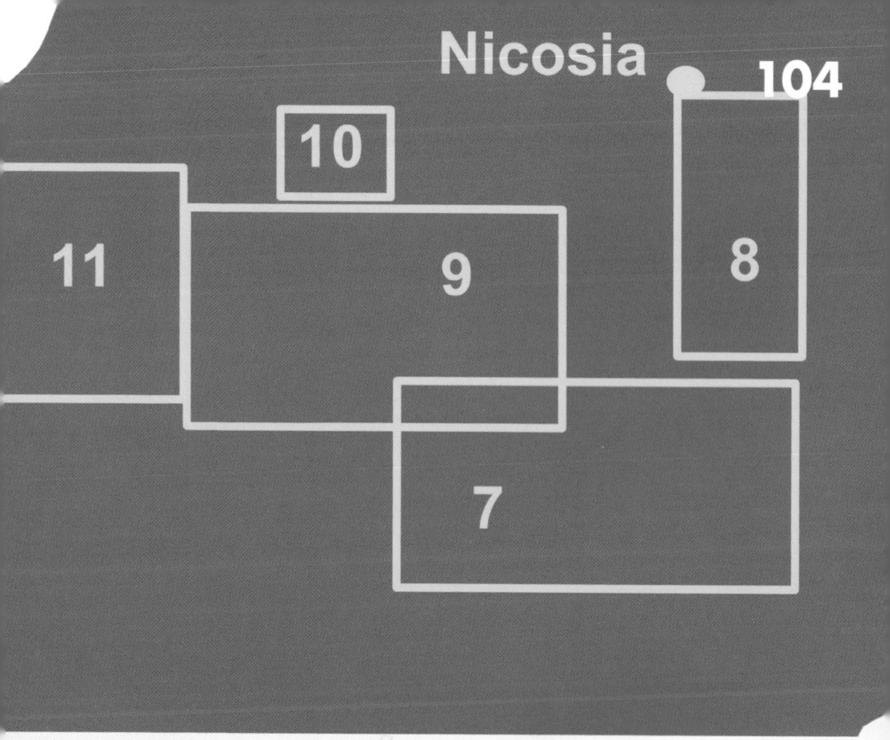

NICOSIA

Divided Walled Nicosia is one of the jewels of Cyprus cultural heritage and an excellent destination for those interested in exploring on foot for a few hours. It is a vibrant part of the divided bicommunal city (a surreal experience in itself) that has a plethora of medieval attractions, including splendid walls and gates, Gothic churches and palaces, old Orthodox churches, mosques, an aqueduct, khans, hammams, renovated quarters and more. It is found in the vast flat Mesaoria plain, rather far from quality beaches. The countryside is scattered with watermills (many of them restored). Nearby there are medieval estates (Agios Sozomenos – Potamia), picturesque villages such as Fikardou and historic monasteries like Machairas. Nicosia is found between two mountain ranges (which are very different geologically and morphologically) and can be a good base to explore (two of the three) medieval castles in Pentadactylos mountains and a few of the UNESCO World Heritage Troodos painted churches. The mountains offer quality walking routes (some of which are quite tough). Birdwatchers and anglers can choose from a selection of wetlands relatively close to Nicosia.

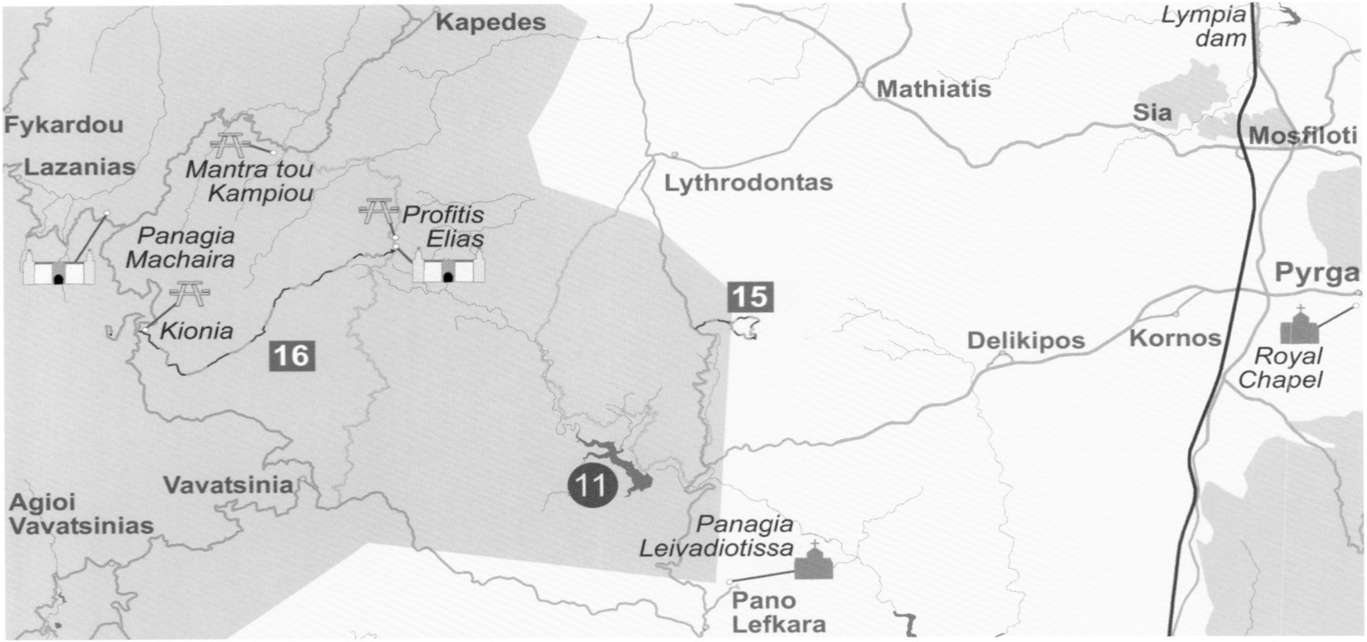

WALKING ROUTES	
15	Lefkothea
16	Kionia picnic area – Profitis Elias church

WETLANDS	
11	Lefkara dam

CHAPELS AND MONASTERIES
Royal Chapel
Panagia Leivadiotissa
Profitis Elias
Panagia Machaira

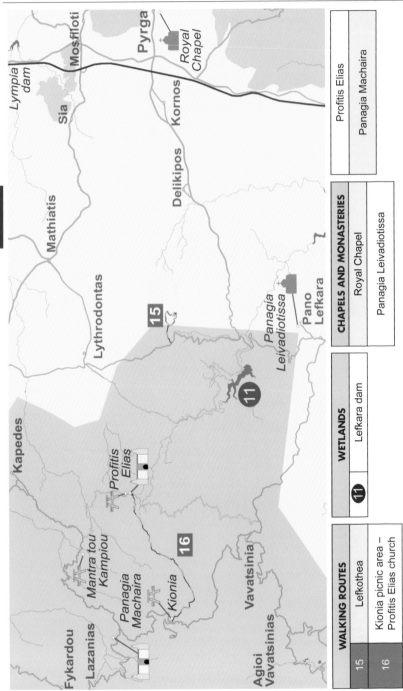

WETLANDS	
7	Athalassa dam

ANCIENT TREES	
7	Cypress tree in Nisou

WATERMILLS	
3	Dali

CHAPELS AND MONASTERIES
Agios Demetrianos
Agioi Apostoloi

OTHER CULTURAL ATTRACTIONS
Agios Sozomenos
Idalion

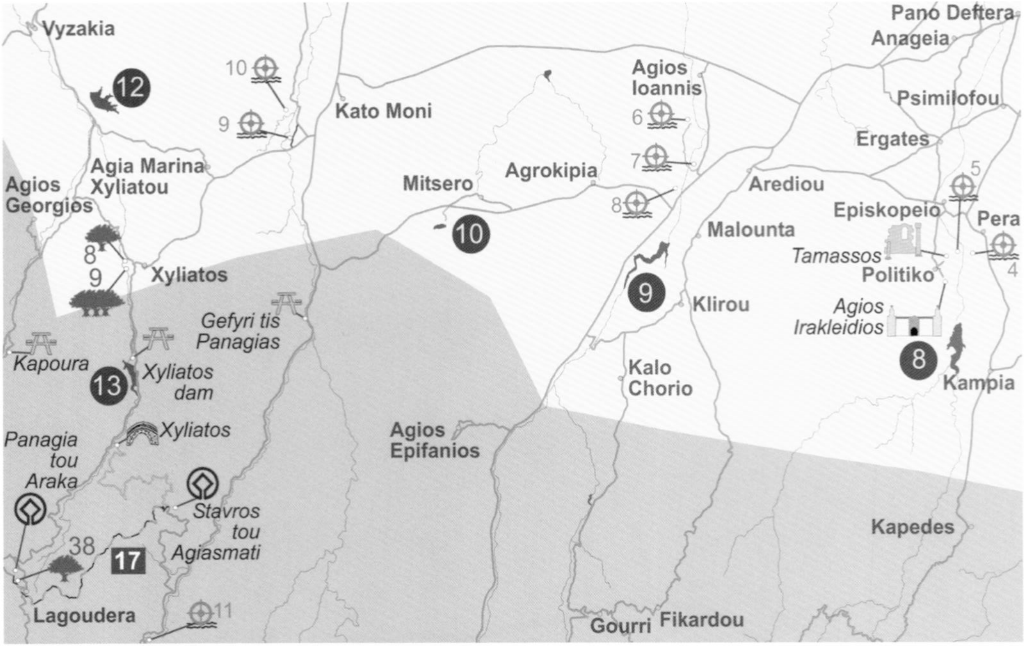

WALKING ROUTES	
17	Stavros tou Agiasmati church - Panagia tou Araka church

WETLANDS	
8	Tamassos dam
9	Klirou dam
10	Mitsero red lake
12	Vyzakia dam
13	Xyliatos dam

ANCIENT TREES	
8	Olive tree in Xyliatos
9	Olives in Xyliatos
38	Oak in Lagoudera

MEDIEVAL BRIDGES
Xyliatos

WATERMILLS	
4, 5	Pera
6, 7, 8	Agios Ioannis
9, 10	Kato Moni
11	Platanistasa

UNESCO WORLD HERITAGE TROODOS PAINTED CHURCHES
Savros tou Agiasmati
Panagia tou Araka

CHAPELS AND MONASTERIES
Agios Irakleidios

OTHER CULTURAL ATTRACTIONS
Tamassos

WATERMILLS	
12, 13	Akaki
14	Orounta

CHAPELS AND MONASTERIES
Apostles Varnavas and Ilarionas
Agios Nicolaos monastery

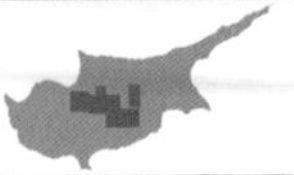

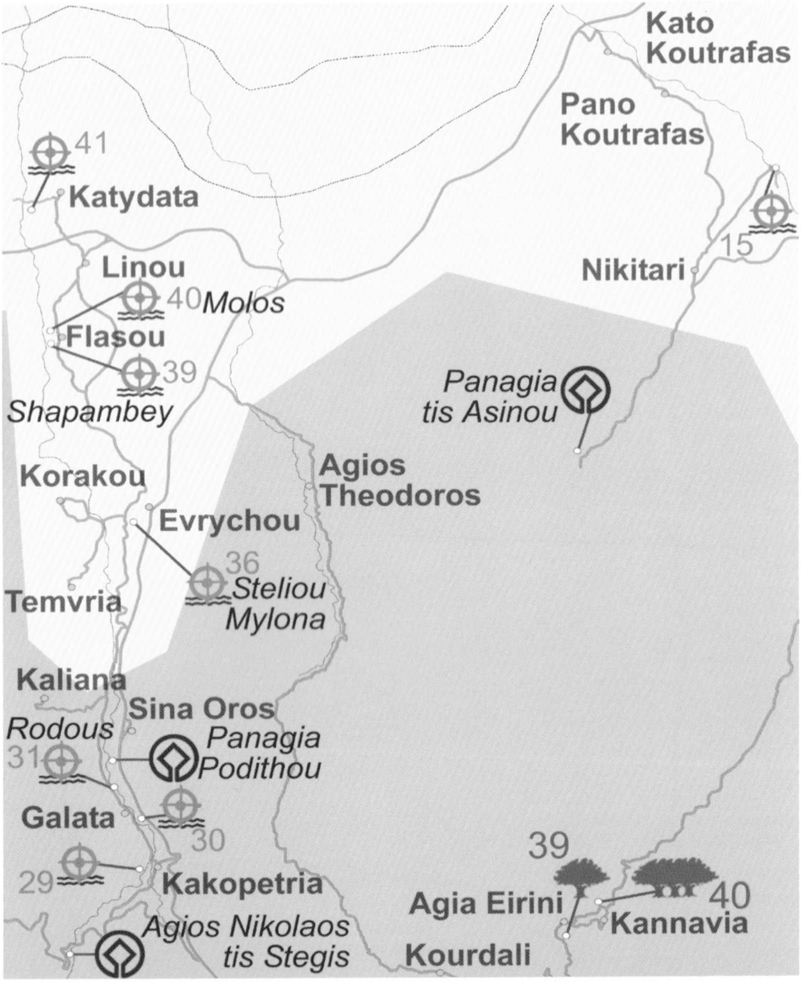

ANCIENT TREES	
39	Cypress in Agia Eirini
40	2 Oaks, 1 Cypress in Kannavia

WATERMILLS	
15	Pano Koutrafas
41	Katydata
40	Flasou
39	Flasou
36	Evrychou
31	Galata
30	Galata
29	Kakopetria

UNESCO WORLD HERITAGE TROODOS PAINTED CHURCHES
Panagia tis Asinou
Panagia Podithou
Agios Nicolaos tis Stegis

LEFKOTHEA WALKING ROUTE

(Map 7 – page 105, 15)

This is an official nature walking trail nearly four km to the south of the village of Lythrodontas (and 28 km south of Nicosia), that can be accessed on the good quality dirt road that connects Lythrodontas village and Lefkara village. According to the sign, the walking trail is 2.5 km long, whereas according to the booklet of the Cyprus Tourism Organisation this is a 1.3 km linear walking trail (which sounds right to me). The trail ascends nearly 150 m to the 670 m high peak called "Aetomoutti" meaning "Eagle's nose" in the Greek Cypriot dialect. Goat herds obviously pass by here, as is evident from goat droppings, and walkers may see samples of the local flora, including pine, wild olive, hawthorn, asphodel, lavender, and other wild plants and flowers. From the peak one enjoys panoramic views of the whole area. Care is needed during the descent as it is rather easy to lose the walking trail. One can combine the walk well with a visit to the excellent Lefkara dam (about seven km south of Lefkothea walking trail), Pano Lefkara (a well preserved stone-built village offering many attractions including a few very old churches and ancient trees – olives and almonds), Kato Lefkara and Lythrodontas villages (all three are picturesque villages), a visit to the historic Machairas monastery or to Kionia peak picnic site. From the picnic site one can try the tough 'Kionia picnic site – Profitis Ilias church' linear seven km long walking route.

Distance (km) : Nicosia : 28 Larnaca: 37 Limassol : 52 Agia Napa : 78
Protaras : 84 Platres : 92 Paphos : 120 Polis : 155

KIONIA PICNIC AREA-PROFITIS ELIAS CHURCH WALKING ROUTE

(Map 7 – page 105, 16)

This linear walking route starts at the Kionia (or 'Djionia' in the Greek Cypriot dialect) picnic site (which is about 35 km south west of Nicosia and can be reached on easily marked paved road from Nicosia, Machairas monastery, Vavatsinia and Kapedes village). The walking route till Profitis Ilias monastery is seven km long and has a considerable elevation variation (the start is at 1,350 m and the end at 700 m), so it can be quite demanding for those that are not very fit. It is one of the most interesting walking routes near Nicosia and among the most composite on the island combining a part at high elevation next to a stream and many rock formations and cliffs, with a part deep inside a forest. The walking route can be loosely divided into two parts; the first higher altitude three-km part, which is the one that I recommend, and the second lower altitude four km part which I would recommend only to the fit adventurers among us. The first part initially passes by a very rocky environment, next to a stream (that dries relatively early in the season) and then it enters the forest. The vegetation is dominated by the endemic golden oak and pines, while one can also see a lot of strawberry trees, hawthorn, olives, rock rose, milk-vetch and asphodels and possibly orchids. After three km, the walking route is met by a well marked dirt road. One may rest on the benches before returning (or continuing). The four km second part is in an environment with poorer vegetation, dominated by rock rose and French lavender. There are good views of the Mesaoria plain. At points it is possible to see Lefkara dam from a distance. The monastery looks uninhabited (but is used as a camping ground in summer) and there is a picnic area. There is a spring there, which we were advised not to use.

It could make sense to combine the walk with a visit to the historic 7th century Machairas monastery (before the walk – about ten km away) and a meal after the walk at a picturesque nearby village (e.g. Fikardou or Lythrodontas).

Distance (km): Nicosia : 34 Platres : 60 Larnaca: 61 Limassol : 101
Agia Napa : 102 Protaras : 108 Paphos : 120 Polis : 154

STAVROS TOU AGIASMATI CHURCH-PANAGIA TOU ARAKA CHURCH WALKING ROUTE

(Map 9 – page 107, 17)

This is a tough (elevation range of 300 m) 7.5 km long linear walking route between two of the UNESCO World Heritage Troodos painted churches. The start (or finish) of the walking route at the church of Stavros tou Agiasmati is about 45 km from Nicosia, while the church of Panagia tou Araka is 54 km from Nicosia. Walkers can reach Stavros tou Agiasmati on a paved road, turning west on the Orounta - Platanistasa road. The beautiful churches are major attractions of the route (but walkers need to ask in Platanistasa village if they want to enter Stavros tou Agiasmati church). The route passes by almond orchards, vineyards, and a forested area mainly with pine trees and the endemic golden oak. There are steep ascents and descents which make the exercise quite tiring. Good walking shoes are a must while a walking stick is recommended for the route. At various places one needs to be very careful as the narrow walking route passes by steep slopes. There are glorious views towards Morphou plain (northwest) and the western Pentadactylos (Keryneia) range and Mesaoria plain (northeast), up to Kionia peak in the east, the villages of Alona and Platanistasa, the village of Lagoudera in the south (west) and Madari peak. Walkers can see rock formations known as Tishia tis Madaris (literally "walls of Madari" in the Greek Cypriot dialect), as well as Xyliatos dam and further north, Vyzakia dam. Rock rose dominates and in March walkers may see orchids in blossom. The last part of the walking route traverses the village of Lagoudera before it reaches Panagia tou Araka church (where there's also an ancient huge oak tree). It is possible to make this a circular 20 – km long walking route, returning via the paved road towards Xyliatos dam and the dirt road to Stavros tou Agiasmati church. On the way one may be able to discover the 'elusive' Venetian medieval bridge, very close to the paved road, near the Xyliatos manmade lake (on the east side of the road, virtually under a modern bridge on the dirt road). There are many attractions in the area, including the beautiful Xyliatos dam, watermills, ancient trees and quality walking routes.

Distance (km): Nicosia : 45 Platres : 46 Limassol : 86 Larnaca: 89 Paphos : 106
Polis : 106 Agia Napa : 125 Protaras : 131

ATHALASSA DAM

(Map 8 – page 106, 7)

The dam is about two km south of Nicosia. It was built in 1962 and has a capacity of 0.8 million cubic meters (and a surface area of about four square km). It is an attractive birdwatchers' spot so close to the capital. Many kinds of birds including egrets and kingfishers may be spotted here. There is a good birdwatchers tower on the manmade lake (next to the paved road, 100 meters from the dam). The lake was devastated in 2005, when as a result of many bird deaths, it was dried completely and cleaned in a way that a lot of the flora was removed. It will take (more) years for the ecosystem to rebound. Nevertheless, it is well worth a visit. It is found inside the Athalassa park (total park area of almost ten square kilometers), with many possibilities for easy walking, biking, nature study (e.g. owls, hares and foxes live there) and photography. There are picnic facilities in the park (including a children's playground) and a few entrances. It is easily accessible through the paved road linking the Nicosia suburb of Aglantzia to the village of Geri and from that road to the new Nicosia General Hospital.

There are cultural and natural attractions about ten km south towards the village of Dali (also in Pera, Agios Sozomenos and Potamia).

Distance (km): Nicosia : 2 Larnaca: 42 Agia Napa : 78 Limassol : 80
Protaras : 84 Platres : 88 Paphos : 148 Polis : 183

TAMASSOS DAM

(Map 9 – page 107, 8)

Tamassos dam is almost 15 km south west of Nicosia and can be accessed on the road from Pera village to Kampia village. It was built in 2002 on the Pediaios river at an altitude of about 400 meters and has a capacity of 2.8 million cubic meters and a surface area of nearly 20 hectares. The shape is relatively regular and its perimeter is about four km long. Fish in the manmade lake include carp, mosquito fish, roach, pumpkinseed sunfish and bass. There are birdwatching possibilities around the lake, and walking routes (dirt roads), especially on the west bank of the lake.

There are picturesque villages in the vicinity (like Pera – less than two km away, towards the north) as well as a couple of watermills a few hundred meters west of Pera village, that are easy to find. Agios Irakleidios monastery and the ancient ruins at Tamassos are less than four km away (in the direction of the watermills).

Distance (km) : Nicosia : 15 Larnaca: 45 Platres : 76 Limassol : 83 Agia Napa : 86 Protaras : 92 Polis : 136 Paphos : 136

KLIROU DAM

(Map 9 – page 107 , 9)

Klirou dam, found in farmland, is about 24 km south west of Nicosia and can be accessed on the road from Nicosia to Palaichori village. It was built in 2010 on the Akaki (Serrachis) river at an altitude of about 400 meters and has a capacity of two million cubic meters. The man-made lake has a somewhat fork-like shape (with one tooth being significantly longer), a surface area of about 15 hectares and a perimeter of around five km. There are birdwatching and angling possibilities in the lake, as it hosts rainbow trout, carp, mosquito fish, bleak and pumpkinseed sunfish. There is no convenient walking route around the manmade lake.

Within a distance of just four kilometers downstream by the Serrachis river (north of the dam), there are three watermills (at a good condition). There are picturesque villages in the vicinity (e.g. Fikardou). Ais Ambelis, one of the better local wineries is just two km further south on the road from Nicosia to Palaichori. Looking south from the dam one enjoys views of the Machairas forest in the Troodos mountains (the forest edge is about four km away from the dam).

Distance (km) : Nicosia : 24 Larnaca: 54 Platres : 67 Limassol : 83
Agia Napa : 95 Protaras : 101 Polis : 127 Paphos : 127

MITSERO RED LAKE

(Map 9 – page 107 , 10)

This is a rather out of place pool that is a leftover from mining operations in the area. It is about 20 km from Nicosia, and can be accessed on a dirt road off the paved road from Agrokipia village past Mitsero village (the pool is just a km south west of Mitsero village), on the left side of the road (in other words towards Troodos in the south). The surface area of the pool is about two hectares. One could walk perimetrically high above the pool partly on dirt roads and partly on unmarked ground for a route that is roughly two km long. Minerals turn the lake colour red and we have been told that the water kills birds that dive for a drink. Maybe this is a monument of man's adverse effect on nature. The red lake makes a good destination for photo safaris.

Within a radius of nine km from the pool, on two different streams there are five relatively easily accessible watermills in good condition. Two (manmade) fresh water wetlands and the UNESCO World Heritage chapel of Stavros tou Agiasmati are marginally further away.

Distance (km) : Nicosia : 20 Platres : 62 Larnaca: 64 Agia Napa : 100
Limassol : 102 Protaras : 106 Polis : 122 Paphos : 122

LEFKARA DAM

(Map 7 – page 105 , 11)

It is almost at an equal distance from Nicosia, Limassol and Larnaca (about 35 km from each of the cities). It can be accessed on a dirt road that connects to the 'Pano Lefkara village to Lythrodontas and Kornos villages' paved road. The dam was built in 1973 on the Pentaschoinos river at an altitude of about 400 meters and has capacity of 13.9 million cubic meters and a surface area of about 40 hectares. Fish in the lake include carp, roach, bass, rainbow trout, bleak, rapfen, pikeperch and silver bream. Because of its shape, location and morphology around it, it may be one of the most beautiful manmade lakes on the island. The perimeter of the lake is about seven km long, however there exists no perimetric walking route around the lake. There is a dirt road on the north side of the lake connecting the dam to Lythrodontas village and Kionia peak. One could walk on the dirt road next to and high above the lake for about five km (in this distance the road ascends by about one hundred meters). In the near future when hopefully using ecological watercrafts (like kayaks) in the lake would be allowed, a route inside the lake, along its perimeter could make a very nice expedition.

Combining an excursion to Lefkara dam with exploration of nearby picturesque villages like Pano Lefkara, Kato Lefkara and Kato Drys is highly recommended.

Distance (km) : Nicosia : 32 Larnaca: 42 Limassol : 48 Agia Napa : 83
Platres : 88 Protaras : 89 Paphos : 116 Polis : 151

VYZAKIA DAM

(Map 9 – page 107 , 12)

Vyzakia dam is about 40 km from Nicosia and can be accessed from the road linking Vyzakia village to Agios Georgios village. It was built in 1994 at an altitude of almost 350 meters and has capacity of 1.7 million cubic meters, a relatively elliptical shape and a surface area of about 15 hectares. Fishing is not allowed. It is found in a relatively flat area and one can easily compose a circular walking route partly on dirt roads and partly on unmarked ground with a length of two to three km (and an elevation range of 30-40 meters).

The breathtaking Panagia tis Asinou church (one of the ten UNESCO World Heritage Troodos painted churches) is just ten km away (south west of Nikitari). On the Elaia river (that runs close to the dam), at the nearby village of Vyzakia one may see parts of an old watermill (there's one in a good condition less than ten km away from the dam, near the village of Pano Koutrafas). More watermills can be found east of Vyzakia on the Elaia river (upstream) and the Peristerona river, (as well as further east, on Akaki river). In the vicinity one can also find Agios Nicolaos monastery in Orounta and the renovated Apostle Varnavas and Ilarionas church in Peristerona (which together with the adjacent mosque constitute a symbol of peaceful bicommunal coexistence on the island). In Akaki village there are also ruins of a medieval tower.

Distance (km) : Nicosia : 40 Platres : 50 Larnaca: 84 Limassol : 90 Paphos : 110
Polis :110 Agia Napa : 120 Protaras : 126

XYLIATOS DAM

(Map 9 – page 107, ⓭)

The dam is found some 45 km from Nicosia, and between the villages of Xyliatos and Lagoudera It was constructed in 1982 on the river of Lagoudera (becoming Elaia river downstream) and has a capacity of 1.43 million cubic meters and a surface area of around ten hectares. It is usually more than 50% full and has an elongated triangular shape (with a perimeter of nearly three km). The Xyliatos dam lake in the center of the forest creates an alpine setting, very atypical of Cyprus. There is a picnic area just downstream and a flat walking route around the perimeter of the lake. On the west bank the route has stretches on a walking trail and on a dirt road, while on the east bank the route is on the paved road. The walk usually takes 30-40 minutes to complete. On the walking route one may see among other plants, pine trees, myrtle and reed (Typha domingensis). The protected grass snake of Cyprus (Natrix natrix cypriaca) lives in the lake. Fish in the lake include carp, roach, bass, crayfish and mosquito fish.

There are some ancient olive trees a few km towards the north. One may be able to discover the 'hidden' Xyliatos medieval bridge just two km south of the manmade lake (next to the modern bridge on the dirt road that leads to UNESCO World heritage Troodos painted church of Stavros tou Agiasmati). Lagoudera village and UNESCO World Heritage Troodos painted church of Panagia tou Araka are seven km to the south of Xyliatos dam, while imposing Madari peak is a few more km further south. There are many ragged mountain peaks towards the south of the manmade lake and a few excellent walking routes.

Distance (km) : Nicosia : 45 Platres : 46 Limassol : 86 Larnaca: 89 Paphos : 106
Polis : 106 Agia Napa : 125 Protaras : 131

CYPRESS TREE IN NISOU

(Map 8 – page 106, 7)

The village of Nisou is about 18 km from Nicosia, 26 km from Larnaca and 64 km from Limassol. Though it is centrally located and easy to reach, very few people stop to see its ancient tree(s). The most impressive is a cypress tree (Cupressus sempervirens) known as 'the cypress of the Frank' and this is an indication of its age (from the time when the Franks/Latins were the rulers in Cyprus). It is one of the tallest trees on the island with a height of 28 meters and a trunk perimeter of over 4.5 meters. It is 500 years old and looks quite lively. It can be spotted north of the road (50 –100 meter further in), on the old Nicosia-Limassol highway. There is another ancient tree in Nisou, a plane tree (Platanus orientalis), but it is in a really bad state now.

There are charming attractions in the area including medieval ruins in Agios Sozomenos (ruins of a medieval royal mansion in Potamia), an ancient watermill next to frescoed 13th century Agios Demetrianos chapel, ruins of the ancient city state of Idalion, the frescoed Agioi Apostoloi chapel, small Lympia dam (six km south, surface area of four hectares), the frescoed medieval Royal Chapel at Pyrga (14 km south) and Panagia Stazousa chapel (7 km further south east on the Pyrga-Klavdia road).

Distance (km) : Nicosia : 18 Larnaca: 26 Limassol : 64 Agia Napa : 67
Protaras : 70 Platres : 104 Paphos : 132 Polis : 167

OLIVE TREE AND GROUP OF OLIVE TREES IN XYLIATOS

(Map 9 – page 107, 8, 9)

The ancient olive tree is described by the Forestry Department as the biggest olive tree on the island. It is found about three km north of the beautiful Xyliatos dam (and about 43 km southwest of Nicosia) and just to the west of Xyliatos village. This Olea europea tree is found in an olive orchard and it is easy to find provided one follows the signs. The tree is 700 years old, six meters high and its trunk has a perimeter of 13 meters. It is found in a group of ancient olive trees.

Other attractions in the area include the UNESCO World Heritage painted churches of Panagia tou Araka and of Stavros tou Agiasmati. Six km south of Stavros tou Agiasmati, by a side road there's a well preserved watermill.

Distance (km) : Nicosia : 43 Platres : 49 Larnaca: 86 Limassol : 89 Paphos : 109 Polis : 109 Agia Napa : 122 Protaras : 128

XYLIATOS MEDIEVAL BRIDGE (Map 9 – page 107)

WATERMILL NEAR DALI (Map 8 – page 106)

WATERMILL NEAR PERA (Map 9 – page 107)

ANOTHER WATERMILL NEAR PERA (Map 9 – page 107)

A WATERMILL NEAR AGIOS IOANNIS MALOUNTAS (Map 9 – page 107)

ANOTHER WATERMILL NEAR AGIOS IOANNIS MALOUNTAS (Map 9 – page 107)

A THIRD WATERMILL NEAR AGIOS IOANNIS MALOUNTAS (Map 9 – page 107)

A WATERMILL NEAR KATO MONI (Map 9 – page 107)

ANOTHER WATERMILL NEAR KATO MONI (Map 9 – page 107)

WATERMILL NEAR PLATANISTASA (Map 9 – page 107)

A WATERMILL INSIDE AKAKI (Map 10 – page 108)

WATERMILL NEAR AKAKI (Map 10 – page 108)

WATERMILL NEAR OROUNTA (Map 10 – page 108)

WATERMILL NEAR PANO KOUTRAFAS (Map 11 – page 109)

CHURCH OF TIMIOS STAVROS (HOLY CROSS) TOU AGIASMATI (Map 9 – page 107)

CHURCH OF PANAGIA (OUR LADY) TIS ASINOU (Map 11 – page 109)

AQUEDUCT IN WALLED NICOSIA (Map 40 – page 365)

ROYAL CHAPEL (Map 7 – page 105)

PROFITIS ELIAS MONASTERY (Map 7 – page 105)

PANAGIA MACHAIRA MONASTERY (Map 7 – page 105)

AGIOS DEMETRIANOS CHAPEL (Map 8 – page 106)

AGIOI APOSTOLOI CHAPEL (Map 8 – page 106)

AGIOS IRAKLEIDIOS MONASTERY (Map 9 – page 107)

APOSTLES VARNAVAS AND ILARIONAS CHURCH (Map 10 – page 108)

AGIOS NICOLAOS MONASTERY (Map 10 – page 108)

AGIOS SOZOMENOS DESERTED MEDIEVAL VILLAGE (Map 8 – page 106)

IDALION ANCIENT KINGDOM (Map 8 – page 106)

TAMASSOS ANCIENT KINGDOM (Map 9 – page 107)

LIMASSOL

The wider Limassol area has a large number of beaches. On the central part of the coastline they are very organised and have wave breakers, while further from the city most of them are less (or not at all) developed (e.g. Lady's mile beach, Paramali coast) and/or have rather wild scenery (Governor's beach, Pissouri beach, Latchi coast, etc). Akrotiri salt like is one of two Cyprus wetlands included in the Ramsar Convention. Together with the connected system of wetlands it is home to thousands of birds and many tens of bird species. Anglers have choices of a few manmade lakes (at least four) from Kalavasos dam in the east part of the district to the huge Kouris dam in the west. The north area was home to ancient oak forests and still hosts a few ancient trees (e.g. in Apesia, which is according to records the home of the oldest tree on the island). There are important cultural attractions dating from Neolithic times (Tenta), to classical times (Curium/Kourion and Amathus), and the medieval era (Kolossi castle, Limassol castle, and medieval bridges in Germasogeia and Akapnou). There are many picturesque villages near Limassol (e.g. Kalavasos, Akapnou and Lofou) and a number of preserved watermills (e.g. in Kantou and Paramytha) mostly downstream from manmade lakes. Commandaria region, where the famous sweet wine is produced, is found north of Limassol.

WETTLANDS	
14	Kalavasos dam
ANCIENT TREES	
10	Olive tree in Eptagoneia
MEDIEVAL BRIDGES	
	Akapnou
WATERMILLS	
16	Kalavasos
17	Kalavasos
OTHER CULTURAL ATTRACTIONS	
	Tenta

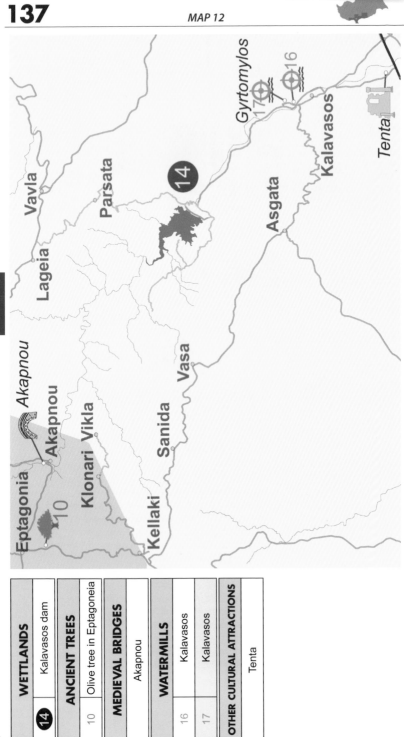

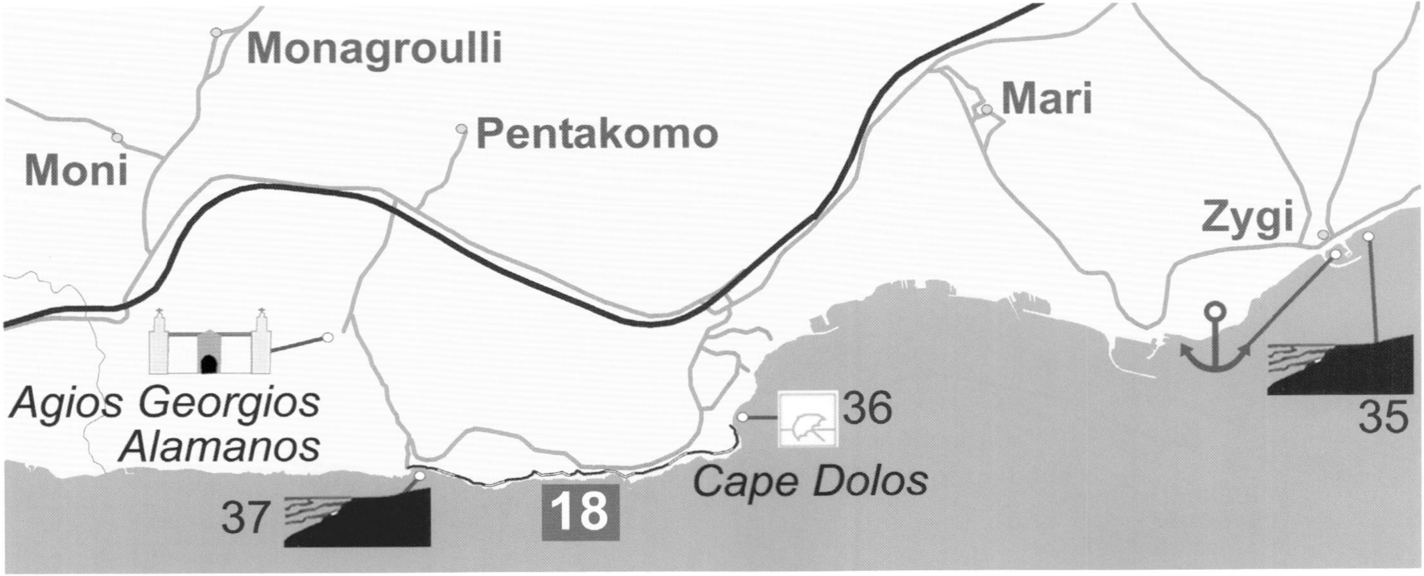

BEACHES/COASTS	
35	Zygi coast
36	Governor's beach
37	Latchi (Agios Georgios Alamanos)

WALKING ROUTES	
18	Governor's beach – Latchi coast

CHAPELS AND MONASTERIES
Agios Georgios Alamanos

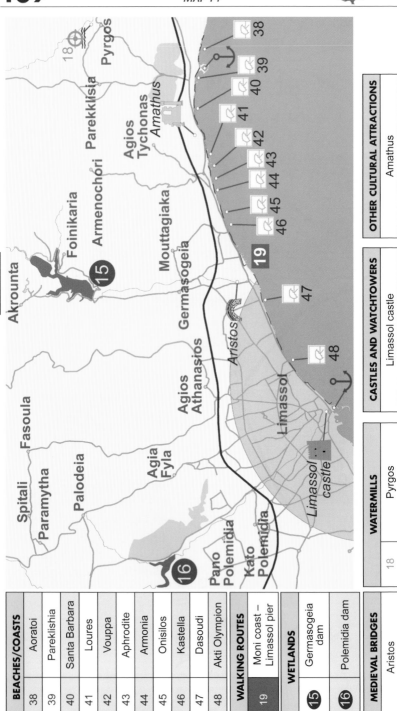

BEACHES/COASTS	
38	Aoratoi
39	Pareklishia
40	Santa Barbara
41	Loures
42	Vouppa
43	Aphrodite
44	Armonia
45	Onisilos
46	Kastella
47	Dasoudi
48	Akti Olympion

WALKING ROUTES	
19	Moni coast – Limassol pier

WETLANDS	
15	Germasogeia dam
16	Polemidia dam

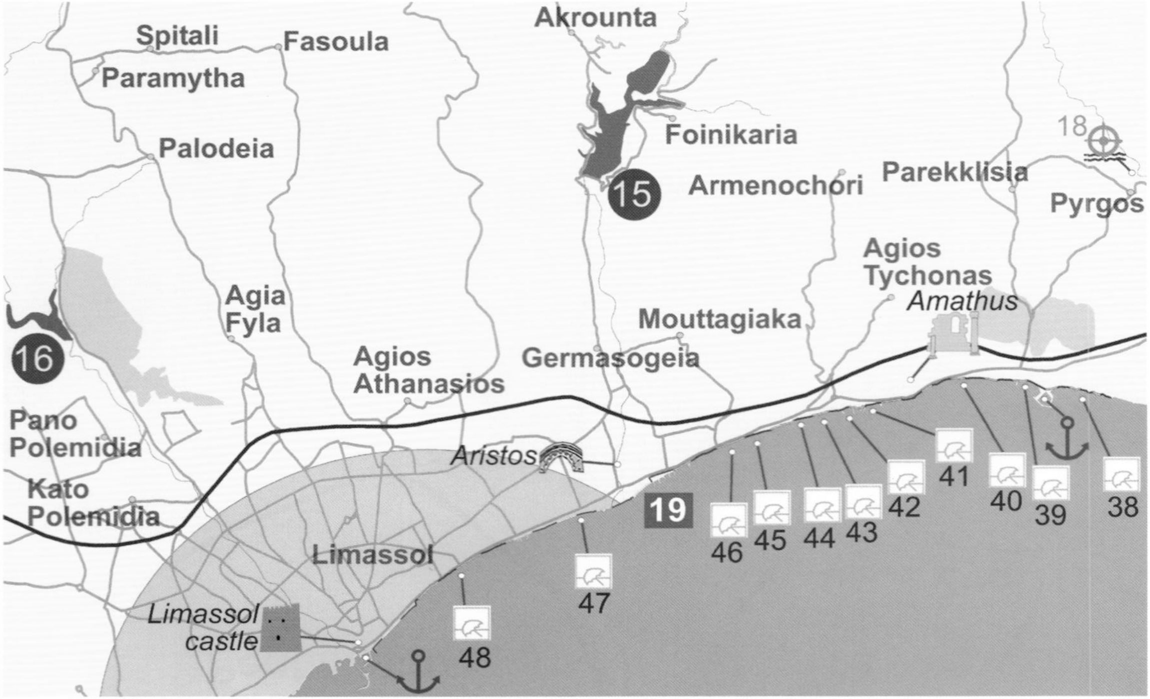

MEDIEVAL BRIDGES
Aristos

WATERMILLS	
18	Pyrgos

CASTLES AND WATCHTOWERS
Limassol castle

OTHER CULTURAL ATTRACTIONS
Amathus

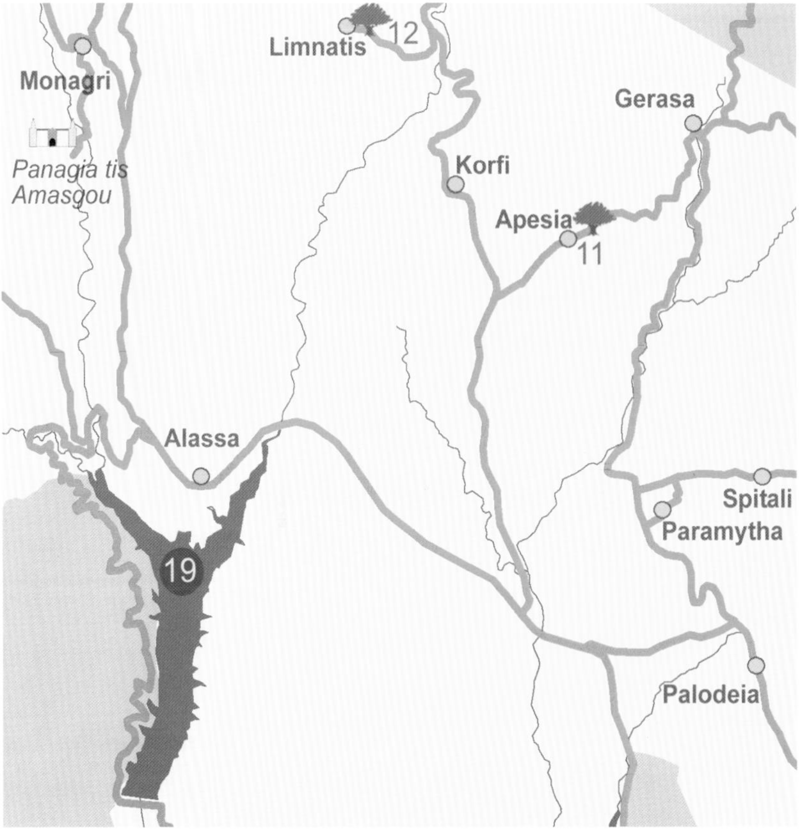

WETLANDS	
19	Kouris dam

ANCIENT TREES	
11	Mastic tree in Apesia
12	Mastic tree in Limnatis (died recently)

CHAPELS AND MONASTERIES
Panagia tis Amasgou

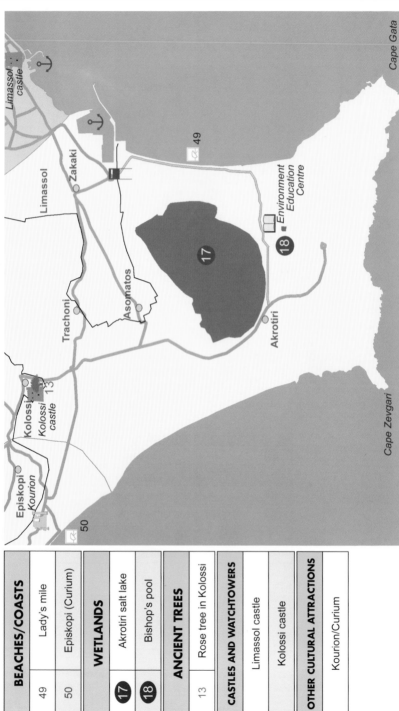

BEACHES/COASTS	
49	Lady's mile
50	Episkopi (Curium)

WETLANDS	
17	Akrotiri salt lake
18	Bishop's pool

ANCIENT TREES	
13	Rose tree in Kolossi

CASTLES AND WATCHTOWERS
Limassol castle
Kolossi castle

OTHER CULTURAL ATTRACTIONS
Kourion/Curium

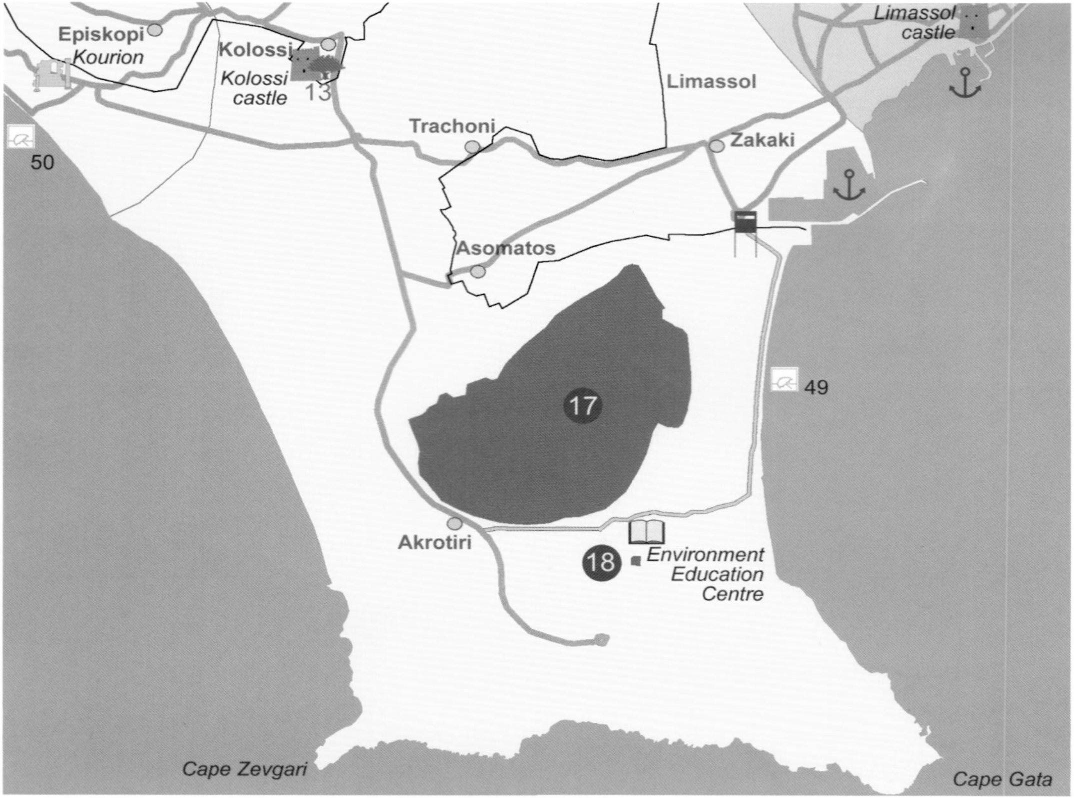

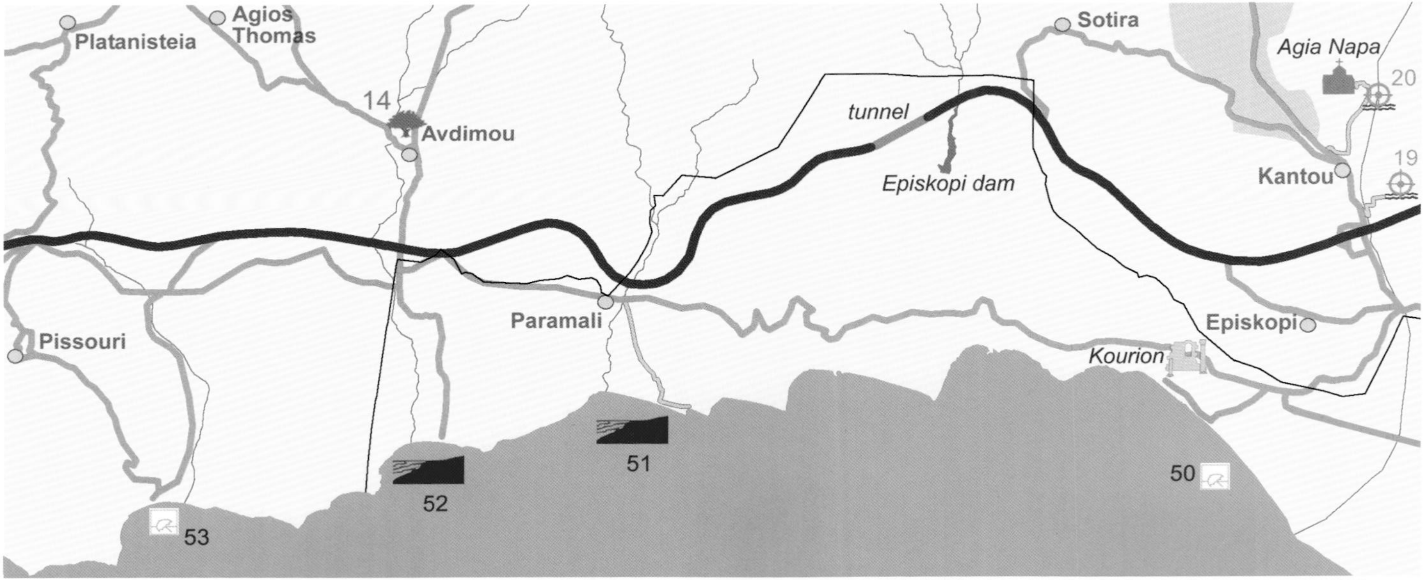

BEACHES/COASTS	
50	Episkopi/Curium
51	Paramali
52	Avdimou
53	Pissouri

ANCIENT TREES	
14	Avdimou olive

WATERMILLS	
19	Kantou
20	Kantou

CHAPELS AND MONASTERIES
Agia Napa

OTHER CULTURAL ATTRACTIONS
Kourion (Curium)

ZYGI COAST

(Map 13 – page 138, 35)

Zygi is some 24 km east of Limassol. I estimate the coast at about two km long. Next to it in the east is the coast of Maroni and Agios Theodoros village whereas to the west is the industrial area of Vasilikos. The coast surface was until recently mostly made of pebble but the construction of the fishing port and of many wave breakers to the east of the port caused the deposition of sand on the coast. There are even records of sea turtles nesting in the area now. The central point of the coast is the port and the many fishing tavernas (which get packed on Sundays) around it. There are accommodation options in this fishing village.

Maybe a stop at Zygi is a good ending to a visit to nearby Kalavasos attractions (Tenta Neolithic site, the watermills and manmade lake), especially if one wants to combine a cultural excursion with a stroll by the sea (or a swim in Zygi or Maroni coast). UNESCO World Heritage Choirokoitia Neolithic site is marginally further (north east) at a distance of ten km. Adventurers may be interested in discovering Kato Drys medieval bridge, which is just about six kilometers further north west of Choirokoitia. A visit to Zygi can also be a good 'gastronomical' destination for those into seafood, especially if they are staying in Zygi or in one of the nearby picturesque villages (e.g. in Psematismenos, Maroni or Tochni).

Distance (km): Limassol : 24 Larnaca: 37 Nicosia : 64 Agia Napa : 78
Protaras : 84 Paphos : 92 Polis : 127

Characteristics: -

GOVERNOR'S BEACH

(Map 13 – page 138, 36)

It is found about 16 km east of Limassol. This is a collection of coves, which together have a length of about 500 meters. The main beach has a length of almost 400 meters, it has been awarded the Blue flag eco-label (www.blueflag.org) and has handicap facilities. Kalymnos beach, a small adjacent 70 m long cove towards the east, has also been awarded the Blue flag eco-label. The beach surface is made up of dark fine sand and white rock. To the east of the beach(es) one can see the industrial complex of Vasilikos; the area is off limits. To the west, there is a lovely four km walking route to Latchi (Agios Georgios Alamanos) coast. Because of the shape of the coast (to the west) Governor's beach is relatively protected from rough seas. It is a destination for those looking for quiet vacations on the coast. There are a number of accommodation options and of fish taverns by the beach.

Nearby attractions include Tenta Neolithic site near Kalavasos, the manmade lake and watermills of Kalavasos, and the Agios Georgios Alamanos monastery. UNESCO World Heritage Choirokoitia Neolithic site is just 15 km to the north east, while the fishing village of Zygi is 11 km away (on the paved road) towards the east.

Distance (km) : Limassol : 16 Larnaca: 50 Platres : 56 Nicosia : 66 Paphos : 84
Agia Napa : 91 Protaras : 97 Polis : 119

Characteristics:  *(Jul-Sep)*

LATCHI COAST (AGIOS GEORGIOS ALAMANOS)

(Map 13 – page 138, 37)

This is a 200 meter long cove in between white rock, about 13 km east of Limassol. The coast surface is made up of medium sized pebble. The coastline on both sides of Latchi coast is ragged. There is easy road access to the sea, as well as a restaurant and umbrella and beach bed rentals. The monastery with the same name (i.e. Agios Georgios Alamanos) is two km north of the coast. The nearby coastal linear walk (from 500 meters west of this coast up to four km east, to Governor's beach) on a dramatic coastline that combines an undeveloped environment, white rock formations, sea caves, tiny sandy coves and rocky islets, is very pleasant and relatively easy. The area constitutes one of the most interesting stretches of Cyprus coastline, especially suited to exploration on ecological watercraft like Waterbikes, sea kayaks or similar. Some of the caves go deep inland (upto fifty or more meters in a couple of cases) and a few have entrances also on land. The coastline with its white rocks and tiny sandy beaches is visited by a few people, who are looking for peace and privacy.

Explorers can compose a trip that includes also the nearby picturesque villages, Tenta and Choirokoitia archaeological sites and Kalavasos dam and watermills.

Distance (km): Limassol : 13 Larnaca: 50 Platres : 53 Nicosia : 66 Paphos : 81
Polis : 116 Agia Napa : 125 Protaras : 131

Characteristics: 

AORATOI BEACH

(Map 14 – page 139, 38)

This is the most eastern of the beaches of the city of Limassol, in a relatively undeveloped (at least the east third of the beach) part of the coast. 'Aoratoi' means juniper (trees) in Greek. The beach is about one km long and predominately sandy. On its east side there is a fence and after that the Moni power generating plant whereas on the west, it ends at a marina. There are a couple of luxury hotels along the beach (the west part of the beach is also called 'Panagies beach'). It has been awarded the Blue flag eco-label (www.blueflag.org) and has handicap facilities. A 14 km long walking trail starts here and connects all the beaches of (central)Limassol (there are a few points on the coast where the walking trail is interrupted). About four kilometers north of the beach, in the village of Pyrgos (which is the Greek word for tower, it seems that one existed here in medieval times) there is a medieval watermill. In medieval times there was a monastery in Pyrgos of the (Catholic) Cistercian order. The watermill was part of the property of the monastery. It is atypical of watermills west of the Keryneia mountains in that instead of using water from streams, it was fed with water from a spring (the water was collected in a pool 300 meters north west of the watermill).

Distance (km): Limassol : 1 Platres : 41 Larnaca: 66 Paphos : 69 Nicosia : 82
Polis : 104 Agia Napa : 107 Protaras : 113

Characteristics: 

(May-Aug)

PAREKLISHIA BEACH

(Map 14 – page 139, 39)

This is one of the three beaches in the eastern coast of the city of Limassol. Even though it is not clear where the border of the beach with the adjacent Santa Barbara beach is, I would put its length at about 800 meters. Out of that, the part on the east end that borders with a marina (about 200 m long), has considerable amounts of sand and a large capacity of visitors (in places, the sandy beach extends 100 meters inland). This beach has been awarded the Blue flag ecolabel (www.blueflag.org) and has handicap facilities. It has a few luxury hotels and villas built on it.

A 14 km long walking trail passes through here that connects all the beaches of (central) Limassol (there are a few points on the route where the walking trail is interrupted). Attractions in the vicinity include the ruins of ancient city of Amathus (two km west of Pareklishia beach) and Pyrgos medieval watermill (four km north east of the beach).

Distance (km) : Limassol : 1 Larnaca: 66 Paphos : 68 Nicosia : 82 Polis : 103
Agia Napa : 107 Protaras : 113

Characteristics:  ***(May-Aug)***

SANTA BARBARA BEACH

(Map 14 – page 139, 40)

There is a small church with the same name in a small eucalyptus forest on the north side of the road, at the western side of the beach, where the walking route (wooden bridge part) continues. Until recently this was a relatively undeveloped part of the coast (except for a few luxury hotels), but now there are high end villas (some are the most expensive on the island) by a large stretch of the beach. I would estimate the length of Santa Barbara beach at about 800 meters. It is predominately sandy, and there is also pebble. A few vertical wave breakers exist. Santa Barbara beach has been awarded the Blue flag eco-label.

There is a good quality constructed walking trail passing by the beach. This 14 km long walking trail connects all the beaches of (central) Limassol (there are a few points on the coast where the walking trail is interrupted). The ancient city of Amathus is next to the beach and makes for a diverting visit.

Distance (km): Limassol : 0 Larnaca: 66 Paphos : 68 Nicosia : 82 Polis : 103
Agia Napa : 107 Protaras : 113

Characteristics: 

(May-Aug)

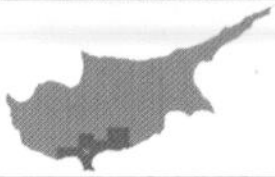

LOURES BEACH

(Map 14 – page 139, 41)

It is a 200 meters long sandy beach in the east side of the Agios Tychonas coastline. It is primarily from here that starts the chain of many wave breakers that define the beaches of central Limassol. The beach capacity is limited as there is only a narrow strip of sand. There are flat rocks in the sea. The beach has been awarded the Blue flag eco-label (www.blueflag.org).

A 14 km long walking trail passes through here that connects all the beaches of (central) Limassol (there are a few points on the coast where the walking route is interrupted). A walk from here towards the east, on the mostly wooden one-km stretch to Santa Barbara beach is highly recommended, as it is next to a rocky, rather wild part of the coast, where the port of ancient Amathus city-state once stood. On the north side of the walking trail there are ruins of the ancient city. The fenced ruins of ancient Amathus city state, which can be visited for a small fee are about 200 m away from the walking trail.

Distance (km): Limassol : 0 Platres : 41 Larnaca: 66 Paphos : 68 Nicosia : 82
Polis : 103 Agia Napa : 107 Protaras : 113

Characteristics:  ***(May-Aug)***

VOUPPA BEACH

(Map 14 – page 139, 42)

This is a 200 meters long sandy beach which is found, like the adjacent Loures beach, in the east side of the Agios Tychonas coastline. It has two 100 m long vertical wave breakers on its two ends, which are largely responsible for the extensive sand quantities deposited here. The beach has a considerable capacity for visitors, as the sand extends inwards at least for 30 meters in the greatest part of the beach. The beach has been awarded the Blue flag eco-label (www.blueflag.org) and has handicap facilities.

A 14 km long walking trail passes through here that connects all the beaches of (central) Limassol (there are a few points on the route where the walking trail is interrupted). There are luxury hotels nearby. A walk from here towards the east, on the mostly wooden one-km stretch (that starts about 700 m east of Vouppa beach) to Santa Barbara beach is highly recommended, as it is next to a rocky, rather wild part of the coast, where the port of ancient Amathus city-state once stood. On the north side of the walking trail there are ruins of the ancient city state. West of the wooden stretch of the walking trail, in a small square on the north side of the paved road there is a replica of a huge ancient monolithic vase from Amathus. The original is exhibited in the Louvre museum.

Distance (km): Limassol : 0 Platres : 40 Larnaca: 66 Paphos : 68 Nicosia : 82 Polis : 103 Agia Napa : 107 Protaras : 113

Characteristics:  ***(Apr-Nov)***

APHRODITE BEACH

(Map 14 – page 139, 43)

Aphrodite sandy beach is found between the two vertical wave breakers and is nearly 500 m long. It sits in the middle part of the Agios Tychonas coastline, in-between Armonia beach in the west and Vouppa beach in the east. It is the eastern part (200 meters long) of the beach that is better organised, and has a lot more sand, which extends inland on an average for more than 30 meters, thus giving this part of the beach a big capacity for sunbathers. The beach has long wave breakers parallel to it and a number of luxury hotels nearby. Aphrodite beach has been awarded the Blue flag eco-label (www.blueflag.org) and has handicap facilities.

A 14 km long walking trail passes through here and connects all the beaches of (central) Limassol (there are a few points on the coast where the walking trail is interrupted).

Distance (km) : Limassol : 0 Platres : 40 Larnaca: 66 Paphos : 68 Nicosia : 82
Polis : 103 Agia Napa : 107 Protaras : 113

Characteristics:  ***(Apr-Nov)***

ARMONIA BEACH

(Map 14 – page 139, 44)

This almost 600 m long sandy beach between two vertical wave breakers (a short 20 m long in the east and a longer 100 m one in the west) sits in the middle part of the Agios Tychonas coastline. It is found in-between Onisilos beach (which is 200 meters away from the western end of Armonia beach) in the west and Aphrodite beach in the east. The eastern part (almost 200 meters long) of the beach is the most organised, and has more sand, which extends inland on an average for 20 meters, thus giving this part of the beach a bigger capacity for sunbathers. The beach has long wave breakers parallel to it and a number of hotels nearby. Armonia beach has been awarded the Blue flag eco-label (www.blueflag.org).

A 14 km long walking trail passes through here and connects all the beaches of (central) Limassol (there are a few points on the coast where the walking trail is interrupted).

Distance (km): Limassol : 0 Platres : 40 Larnaca: 66 Paphos : 68 Nicosia : 82
Polis : 103 Agia Napa : 107 Protaras : 113

Characteristics: *(Apr-Nov)*

ONISILOS BEACH

(Map 14 – page 139, 45)

Together with the adjacent Kastella beach on its west side (there is no clear border between the two) they make an 800 meter long continuous sandy beach. The 600 meters long eastern part of the continuous beach goes on average 25 meters inland, thus giving it a very large capacity for visitors, whereas the western part has a depth of no more than 10 meters. The beach is found in the western part of the Agios Tychonas coastline, and the next public organised beach in the east (250 meters away) is Armonia beach. There are long wave breakers, beach volley facilities and a small outdoor theatre by the beach. Onisilos beach has been awarded the Blue flag eco-label (www.blueflag.org) and has handicap facilities. There are luxury hotels nearby.

A 14 km long walking trail passes through here and connects all the beaches of (central) Limassol (there are a few points on the route where the walking trail is interrupted).

Distance (km): Limassol : 0 Platres : 40 Larnaca: 66 Paphos : 68 Nicosia : 82
Polis : 103 Agia Napa : 107 Protaras : 113

Characteristics:  ***(Apr-Nov)***

KASTELLA BEACH

(Map 14 – page 139, 46)

Together with the adjacent Onisilos beach on its east side (there is no clear border between the two), they make an 800 meter long continuous sandy beach. The 600 meter long eastern part of the continuous beach goes on the average 25 meters inland, thus giving it a very large capacity for visitors, whereas the western part has a depth of no more than 10 meters. The beach is found in the western part of the Agios Tychonas coastline, and the next public organised beach in the west (more than two km away) is Dasoudi beach. There are long wave breakers. Kastella beach has been awarded the Blue flag eco-label (www.blueflag.org) and has handicap facilities. There are luxury hotels nearby.

A 14 km long walking trail passes through here and connects all the beaches of (central) Limassol (there are a few points on the route where the walking trail is interrupted).

Distance (km) : Limassol : 0 Platres : 41 Larnaca: 66 Paphos : 68 Nicosia : 82
Polis : 103 Agia Napa : 107 Protaras : 113

Characteristics:  ***(Apr-Nov)***

DASOUDI BEACH

(Map 14 – page 139, 47)

Dasoudi beach is a one km plus long sandy beach in the middle of the coastline of the city of Limassol and is characterised by a eucalyptus forest ("Dasoudi" means small forest in the Greek Cypriot dialect) that is found behind the beach. On average the sand goes up to 25 meters inland, and the beach thus has a significant capacity for visitors. There are long wave breakers covering the whole length of the beach. There are amenities and luxury hotels in the vicinity. On the east side of the beach, there are many vertical wave breakers, and small coves in front of hotels, while to the west, the public Akti Olympion beach is only 200 meters away.

A 14 km long walking trail starts here and connects all the beaches of (central) Limassol (there are a few points on the coast where the walking trail is interrupted). The historic center of Limassol, much of which has been renovated, is found just a couple hundred meters away towards the north west. Limassol castle is 1,300 meters south west of the west end of the beach.

Distance (km): Limassol : 0 Platres : 40 Larnaca: 66 Paphos : 68 Nicosia : 82
Polis : 103 Agia Napa : 107 Protaras : 113

Characteristics:  ***(Apr-Nov)***

AKTI OLYMPION BEACH

(Map 14 – page 139, 48)

This is a two km long sandy beach on the east of the sea front promenade of Limassol. Officially there are two beaches, Akti Olympion, and Akti Olympion B, both of which have been awarded the Blue flag eco-label and have handicap facilities. They are divided into two almost equal-length parts by the wooden pier that is found there. Wave breakers exist along the whole stretch.

A 14 km long walking trail starts here and connects all the beaches of (central) Limassol (there are a few points on the coast where the walking trail is interrupted). The historic center of Limassol, much of which has been renovated, is found just a couple hundred meters away towards the north west. Limassol castle is 1,300 meters south west of the west end of the beach.

Distance (km) : Limassol : 0 Platres : 40 Larnaca: 66 Paphos : 68 Nicosia : 82
Polis : 103 Agia Napa : 107 Protaras : 113

Characteristics:  *(May-Oct)*

LADY'S MILE BEACH

(Map 16 – page 141, 49)

This is unlike any other of the beaches of Limassol city. It is very long by comparison (five km long), has no wave breakers and is found in an area where there is almost no human construction (apart from very few restaurants on the beach). It is right next to the Akrotiri salt lake (a 15 sq. km, very important habitat for birds, that is one of the wetlands under the Ramsar Convention - www.ramsar.org). The beach is found to the west side of Limassol's port and access is on a passable dirt road. There are (some) amenities on the beach.

Distance (km) : Limassol : 2 Platres : 42 Larnaca: 68 Paphos : 70 Nicosia : 84
Polis : 105 Agia Napa : 109 Protaras : 115

Characteristics:  *(Jul-Aug)*

EPISKOPI COAST

(Map 17 – page 142, 50)

Episkopi coast is about 20 km to the west of Limassol. The coast is more than three km long. The 'beach' at the west part of the coast, below the cliffs and Kourion ancient city state, is about one km long; its surface is mostly sandy or a mixture of sand and pebble. Unlike the beaches of the city of Limassol this is a coast in an undeveloped area, with few amenities. The water needs caution (especially in the two km long east part) because of currents and because it gets rough often.

Other natural and cultural attractions in the area include the ancient city of Kourion and its excellent mosaics, medieval Kolossi castle (and its ancient rose tree - Tipuana tipu), the watermills of Kantou and Agia Napa chapel, Kouris dam and nearby ancient trees, the medieval Panagia tis Amasgou monastery, or one of the nearby picturesque villages.

Distance (km) : Limassol : 20 Paphos : 50 Platres : 60 Polis : 85 Larnaca: 86 Nicosia : 102 Agia Napa : 127 Protaras : 133

Characteristics: 

(Jun-Sep)

PARAMALI COAST

(Map 17 – page 142, 51)

Paramali coast is about 25 km to the west of Limassol. There are two beaches in close proximity, with the east one being 0.3 km long and the west one 1.2 km long. These are quite good sandy (with some pebble) beaches, very close to Limassol with no infrastructure and with limited crowds. Sea turtles nest here in summer. It is popular with expatriates and kite surfers. Access is on a dirt road.

Other natural and cultural attractions in the area include the ancient city of Kourion and its excellent mosaics, Kolossi castle (and its ancient rose tree - Tipuana tipu), the Avdimou ancient olive tree, the Kantou watermills and Agia Napa chapel, Kouris dam and nearby picturesque villages.

Distance (km): Limassol : 25 Paphos : 45 Platres : 58 Polis : 80 Larnaca: 91 Nicosia : 107 Agia Napa : 132 Protaras : 138

Characteristics: -

AVDIMOU COAST

(Map 17 – page 142, 52)

It is found about 30 km west of the city of Limassol. There is a main sand (and pebble) 'beach' more than one km long, another sandy stretch more than 200 meters long, as well as other smaller coves. Access is on good dirt roads, and there are tavernas on the coast. Unlike the busy, people-packed and organised beaches of Limassol city, this is a place for people looking for a more peaceful stay by the sea.

Other natural and cultural attractions in the area include the Avdimou ancient olive tree, the (ruins of the) ancient city of Kourion and its excellent mosaics, Aphrodite's Rock, Kolossi castle (and its ancient rose tree - Tipuana tipu), the Kantou watermills and Agia Napa chapel and nearby picturesque villages.

Distance (km) : Limassol : 30 Paphos : 38 Platres : 45 Polis : 73 Larnaca: 96
Nicosia : 112 Agia Napa : 137 Protaras : 143

Characteristics:  *(Jul-Aug)*

PISSOURI BEACH

(Map 17 – page 142, 53)

Pissouri beach is the most organised of those beaches in the district of Limassol that are relatively far from the city. It is found about halfway between Limassol and Paphos (about 30 km from each). The surface is made up of a mixture of sand and pebble and the beach is over a km long. It is very popular, and has restaurants and luxury hotel(s) on it. There are cliffs on the two ends of the beach (towards the west there is a six km long stretch of 100-m high white cliffs, well-suited for coastal sea exploration). Pissouri beach has been awarded the Blue flag eco-label
(www.blueflag.org) and has handicap facilities.

The area near it is very developed touristically. Aphrodite's Rock (or Petra tou Romiou in Greek, meaning 'the Rock of the Greek') which is thought of being Aphrodite's birthplace, is about 13 km to the west. Aphrodite's sanctuary at Palaipaphos, a UNESCO World Heritage site is 20 km away towards Paphos. The ruins of the ancient city of Kourion and its exquisite mosaics are about 23 km away towards Limassol. There are also picturesque villages nearby.

Distance (km): Limassol : 30 Paphos : 30 Platres : 60 Polis : 65 Larnaca: 96
Nicosia : 112 Agia Napa : 137 Protaras : 143

Characteristics:  ***(Jul-Aug)***

GOVERNOR'S BEACH – LATCHI COAST (AGIOS GEORGIOS ALAMANOS) WALKING ROUTE

(Map 13 – page 138, 18)

This is a four km long, rather easy linear coastal route, connecting the two natural attractions (Governor's beach is about 16 km east of Limassol). The coastline is ragged, composed of white rock and mostly undeveloped (still). I suggest that walkers extend their walk at least 500 meters further to the west of Latchi beach; the coast continues to be ragged with tiny sandy coves in between white rocks. Walkers may pass by a fenced cave (its "roof" entrance from the land has been filled up in late 2007) called "Hostospilios", whose entrance is reached from the sea (about 50 meters deep inland). Further west (800 meters from the beach) there is a rock that the locals call "Karavopetra" i.e. boat stone because of its shape. Walkers may see the dirt road (which for the next 1.5 km runs parallel to the coast) that was used to carry material from the nearby quarry. The quarry closed recently and a reforestation effort is underway in the area. There is an industrial complex further west (no access from the coast) and a pool (in the old quarry complex) further inland. On the west side of the industrial complex begins the chain of beaches of the city of Limassol.

Distance (km) : Limassol : 16 Larnaca: 50 Platres : 56 Nicosia : 66 Paphos : 84
Polis : 119 Agia Napa : 123 Protaras : 129

MONI COAST – LIMASSOL PIER WALKING ROUTE

(Map 14 – page 139, 19)

This is a 14 km long walking trail that starts where Aoratoi beach begins to the west of the electricity generating plant of Moni and finishes at the pier of Limassol. Much of the route is paved and walkers pass by many organised (eleven blue flag awarded) beaches, other (wave breaker produced) coves, and wooden bridges at the ancient city of Amathus. There is a 1.5 km stretch on the coast between Kastella beach and Dasoudi beach that may prove difficult to walk (at places either there is no access at all, or it is very difficult to walk on the rocks or pebbles). Walkers may prefer to skip this stretch and take the adjacent walking route on the coastal October 28 avenue. Besides beaches, attractions within walking distance of the walking route include the ruins of the ancient city of Amathus, the medieval Venetian bridge of Aristos and Limassol castle.

Distance (km) : Limassol : 0 Larnaca: 32 Nicosia : 68 Paphos : 68 Agia Napa : 93 Protaras : 99 Polis : 103 Platres : 108

KALAVASOS DAM

(Map 12 – page 137, 14)

Kalavasos dam is found almost 25 km north west of the city of Limassol and can be accessed on the road from Kalavasos village to Asgata village. It was built in 1985 on the Vasilikos river at an altitude of about 200 meters and has capacity of 17.1 million cubic meters and a maximum surface area of about 60 hectares. Unfortunately there is no convenient walking route around it. Fish in the lake include carp, mosquito fish, roach, bass, catfish, pumpkinseed sunfish and tilapia.

There are many natural and especially cultural attractions in the area including the Neolithic settlement of Tenta (the word is derived from the English 'Tent' – the Tent that covers the Neolithic settlement is an attraction by itself), the picturesque village of Kalavasos (and others), two watermills in or close to Kalavasos (and one in a poorer condition very close to Tenta), medieval Venetian bridges by Akapnou and near Kato Drys, ancient trees and more.

Distance (km): Limassol : 25 Larnaca: 57 Platres : 65 Nicosia : 73 Paphos : 93
Agia Napa : 98 Protaras : 104 Polis : 128

GERMASOGEIA DAM

(Map 14 – page 139, 15)

Germasogeia dam is found less than four km north (east) of the city of Limassol, on the road linking the village of Germasogeia to the village of Foinikaria. It was built in 1968 on Germasogeia river, at an altitude of about 100 meters and has capacity of 13.5 million cubic meters and a maximum surface area of about 70 hectares. Fish in the lake include carp, mosquito fish, roach, bass, catfish, bleak, silver bream and perch. Canoe and kayak clubs are practicing in the manmade lake. There are walking possibilities in the area.

The natural and cultural attractions in the area include ancient olive trees in the village of Germasogeia, 12th century Saint. Christina church in the old village center, Aristos medieval Venetian bridge on the river near the sea, nearby beaches and more.

Distance (km) : Limassol : 4 Platres : 44 Larnaca: 66 Paphos : 72 Nicosia : 82
Agia Napa : 107 Polis : 107 Protaras : 113

POLEMIDIA DAM

(Map 14 – page 139, 16)

Polemidia dam is found six km north of the city of Limassol and it is on the road from Limassol to Platres and Troodos Square. It was built in 1965 on Garyllis river at an altitude of about 130 meters and has capacity of 3.4 million cubic meters and maximum surface area of about 15 hectares. Unfortunately there is no convenient walking route around it. This manmade lake is used for canoeing/kayaking practicing by local clubs. Fish in the lake include carp, mosquito fish, roach and catfish.

Attractions in the area include an ancient olive tree in Kato Polemidia village (and other ancient trees nearby), old Limassol (the medieval castle and the renovated city quarter) and Limassol beaches, 12th century Panagia tis Amasgou monastery near Monagri village, picturesque villages (and wineries in Commandaria region, home of the famous dessert wine) and other wetlands.

Distance (km) : Limassol : 6 Platres : 42 Larnaca: 68 Paphos : 74 Nicosia : 84
Agia Napa : 109 Polis : 109 Protaras : 115

AKROTIRI SALT LAKE

(Map 16 – page 141, 17)

It is found near Akrotiri village and only two km from Limassol. It is three times larger than the Larnaca salt lakes, covering an area of more than 15 sq. km. In maps as recently as 1600 A.D. Akrotiri salt lake was shown to be connected to the sea. Many thousands of flamingos and other bird species are found here in winter. It is part of a collection of very important birdwatching areas that includes also the Phasouri reed beds and the Zakaki Marsh. It is one of the wetlands under the Ramsar Convention (www.ramsar.org). Akrotiri salt lake is dry in summer and it is adjacent to Lady's mile beach, a five km long sandy beach to the west of the city of Limassol.

Nearby attractions include amongst others, Kolossi castle (originally built in the 13th century, the existing castle was rebuilt in the 15th century by the Knights of the Order of St John of Jerusalem, otherwise known as the Hospitallers).

Distance (km) : Limassol : 2 Platres : 46 Paphos : 68 Larnaca: 70 Nicosia : 86
Polis : 103 Agia Napa : 111 Protaras : 117

BISHOP'S POOL

(Map 16 – page 141, 18)

Bishop's pool was constructed in 1960 to facilitate the irrigation of the nearby plantation. It has taken its present form in 1998. It has an area of one hectare (10,000 sq.m.) and a depth of ten metres, while it is enriched with fresh water from the Kouris dam. It is found inside the estate of Saint Nicolaos monastery (of the Cats) which belongs to Limassol Bishopric. It constitutes the most southern collection facility for fresh water in Cyprus and though it is an artificial lake, the vegetation on its banks is progressively becoming natural. Bishop's Pool constitutes an important stop station for migratory birds but also for the predatory birds in the region. 50 species of birds have been recorded to date, including one endemic, and six nesting species, the remaining being migratory bird species. The presence of two birdwatching towers around it makes Bishop's Pool one of the best destinations for casual birdwatchers in the area.

The towers can be visited throughout the week.

The adjacent Environmental Education and Research center is open Monday - Friday from 8:00 up to 14:00). Tel No: 25954954 Email: kykpee@cytanet.com.cy

Distance (km): Limassol : 7 Platres : 46 Paphos : 68 Larnaca: 70 Nicosia : 86
Polis :103 Agia Napa : 111 Protaras : 117

KOURIS DAM

(Map 15 – page 140, 19)

Kouris dam is by far the largest dam in Cyprus with a capacity of 115 million cubic meters and a surface area of about two square kilometers. It is just ten km from Limassol and close to the village of Alassa. It was built in 1988 on the Kouris river at an altitude of 200 meters. There is a paved road going from the dam round and west of the lake to the village of Alassa. There are also some walking routes on the north east bank of the lake. Fish in the lake include carp, mosquito fish, roach, silver bream, bass, catfish, pikeperch, perch, bleak and pumpkinseed sunfish.

Attractions in the area include the excellent birdwatching area nearby (Akrotiri salt lake, Phasouri reed beds, etc), medieval Kolossi castle and ancient Curium, the watermills of Kantou and Agia Napa chapel, the monastery of Panagia tis Amasgou, ancient trees in the vicinity, the picturesque "Krasohoria" (meaning 'wine villages' in Greek) villages to the north and the beaches in the south.

Distance (km) : Limassol : 10 Platres : 34 Paphos : 63 Larnaca: 76 Nicosia : 92
Polis : 98 Agia Napa : 117 Protaras : 123

OLIVE TREE IN EPTAGONEIA

(Map 12 – page 137, 10)

Eptagoneia is a picturesque village built at an altitude of 500 meters, about 25 km north east of Limassol. There is a 600 years old olive tree (Olea europaea) living near the village. The tree is found on the left side of a dirt road, which one takes on the left side of the road leading from Eptagoneia village to Kellaki village. It's a good idea to ask locals for directions. The olive tree is five meters tall and has a trunk perimeter of seven meters. Four km east of Eptagoneia village stands the double arched medieval Venetian bridge of Akapnou (village), while about six km south east, near the small village of Klonari there is an ancient oak tree (it is found on the right side of the road from Kellaki village to Klonari, explorers need to ask locals for direction).

Other attractions in the area include Kalavasos dam, Kalavasos watermills and the ancient Neolithic settlement of Tenta.

Distance (km) : Limassol : 25 Platres : 30 Larnaca: 91 Paphos : 93 Nicosia : 106
Polis : 128 Agia Napa : 132 Protaras : 138

MASTIC TREE IN APESIA

(Map 15 – page 140, 11)

Apesia is a small picturesque village about 17 km north of Limassol, at an altitude of 500 meters. In the village center, on the right side of the road to Gerasa village, one finds what is probably the oldest living tree on the island. It is an Atlas pistache (or mastic tree, scientific name: Pistacia atlantica) whose age is estimated at 1,500 years. It is ten meters tall, and its trunk has a perimeter of 6.80 meters. It is not the dimensions of the tree that are amazing, but rather its age.

Attractions in the vicinity include the excellent birdwatching area nearby (Akrotiri salt lake, Phasouri reed beds, etc), medieval Kolossi castle and ancient Curium (with its exquisite mosaics), Kouris which is by far the largest manmade lake in Cyprus, the watermills of Kantou and Agia Napa chapel, the monastery of Panagia tis Amasgou, ancient trees nearby, the picturesque "Krasohoria" (meaning 'wine villages' in Greek) villages and the beaches in the south.

Distance (km) : Limassol : 17 Platres : 20 Larnaca: 83 Paphos : 85 Nicosia : 99
Polis : 120 Agia Napa : 124 Protaras : 130

ROSE TREE IN KOLOSSI

(Map 16 – page 141, 13)

This huge and exotic tree is found in the yard of well preserved medieval Kolossi castle, which is one of the main cultural attractions in Cyprus. Kolossi village (and Kolossi castle) is about nine km west of Limassol. It is a tree of the species Tipuana tipu, 200 years old, 26 meters high and its trunk has a perimeter of 4.5 meters. In the yard of the impressive Kolossi castle next to the rose tree there is also a very tall cypress tree, estimated to have the same age as the rose tree. There are also ruins of a sugar cane processing plant. It is noteworthy and maybe somewhat strange that during medieval times sugar cane was cultivated in coastal areas of Cyprus. There are also ruins of a medieval aqueduct (channeling water from Kouris river) and of a watermill at the site of the sugar processing plant.

Besides beaches and the excellent wetland system at Akrotiri, other attractions in the area include the ruins of the ancient city of Curium and its mosaics, watermills, chapels, other ancient trees and picturesque villages in the vicinity.

Distance (km): Limassol : 9 Platres : 48 Paphos : 60 Larnaca: 75 Nicosia : 91
Polis : 95 Agia Napa : 116 Protaras : 122

OLIVE TREE IN AVDIMOU

(Map 17 – page 142, 14)

Avdimou is a picturesque village built at an altitude of 100 meters, about 30 km east of Limassol. There is a 700 years old olive tree (Olea europaea) in the village. The tree is found on the left side of the main road that leads north to Pachna village. The olive tree is nearly five meters tall, and has a trunk perimeter of nearly nine meters. There is another ancient olive tree in the area, towards the sea, but that's hard to find.

Avdimou coast is a few km south, while the undeveloped Paramali coast towards the south east and the Blue flag Pissouri beach towards the south west are marginally further. The ruins of ancient Kourion and its excellent mosaics are further east (very close to medieval Kolossi castle and the watermills of Kantou), while the legendary birthplace of Aphrodite, i.e. Aphrodite's Rock is a few km west of Pissouri village.

Distance (km) : Limassol : 30 Platres : 35 Paphos : 38 Polis : 73 Larnaca: 96
Nicosia : 112 Agia Napa : 137 Protaras : 143

AKAPNOU MEDIEVAL BRIDGE

(Map 12 – page 137)

ARISTOS MEDIEVAL BRIDGE

(Map 14 – page 139)

A WATERMILL IN KALAVASOS

(Map 12 – page 137)

A WATERMILL NEAR KALAVASOS

(Map 12 – page 137)

WATERMILL IN PYRGOS LEMESOU (Map 14 – page 139)

WATERMILL NEAR KANTOU (Map 17 – page 142)

ANOTHER WATERMILL NEAR KANTOU (Map 17 – page 142)

LIMASSOL CASTLE (Map 14 – page 139)

KOLOSSI CASTLE (Map 16 – page 141)

AGIOS GEORGIOS ALAMANOS MONASTERY (Map 13 – page 138)

PANAGIA TIS AMASGOU MONASTERY (Map 15 – page 140)

AGIA NAPA CHAPEL (Map 17 – page 142)

TENTA NEOLITHIC SETTLEMENT (Map 12 – page 137)

AMATHUS ANCIENT KINGDOM (Map 14 – page 139)

CURIUM/KOURION ANCIENT KINGDOM

(Map 16 – page 141)

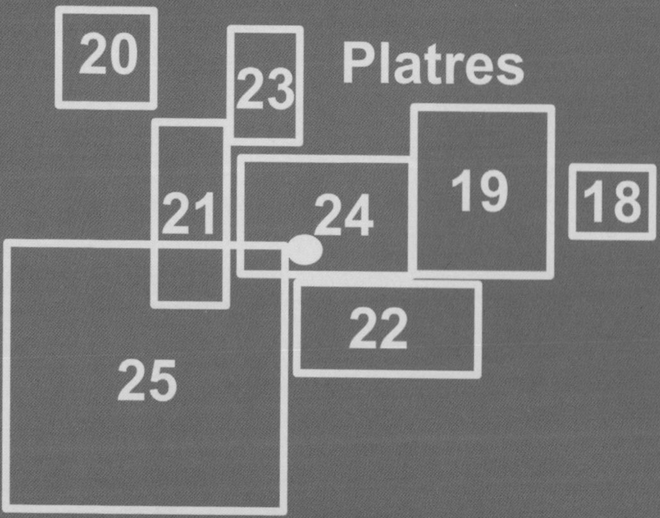

PLATRES

The resort village of Platres (Pano Platres, to be distinguished from the adjacent village of Kato Platres – 'Pano' means 'Upper' in Greek while 'Kato' means 'Lower') is found on the mountainous, less developed Troodos region. The area is ideal for those seeking to explore the forests of Cyprus and to discover green valleys, many tens of endemic plants, streams with water flowing all year round, waterfalls and Venetian bridges, magnificent Byzantine churches, monasteries, vineyards and wineries and traditional villages. There are superb walking routes in Paphos Forest, in Troodos Forest as well as on the peak of Madari. In the area there are many ancient trees. Troodos is fascinating for those into geology as it is one of the few places on earth where very ancient rock can be observed on the surface rather than kilometers below ground. Lucky visitors may spot shy moufflon in Paphos Forest.

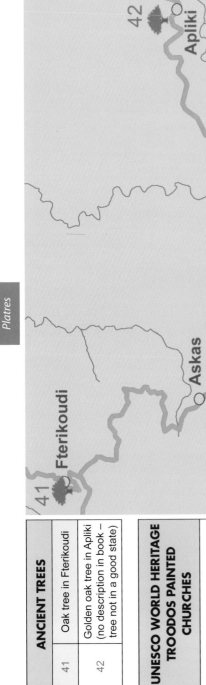

ANCIENT TREES	
41	Oak tree in Fterikoudi
42	Golden oak tree in Apliki (no description in book – tree not in a good state)

UNESCO WORLD HERITAGE TROODOS PAINTED CHURCHES
Metamorfosis tou Sotiros

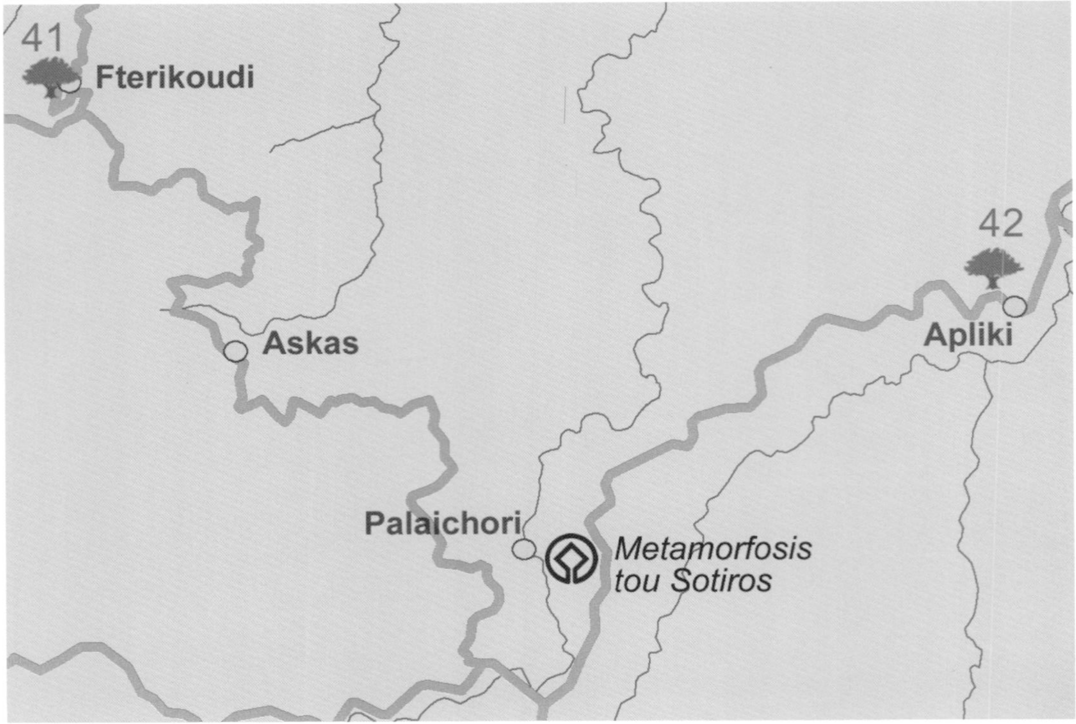

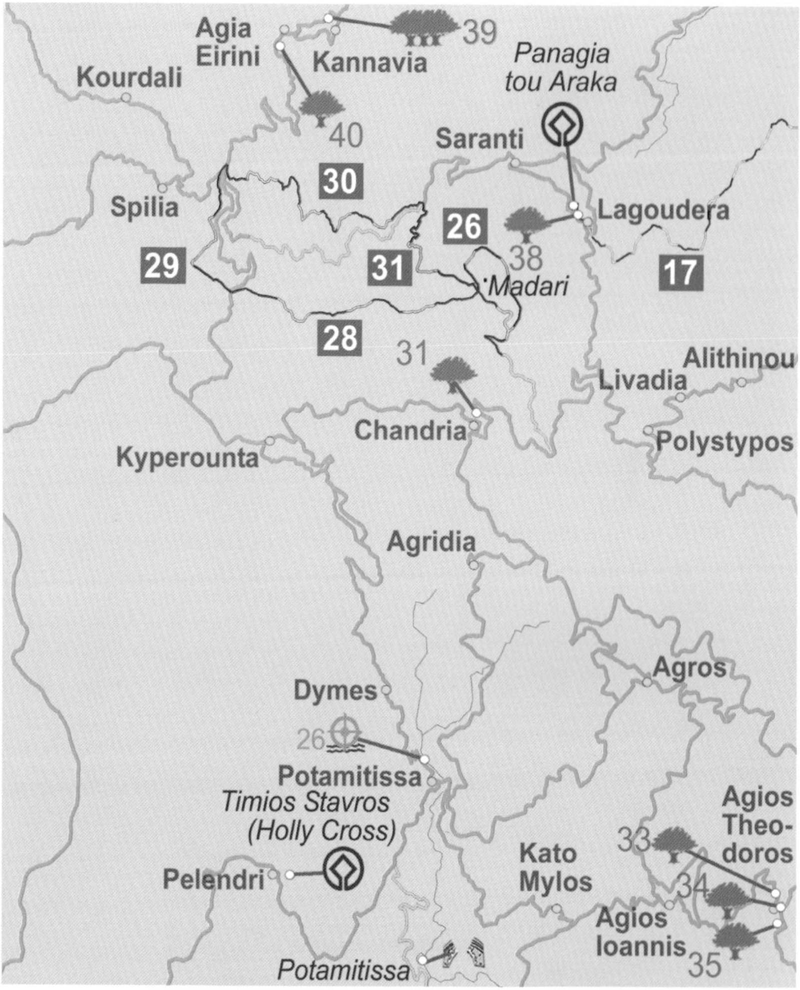

WALKING ROUTES	
17	Stavros tou Agiasmati church - Panagia tou Araka church
26	Teichia tis Madaris
27	Madari Circular (28-31)
28	Madari - Doxa si o Theos
29	Doxa si o Theos - Moutti tis Choras
30	Moutti tis Choras - Selladi tou Karamanli
31	Madari - Selladi tou Karamanli

ANCIENT TREES	
31	Pine tree in Chandria
33	Pine tree in Agios Theodoros Agrou
34	Oak tree in Agios Theodoros Agrou
35	Terebinth in Agios Theodoros Agrou
38	Oak in Lagoudera
39	2 Oaks,1 Cypress in Kannavia
40	Cypress in Agia Eirini

MEDIEVAL BRIDGES
Potamitissa bridge (damaged)

WATERMILLS	
26	Potamitissa

UNESCO WORLD HERITAGE TROODOS PAINTED CHURCHES
Timios Stavros (Holly Cross)
Panagia tou Araka

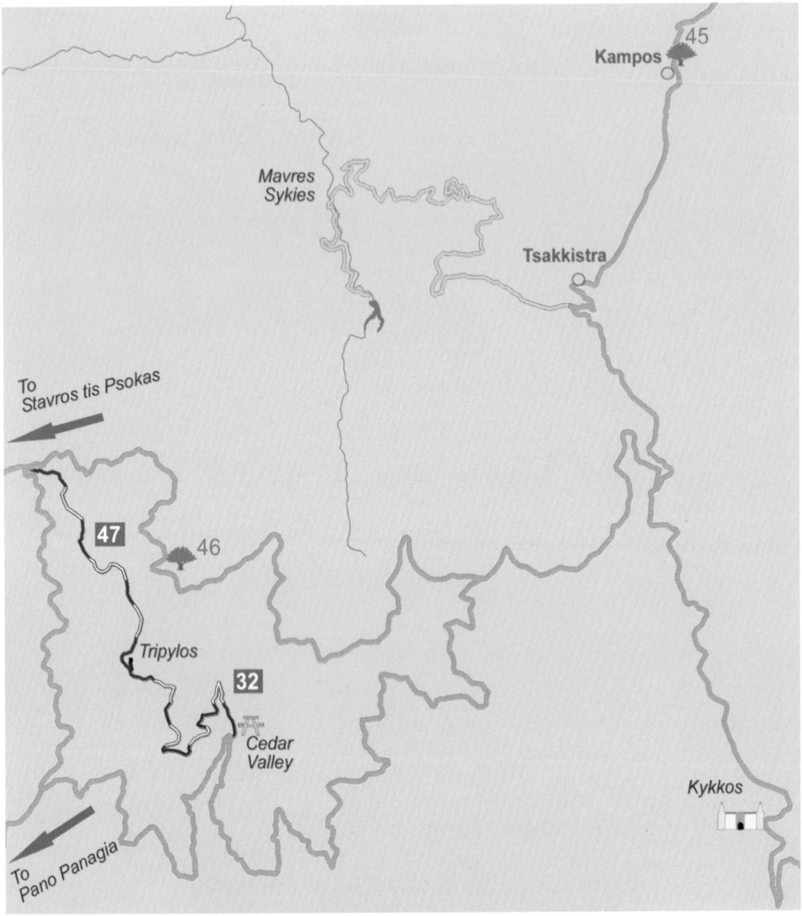

WALKING ROUTES	
32	Cedar Valley – Tripylos peak
47	Panagia village junction – Tripylos peak

ANCIENT TREES	
45	Oak tree in Kampos
46	Golden Oak in Kremmos tis Pellis

CHAPELS AND MONASTERIES
Kykkos

WALKING ROUTES	
25	Platy valley – Kelefos bridge

WETLANDS	
20	Arminou dam

ANCIENT TREES	
25	Oak tree in Agios Nikolaos

MEDIEVAL BRIDGES
Mylos
Treis Elies
Elia
Kelefos

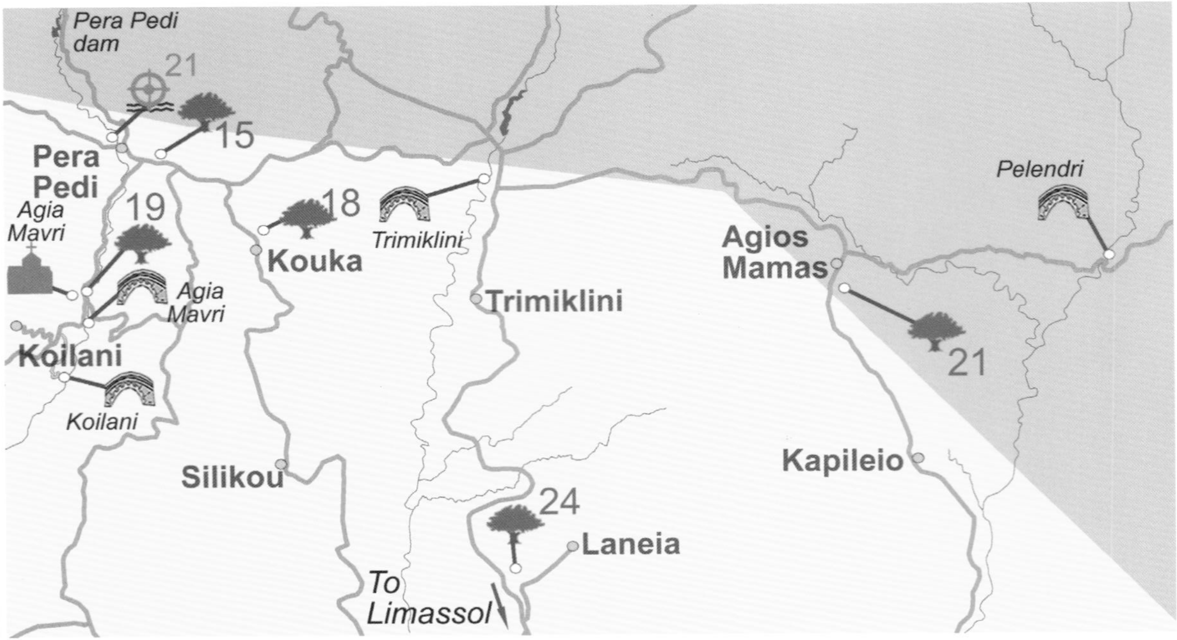

ANCIENT TREES	
15	Oak tree in Pera Pedi
18	Oak tree in Kouka
19	Plane tree at Agia Mavri
21	Oak tree in Agios Mamas
24	Oak tree in Laneia

MEDIEVAL BRIDGES
Trimiklini
Agia Mavri
Koilani
Pelendri

WATERMILLS	
21	Pera Pedi

CHAPELS AND MONASTERIES
Agia Mavri

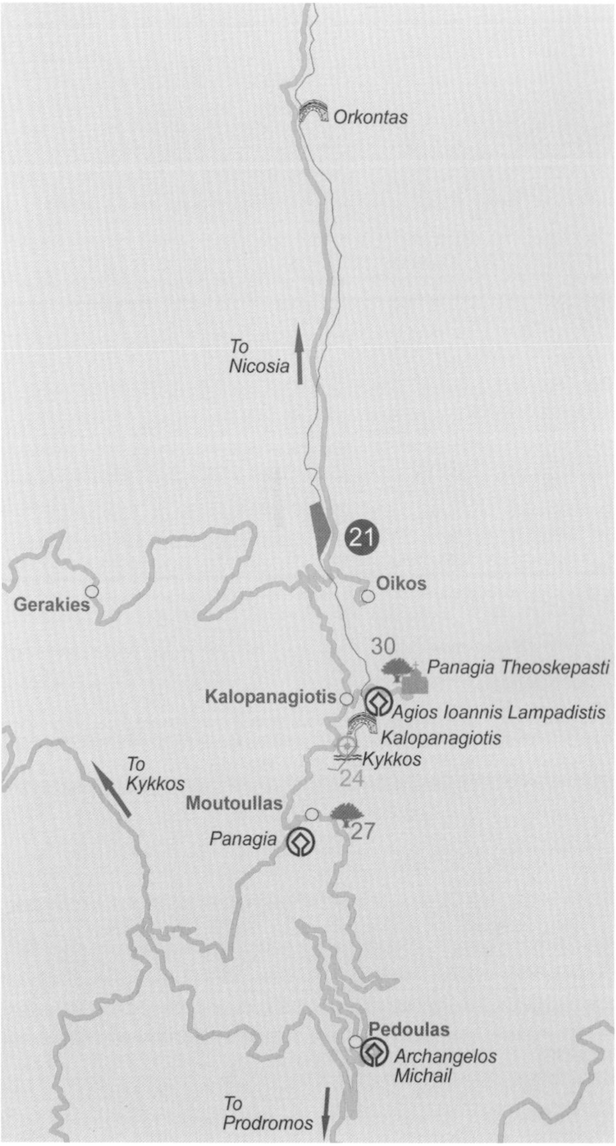

UNESCO WORLD HERITAGE TROODOS PAINTED CHURCHES
Archangelos Michail
Agios Ioannis Lampadistis
Panagia tou Moutoulla

CHAPELS AND MONASTERIES
Panagia Theoskepasti

WETLANDS	
21	Kalopanagiotis dam

ANCIENT TREES	
27	Oak in Moutoullas
30	Kermes oak in Kalopanagiotis

MEDIEVAL BRIDGES
Kalopanagiotis
Orkontas

WATERMILLS	
24	Kykkos

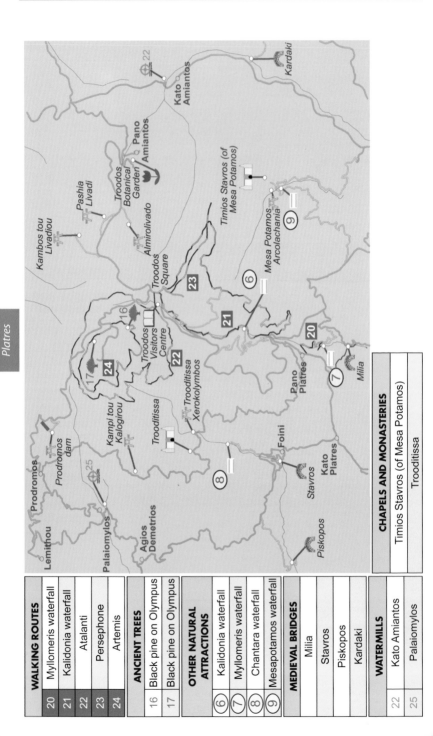

WALKING ROUTES	
20	Myllomeris waterfall
21	Kalidonia waterfall
22	Atalanti
23	Persephone
24	Artemis

ANCIENT TREES	
16	Black pine on Olympus
17	Black pine on Olympus

OTHER NATURAL ATTRACTIONS	
6	Kalidonia waterfall
7	Myllomeris waterfall
8	Chantara waterfall
9	Mesapotamos waterfall

MEDIEVAL BRIDGES
Milia
Stavros
Piskopos
Kardaki

WATERMILLS	
22	Kato Amiantos
25	Palaiomylos

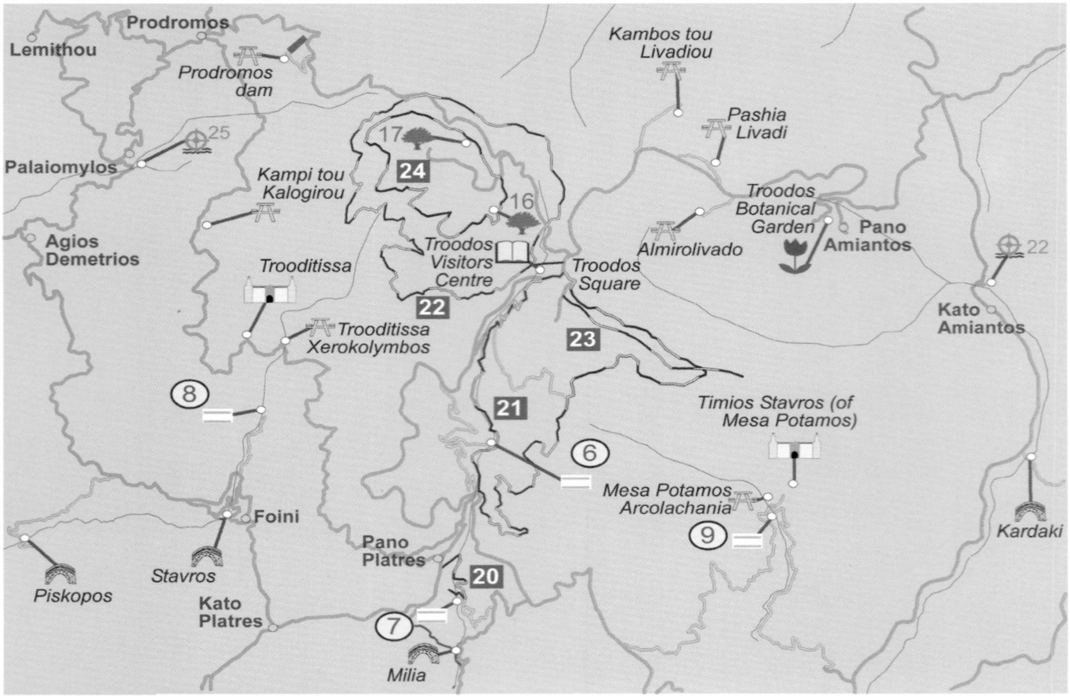

CHAPELS AND MONASTERIES
Timios Stavros (of Mesa Potamos)
Trooditissa

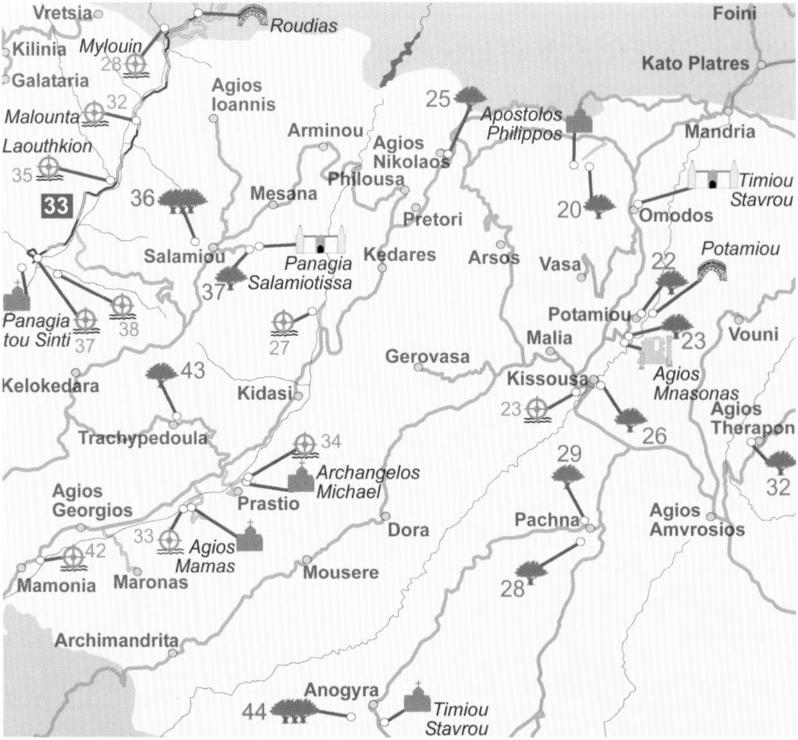

WALKING ROUTES	
33	Panagia tou Sinti - Roudias medieval bridge

ANCIENT TREES	
20	Laurel in Omodos
22	Olive in Potamiou
23	Mastic in Potamiou
25	Oak tree in Agios Nikolaos
26	Mastic in Kissousa
28	Oak tree in Pachna
29	Kermes oak in Pachna
32	Mastic in Agios Therapon
36	Three Cypresses in Salamiou
37	Storax in Salamiou
43	White mulberry in Trachypedoula
44	Olive trees in Anogyra

MEDIEVAL BRIDGES
Potamiou
Roudias

WATERMILLS	
23	Kissousa
27	Kedares
28	Vretsia
32	Agios Ioannis
33	Agios Mamas
34	Archangelos Michail
35	Galataria
37	Pentalia
38	Salamiou
42	Mamonia

CHAPELS AND MONASTERIES
Timiou Stavrou (Omodos)
Apostolos Philippos
Archangelos Michael
Agios Mamas
Panagia Salamiotissa
Timiou Stavrou (Anogyra)
Panagia tou Sinti

OTHER CULTURAL ATTRACTIONS
Agios Mnasonas

MYLLOMERIS WATERFALL WALKING ROUTE

(Map 24 – page 189, 20)

This linear walking route starts at the center of (Pano) Platres village and ends at the Myllomeris waterfall. The walking trail is just 1.2 km long with an elevation range of nearly 150 meters. The first half of the walking route goes parallel to the Kryos Potamos river while the second part ascends a steep slope before descending to the waterfall. The Myllomeris waterfall is the tallest of the four waterfalls in the area with a height of 15 meters.

Downstream and within a distance of about five km one finds three medieval Venetian bridges, a small manmade lake, an atypical restored watermill, ancient trees and the small 12th century chapel of Agia Mavri. Besides excellent walks, the area boasts picturesque villages like Koilani, Vouni and Foini, wineries (e.g. in Kato Platres, Pera Pedi, Koilani) and monasteries (e.g. Trooditissa and Timios Stavros of Mesa Potamos).

Distance (km): Platres : 0 Limassol : 40 Paphos : 60 Polis : 72 Nicosia : 86
Larnaca: 106 Agia Napa : 147 Protaras : 153

KALIDONIA WATERFALL WALKING ROUTE

(Map 24 – page 189, 21)

The route is on an official linear walking trail that starts at about three km from Troodos Square and ends in Platres village (elevation change of about 300 meters). Both of its ends can be accessed on paved roads. The trail has a length of three km and can be divided into two parts, the higher part until the waterfall, and the lower one, from the waterfall to Platres. The higher one is the most dramatic as one walks next to cliffs at places, smaller waterfalls and pools (whose icy water can be very refreshing in hot weather). The walking route is very steep at places so walking here can be very tiring. It is also slippery so caution is needed. The walking route is open year round and can be quite difficult after heavy rains and when the snow from the peaks above is melting. Walkers may see many representatives of the local flora and (mostly hear) many birds. The route is excellent and a stop at the waterfall for a view is highly recommended.

It is possible to compose a 14 km long circular route (with an elevation range of 500 meters) that takes one to Troodos via Pouziaris locality to the east of the waterfall. To go to Pouziaris one walks east from the low end of the Kalidonia waterfall walking route (at Psilon Dendron locality).

Distance (km) : Platres : 0 Limassol : 40 Paphos : 60 Nicosia : 81 Polis : 95
Larnaca: 106 Agia Napa : 147 Protaras : 153

ATALANTI WALKING ROUTE

(Map 24 – page 189, 22)

Atalanti walking route is 14 km long and circular. The walking route starts at Troodos Square. Nine km on, it reaches the Prodromos - Troodos paved road, at which point walkers can either cross the road and find the walking trail again, or return to Troodos Square by the paved road. The route is relatively easy, but care is needed as at some points there are cliffs. The vegetation is dominated by juniper and black pine. Walkers pass by an old mine which is not used any more. This is one of the official nature walking trails and travellers see many signs explaining the flora and geology on the route.

There are a few other excellent nature walking routes in the vicinity and a Visitors' Centre at Troodos Square. In Troodos Square one can find restaurants, cafes and a couple of hotels. A few km north east one finds a couple of picnic places and the Troodos Botanical Garden.

Distance (km): Platres : 6 Limassol : 46 Polis : 66 Paphos : 66 Nicosia : 80
Larnaca: 112 Agia Napa : 153 Protaras : 159

PERSEPHONE WALKING ROUTE

(Map 24 – page 189, 23)

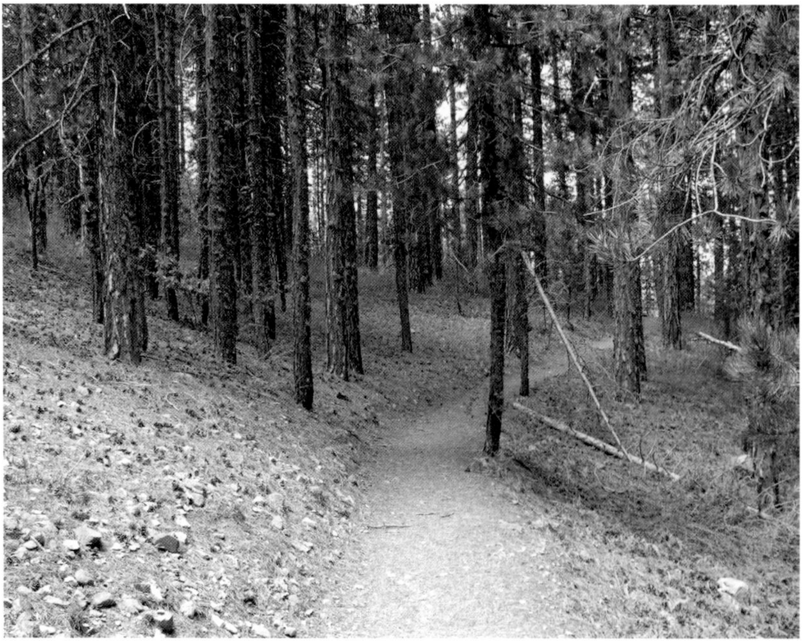

Persephone nature walking trail is the easiest of the three highest altitude Troodos walking trails. A few points on the way need care as they are close to steep slopes. It is linear and three km long, in the direction of Amiantos village (Amiantos means 'asbestos' in Greek - the village took its name from the nearby mine). The walking route can be accessed from the paved road going to the local police station near Troodos Square. On the way walkers may see wild apple trees and many pine trees, junipers and wild rose bushes. Walkers may very likely meet jay birds. Towards the east one may see parts of the asbestos mine (no longer used) and a small pool. At the end there is a vista point towards Limassol in the south. Persephone makes a good combination with Artemis, the circular nature walking trail near Olympus peak, as the combined length of the walking route is about 16 km (alternatively one can use a car to cover the two-km distance on the paved road from the end of the one to the start of the other).

Persephone could also together with Kalidonia waterfall nature walking trail compose a circular, rather tough 14 km route via Pouziaris locality.

Distance (km): Platres : 6 Limassol : 46 Polis : 66 Paphos : 66 Nicosia : 80
Larnaca: 112 Agia Napa : 153 Protaras : 159

ARTEMIS WALKING ROUTE

(Map 24 – page 189, 24)

It is the highest altitude walking trail in Cyprus. It is a circular, seven km long walking trail starting and finishing on the road to Chionistra (officially known as Olympus peak). There are signs indicating particular flora species and geological attractions on the walking route. The walk is not tiring, but considerable caution is needed as in many places it is next to cliffs. Walkers may see the black pines and junipers of the region growing out of the barren rocks, as well as wild apple trees, a number of rare flowers, and possibly jay birds. When there is snow in Cyprus in winter, the walking trail is completely covered by snow. The walking trail traverses ski pistes. The walk offers glorious vistas, especially towards the south (west). There are two ancient black pine trees on (or very near) the nature walking trail.

Artemis can make a good combination with easy three km long linear Persephone nature walking trail that starts near Troodos Square, or even with the more difficult three km long Kalidonia waterfall walking trail (which has an elevation range of 300 m). Those into more extreme walking experiences may combine Artemis with a twelve km long walking route to Agios Nicolaos tis Stegis UNESCO World Heritage Troodos Painted Church (towards the north east, the route descends 1,000 meters). Kakopetria village is three kilometers further north east (a further 200m descent).

Distance (km): Platres : 8 Limassol : 48 Polis : 68 Paphos : 68 Nicosia : 82
Larnaca: 114 Agia Napa : 155 Protaras : 161

PLATY VALLEY – KELEFOS BRIDGE WALKING ROUTE

(Map 21 – page 186, 25)

The route is some 15 km from Platres and between the villages of Mylikouri, Kaminaria and Agios Nikolaos. Platy valley is fantastic and offers great walking and mountain biking (and photo safari) possibilities. The recommended route starts from the paved road about 1.5 km north of Kaminaria village. Walking is mostly on the dirt road in the valley, which ends in the south where the river Diarizos (which means 'having two roots' in Greek) is born. On this walking route travellers may have to cross the stream up to three times (in summer usually just once). Nearly six km from the start one comes to Komititzi (or Komitidji) picnic area, a good place to have a lunch break (there's an ancient plane tree there). Nearly four km further south there is a spring. In the valley one may see many plane trees, ferns, maples, storax, pines and fig trees, while they are likely to see the elusive moufflon (especially in summer) early in the morning or late in the afternoon. Please do not drive through the valley. Unfortunately in summer one may meet a few cars driving in the valley. Once walkers reach the road connecting Kaminaria to Agios Nicolaos village and turn right on the paved road, they have two options: Either to continue to walk on the paved road for nearly two km to beautiful Kelefos medieval Venetian bridge or complete the route by turning left on a dirt road and then after about 400 m to turn right on the walking trail connecting the three medieval bridges in the area. The second option adds splendid views and variety to the walk, but locating the walking trail can be difficult.

Distance (km) : Platres : 14 Paphos : 56 Limassol : 56 Polis : 76 Nicosia : 104
Larnaca: 122 Agia Napa : 163 Protaras : 169

TEICHIA TIS MADARIS WALKING ROUTE

(Map 19 – page 184, 26)

The Greek Cypriot name of the walking trail means 'the Walls of Madari' (Madari is the name of this mountain peak). Indeed the rock formations in the vicinity are extraordinary and walkers have the chance to observe them throughout the short three km long journey on the circular walking trail. The walking route is about 22 km from Platres and offers panoramic views of the west part of Mesaoria plain including Nicosia, Morphou and even the Pentadactylos (or Keryneia) range. The flora includes (amongst others) golden oaks and junipers and walkers may also see wild roses (in bloom in late spring). The walking trail has its ups and downs, and caution is a must, as some slopes are quite steep. The walking trail is part of a chain of walking trails and it makes a good small addition to those who want longer walks than the adjacent excellent 13 km long Madari circular walking route.

The walking trail is found near a part of Pitsilia region known for its hazelnut 'forests' (plantations really - the trees are between 50 and 100 years old and the area is protected). Panagia tou Araka UNESCO World Heritage Troodos painted church is a very important cultural attraction nearby between the villages of Lagoudera and Saranti. There's also an ancient oak tree near the church.

Distance (km) : Platres : 22 Limassol : 62 Nicosia : 78 Paphos : 82 Polis : 88
Larnaca: 128 Agia Napa : 169 Protaras : 175

MADARI CIRCULAR WALKING ROUTE

(Map 19 – page 184, 27)

Platres

This is a superb 13 km long circular walking route that is a composition of four smaller walking routes (described in the pages below) near Madari mountain peak (in the area of Pitsilia, on the Troodos mountain range). The walking route is of medium difficulty and without very steep ascents and descents. Nevertheless it is quite tiring and walkers may choose to do one of the component walking routes, as a number of them meet roads on both ends (so an arrangement could be made for a car pick up at the end of a shorter trip). Walkers enjoy great views towards the north, including Morphou bay, and to the south, including the village of Kyperounta and Troodos peak. To the west there is view towards the village of Spilia. There is great variety in the vegetation as it includes golden oak, wild rose and mastic bushes, junipers, pine, strawberry trees, rock rose and sage and even cedar, plane trees and fern. Walkers may observe the intriguing rock formations in the area. Though the usual start (and finish) of the walking route is at Madari peak (which one can reach by car from the 'Polystypos village – Chandria village' road), walkers could also take the walking route on two intersections with the paved road that connects Spilia village to Kyperounta village. Madari peak is about 22 km north east of Platres village.

In the vicinity there are other pretty walking routes, as well as the two UNESCO WorldHeritage painted churches of Panagia tou Araka and Stavros tou Agiasmati, picturesque villages, ancient trees and the beautiful Xyliatos dam. Good walking shoes are recommended, as are walking poles.

Distance (km): Platres : 22 Limassol : 62 Nicosia : 78 Paphos : 82 Polis : 88
Larnaca: 128 Agia Napa : 169 Protaras : 175

MADARI – DOXA SI O THEOS WALKING ROUTE

(Map 19 – page 184, 28)

This is a four km long linear walking trail from Madari peak to Doxa si o Theos locality. Madari peak is about 22 km north east of Platres village. The walking trail has an altitude range of about 200 meters. The walking route is easy, without too steep ascents and descents. Walkers enjoy great views towards the south, including Morphou bay, and to the north, including the village of Kyperounta and Troodos peak. There is considerable variety in the vegetation which includes golden oak, wild rose and mastic bushes, junipers, pine, strawberry trees, rock rose, sage and even cedar. Its Madari peak end can be reached by car from the 'Polystypos village – Chandria village' road while the Doxa si o Theos locality ends at the paved road that connects Spilia village to Kyperounta village. The walking trail can be combined with adjacent walking trails to form the excellent, 13 km long Madari Circular walking route.

In the vicinity there are also other pleasant walking routes, as well as the two UNESCO World Heritage painted churches of Panagia tou Araka and Stavros tou Agiasmati, picturesque villages, ancient trees, the beautiful Xyliatos dam and a 'hidden' medieval bridge nearby, and a number of watermills.

Distance (km) : Platres : 22 Limassol : 62 Nicosia : 78 Paphos : 82 Polis : 88
Larnaca: 128 Agia Napa : 169 Protaras : 175

DOXA SI O THEOS – MOUTTI TIS CHORAS WALKING ROUTE

(Map 19 – page 184, 29)

This is an easy, 1.6 km long linear walking trail from the locality 'Doxa si o Theos' to the locality 'Moutti tis Choras'. It runs parallel and next to the paved road that connects Spilia village to Kyperounta village. The walking trail has an altitude range of almost 200 meters. To the west walkers may see the village of Spilia. The vegetation is dominated by pine and there are also many golden oaks and strawberry trees, as well as rock rose and sage. I suggest that this walking trail is combined with adjacent walking trails to form the excellent 13 km long Madari Circular walking route.

In the vicinity there are also other lovely walking routes, as well as the two UNESCO World Heritage painted churches of Panagia tou Araka and Stavros tou Agiasmati, picturesque villages, ancient trees, the beautiful Xyliatos dam and a 'hidden' medieval bridge nearby, and a number of watermills.

Distance (km) : Platres : 20 Limassol : 60 Nicosia : 78 Paphos : 80 Polis : 86
Larnaca: 126 Agia Napa : 169 Protaras : 175

MOUTTI TIS CHORAS – SELLADI TOU KARAMANLI WALKING ROUTE

(Map 19 – page 184, 30)

This is a four km long linear walking trail from the locality 'Moutti tis Choras' to the locality 'Selladi tou Karamanli'. The two ends of the walking trail have an altitude difference of only 100 meters and the walking route starts and ends at the dirt road that connects at paved roads near the villages of Spilia and Lagoudera. The altitude range of the walking trail is about 200 meters. There are great views of strange rock formations. The vegetation is dominated by pine and golden oak. Walkers can also see strawberry trees, myrtle, some plane trees, as well as rock rose and sage. The walking trail can be combined with adjacent walking trails to form the excellent 13 km long Madari Circular walking route.

In the vicinity there are also other attractive walking routes, as well as the two UNESCO World Heritage painted churches of Panagia tou Araka and Stavros tou Agiasmati, picturesque villages, ancient trees, the beautiful Xyliatos dam and a 'hidden' medieval bridge nearby, and a number of watermills.

Distance (km) : Platres : 20 Limassol : 60 Nicosia : 78 Paphos : 80 Polis : 86
Larnaca: 126 Agia Napa : 169 Protaras : 175

MADARI – SELLADI TOU KARAMANLI WALKING ROUTE

(Map 19 – page 184, 31)

This is a 3.6 km long linear walking trail from Madari peak to 'Selladi tou Karamanli' locality Madari peak is about 22 km north east of Platres village. The altitude range of this walking route is about 300 meters. The walking route is of medium difficulty, without relatively steep ascents and descents. Walkers can enjoy great views of barren peaks and rock formations in the area. The vegetation is dominated by pine and golden oak. The walking trail passes inside a cedar forest. There are also strawberry trees, wild rose and mastic bushes, rock rose, sage and even plane trees and ferns. The walking route's Madari peak end can be reached by car from the 'Polystypos village – Chandria village' road while the 'Selladi tou Karamanli' locality is on the dirt road that connects at paved roads near the villages of Spilia and Lagoudera. The walking trail can be combined with adjacent walking trails to form the excellent 13 km long Madari Circular walking route.

In the vicinity there are also other interesting walking routes, as well as the two UNESCO World Heritage painted churches of Panagia tou Araka and Stavros tou Agiasmati, picturesque villages, ancient trees, the beautiful Xyliatos dam and a 'hidden' medieval bridge nearby, and a number of watermills.

Distance (km) : Platres : 22 Limassol : 62 Nicosia : 78 Paphos : 82 Polis : 88
Larnaca: 128 Agia Napa : 169 Protaras : 175

CEDAR VALLEY – TRIPYLOS PEAK WALKING ROUTE

(Map 20 – page 185, 32)

Cedar Valley is found about 30 km north west of Platres. It is easily accessible through paved road, either from the 'Kykkos monastery to Stavros tis Psokas forest station' road, or from Panagia village. It has picnic facilities. The walking route which is on a dirt road is linear, 2.5 km long and has an altitude range of about 250 meters. It ascends to Tripylos peak from where one can have a panoramic view of the north coast, all the way from the Akamas peninsula to Morphou bay and beyond. The walk is through the cedar forest of Cyprus which has 130,000 cedar trees. The fauna includes many jay birds. Early in the morning or late in the afternoon walkers have good chances of spotting some of the elusive moufflon of Cyprus.

Cedar Valley is deep inside the vast Paphos Forest, a huge uninhabited part of Troodos mountains that offers great walking and cycling opportunities on its network of forest dirt roads.

There are no villages or other facilities for many kilometers away. Stavros tis Psokas forest station where there is a restaurant and rooms to let is 16 km away towards the north west. The village of Pano Panagia which has a number of accommodation options is about 20 km away towards the south west. The small village of Tsakkistra and Kykkos monastery are about 15 km away from Cedar Valley towards the north east and south east respectively.

Distance (km) : Platres : 30 Polis : 50 Paphos : 55 Limassol : 70 Nicosia : 104 Larnaca: 136 Agia Napa : 152 Protaras : 158

PANAGIA TOU SINTI - ROUDIAS MEDIEVAL BRIDGE WALKING ROUTE

(Map 25 – page 190, 33)

It is a ten km long linear route mainly on dirt roads connecting Panagia tou Sinti church and Roudias Venetian medieval bridge. Roudias bridge is about 25 km west of the village of Platres and just inside Paphos Forest while the church is 34 km south west in Xeros Potamos valley. As the elevation difference is just 100 m, it does not matter at which end walkers start their walk. On the way they pass by three watermills (and close to a fourth), below the imposing cliffs near Ais Yiannis village and next to other peculiar rock formations (e.g. Rotsos ton Laouthkion, whose Greek Cypriot name means 'the Rock of the hares'). The vegetation by the river, especially on the northern part of the route is very rich, and dominated by alder trees. The route in this uninhabited valley showcases beautiful pieces of the island's nature and cultural heritage. This is likely the most adventurous walk in the Book, as it crosses (the northern part of) Xeros Potamos river a few times. The river sometimes has a lot of water and extreme care is absolutely necessary after heavy rains.

Another splendid chapel of Xeros Potamos valley, found on the west slope at a rock formation about four km south east of Galataria village is frescoed 16th century Agios Nicolaos.

Distance (km) : Platres : 25 Paphos : 41 Polis : 46 Limassol : 59 Larnaca: 125
Nicosia : 141 Agia Napa : 166 Protaras : 172

ARMINOU DAM

(Map 21 – page 186, 20)

It is about 15 km west of Platres and within four km from the villages of Arminou, Filousa and Agios Nikolaos. It was built in 1998 on the river Diarizos ('Diarizos' is derived from the Greek word for 'the one who has two roots') at an altitude of about 300 meters, it has capacity of 4.3 million cubic meters and a surface area of about 25 hectares. Fish in the lake include carp, mosquito fish, roach, silver bream, rainbow trout and brown trout. The landscape is very pretty with pines and other wild trees and bushes on the banks of the manmade lake. Unfortunately there are no good walking opportunities around the lake. The roads around it are at a distance of on average a kilometer from the lake and are usually 150 m to 250 m higher than the lake. The north end of Arminou manmade lake is just 500 meters south of Kelephos medieval Venetian bridge. It is not unusual to spot moufflon here.

The villages in the vicinity have stone built houses and are well preserved. There are many vineyards, wineries, old chapels, medieval bridges and watermills relatively near.

Distance (km): Platres : 15 Paphos : 50 Limassol : 50 Polis : 85 Nicosia : 101
Larnaca: 116 Agia Napa : 157 Protaras : 163

KALOPANAGIOTIS DAM

(Map 23 – page 188, 21)

Kalopanagiotis dam is built at an altitude of about 600 meters and is thus the dam at the highest elevation out of all (big) dams in Cyprus. It is found nearly 30 km north of Platres in Marathasa valley and can be accessed on the road from Kalopanagiotis village towards Morphou and Nicosia. It was built in 1966 on the Setrakhos (Marathasas) river and has a capacity of just 0.4 million cubic meters and a surface area of about five hectares. Fish in the lake include mosquito fish, bleak, rainbow trout and brown trout.

Marathasa valley has some outstanding cultural attractions including three UNESCO World Heritage churches, the impressive renovated Kykkos watermill, more ancient chapels and a couple of medieval Venetian bridges. Most of these as well as a few ancient trees in the valley (in Kalopanagiotis and in Moutoullas) can be combined in walking routes.

Distance (km) : Platres : 28 Limassol : 68 Polis : 73 Nicosia : 74 Paphos : 88
Larnaca: 134 Agia Napa : 175 Protaras : 181

OAK TREE IN PERA PEDI

(Map 22 – page 187, 15)

The village of Pera Pedi is about eight km south of Platres, at an altitude of 800 meters. There are two oak trees (Quercus infectoria subsp. veneris) very close to each other. Visitors may spot at least the younger one, inside the village, on the right side of the main road coming from Trimiklini village. The older oak tree is just tens of meters further to the right (at a higher elevation). It is 200 years old, 22 meters tall and its trunk has a perimeter of almost three meters.

A stop here can be combined with the many natural and cultural attractions in the area, including the renovated atypical watermill at Pera Pedi, the small Pera Pedi manmade lake just kilometers to the north, four medieval bridges in close proximity, small wineries, Agia Mavri ancient chapel, picturesque villages and other ancient trees in the area.

Distance (km) : Platres : 8 Limassol : 37 Paphos : 60 Polis : 80 Nicosia : 94 Larnaca: 103 Agia Napa : 144 Protaras : 150

TWO BLACK PINES ON OLYMPUS

(Map 24 – page 189, 16-17)

Both of these black pines are ancient, huge trees. They range between 450 and 500 years old, with a height of 18 and 20 meters respectively and a trunk perimeter of about 4.5 meters. One is found on (the north stretch of) Artemis Nature walking trail and the other quite near the (south stretch of the) walking trail. While it makes great sense to visit the trees while walking on Artemis walking trail, they are not far from the paved road, so it is quite easy to visit even for those who are not walking the walking trail (especially in winter when the walking trail is often covered in snow and dangerous).

Troodos has exceptional geology in that, ancient rock layers may be observed at the surface instead of kilometers underground. The area which is at the highest elevation of the island (1,600 – 1,950 m) offers a selection of nature walking routes in alpine surrounding, dramatic settings and exceptional vistas. There's an environmental information center at Troodos Square and a botanical garden a few km north east from Troodos Square.

Distance (km) : Platres : 9 Limassol : 38 Paphos : 61 Polis : 81 Nicosia : 95 Larnaca: 104 Agia Napa : 145 Protaras : 151

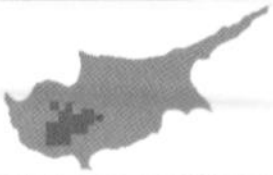

OAK TREE IN KOUKA

(Map 22 – page 187, 18)

Kouka is a small village about nine km south of Platres, at an altitude of 700 meters. The ancient oak tree (Quercus infectoria subsp. veneris) is on the left side of the road from Pera Pedi village, a few hundred meters before the village. It is 400 years old, 16 meters tall and its trunk has a perimeter of about 4.5 meters. A stop here can be combined with the exploration of many of the natural and cultural attractions in the area, including the renovated atypical watermill at Pera Pedi, the small Pera Pedi manmade lake to the north, four medieval bridges in close proximity (Trimiklini, Agia Mavri, Milia, Koilani), small wineries, Agia Mavri ancient chapel, picturesque villages and other ancient trees in the area.

Distance (km) : Platres : 9 Limassol : 36 Paphos : 61 Polis : 81 Nicosia : 95 Larnaca: 102 Agia Napa : 143 Protaras : 149

PLANE TREE AT AGIA MAVRI (NEAR KOILANI VILLAGE)

(Map 22 – page 187, 19)

The ancient Agia Mavri chapel (believed to have been built in the 12th century) and the plane tree are just ten km from the resort of Platres, and easily accessible on the road between the villages of Pera Pedi and Koilani. This huge plane tree (Platanus orientalis) has a height of 36 meters and a trunk circumference of 5.5 meters. It is estimated to be 800 years old. It is right on the Kryos Potamos river.

The Agia Mavri medieval bridge is just 400 meters to the south of the church (there's also a damaged watermill close to the bridge) and easily accessed while the Koilani medieval bridge is 1,200 meters south of Agia Mavri church.

Other charming attractions in the area include small wineries (e.g. in Koilani and near Pera Pedi), splendid picturesque villages (e.g. Koilani, Vouni), more medieval Venetian bridges, an unusual watermill in Pera Pedi, the small Pera Pedi manmade lake and more ancient trees.

Distance (km) : Platres : 10 Limassol : 38 Paphos : 60 Polis : 95 Nicosia : 96 Larnaca: 104 Agia Napa : 145 Protaras : 151

LAUREL IN OMODOS

(Map 25 – page 190, 20)

Omodos is one of the largest villages in the Krasohoria region (the word 'Krasohoria' comes from the Greek word that means 'wine villages'), which is found north west of Limassol. The village is some eight km south west of (Pano) Platres village. It is a picturesque and to some extent commercialized village whose major attraction is the historic monastery of the Holy Cross, which dates back to the time Saint Helen was on the island (4th century AD). The ancient laurel tree (Laurus nobilis) is about three km west of the village, close to the road to Agios Nikolaos village. Explorers need to take the second dirt road on their left, on the road to Agios Nikolaos village (the dirt road is a few hundred meters long). The tree is in the courtyard of the very pretty renovated Apostle Philip chapel. It has an age of 1,000 years, a height of ten meters and its trunk has a perimeter of eight meters. The tree is used as the chapel's belfry. Laurel is connected with the worship of Greek mythology god Apollo and it is possible that a shrine to Apollo existed here in antiquity. There are vineyards all around.

Other attractions in the area include small wineries (e.g. in Vasa, Omodos), picturesque stone built villages (e.g. Arsos, Vasa, Kedares, Filousa), medieval Venetian bridges (in Potamiou village or Kelefos), and many more.

Distance (km): Platres : 11 Limassol : 48 Paphos : 52 Polis : 87 Nicosia : 97 Larnaca: 114 Agia Napa : 155 Protaras : 161

OAK TREE IN AGIOS MAMAS

(Map 22 – page 187, 21)

Agios Mamas is a village in the Commandaria region (an area in the mountains above Limassol where the famous Commandaria dessert wine is produced), about 13 km southeast of Platres, at an altitude of 600 meters. The ancient oak tree (Quercus infectoria subsp. veneris) is on the outskirts of the village, just behind the football pitch, on the road that leads to Kapilio village. It is a very large 500 years old tree, 22 meters tall and its trunk has a perimeter of about 5.5 meters.

One could stop here on the way to the nearby medieval bridge, which is found about three km east of Agios Mamas village next to a quarry, by the side of the road that leads to Kalo Chorio village. The bridge has seen better, dust free days. Hopefully it will be restored and protected. Luckily cars and trucks do not run over it but instead, on the adjacent modern bridge.

There are a few more medieval bridges in the vicinity as well as other ancient trees, watermills, a UNESCO World Heritage church in Pelendri (Holly Cross), small wineries and picturesque villages.

Distance (km): Platres : 13 Limassol : 38 Paphos : 63 Polis : 98 Nicosia : 99 Larnaca: 102 Agia Napa : 143 Protaras : 149

OLIVE AND MASTIC TREE IN POTAMIOU

(Map 25 – page 190, 22-23)

Olive tree

Mastic tree

Potamiou is a small picturesque village about 13 km southwest of Platres, and three km south of Omodos village (a large village in the area) at an altitude of 670 meters. Though it is hardly on the tourist map, it offers the explorer welcomed surprises. There are two ancient trees in the village. The olive tree (Olea europaea), on the right side of the downhill road that leads to the cemetery and a mastic tree (Pistacia atlantica) at the Agios Mnasonas church ruins (on the downhill road to the south of the village). The olive tree lives on private land, it's 700 years old, eight meters tall and its trunk has a perimeter of about 7.3 meters. 150 meters on the dirt road past the cemetery the explorer finds the medieval bridge. The bridge is in a quite decent state and near orchards.

There are many other worthy destinations in the area, including Omodos village (a main tourist attraction, with the historic Timiou Stavrou – Holly Cross - monastery and cobblestone alleys), other pretty villages like Vasa and Arsos, small wineries, chapels, ancient trees and many other attractions.

Distance (km) : Platres : 13 Limassol : 45 Paphos : 51 Polis : 86 Nicosia : 99 Larnaca: 111 Agia Napa : 152 Protaras : 158

OAK TREE IN LANEIA

(Map 22 – page 187, 24)

Laneia is a very picturesque village in the Commandaria region (an area in the mountains above Limassol where the famous Commandaria dessert wine is produced). It sits about 15 km southeast of Platres, at an altitude of 600 meters. The ancient oak tree (Quercus infectoria subsp. veneris) is outside the village, about 300 meters east of the main road from Limassol to Platres. There are relevant signs (3rd turn right, after the police station which is on the left side of the road) by the road. It is a majestic 800 years old tree, 26 meters tall and its trunk has a perimeter of about 8.5 meters. In Laneia village there was until some years ago also another very impressive ancient oak tree in the yard of a coffee shop. Sadly it does not exist anymore. There are many other younger oak trees close to the village.

Other attractions in the area include the monastery of Panagia tis Amasgou near Monagri, the medieval bridges of Trimiklini (and east of Agios Mamas), local wineries, preserved villages and ancient trees.

Distance (km): Platres : 14 Limassol : 26 Polis : 86 Larnaca: 92 Paphos : 94 Nicosia : 100 Agia Napa : 133 Protaras : 139

OAK TREE IN AGIOS NIKOLAOS

(Map 21 – page 186, 25)

Agios Nikolaos village is about 15 km to the (south) west of the village of Platres, at an altitude of 800 meters. The ancient oak tree (Quercus infectoria subsp. veneris) is found in the outskirts of the village, north west of the Forest Department office. The tree is in a private yard so explorers may not be able to get too close. It is 400 years old, ten meters tall and its trunk has a perimeter of almost 4.5 meters.

Visitors could stop here while exploring other attractions of this, very rich in natural beauty, part of Cyprus. The valley of Diarizos where the village is found has an abundance of watermills, and well preserved stone built villages surrounded by vineyards (there are also a few wineries in the area e.g. near Praitori, in Arsos and in Salamiou). Arminou dam is close by, and so is the huge Paphos Forest, Kelephos medieval Venetian bridge and shaded Platy valley.

Distance (km) : Platres : 15 Paphos : 45 Limassol : 45 Polis : 80 Nicosia : 96 Larnaca: 111 Agia Napa : 152 Protaras : 158

MASTIC IN KISSOUSA

(Map 25 – page 190, 26)

Kissousa is a minute village about 15 km southwest of Platres, at an altitude of nearly 600 meters. The ancient mastic tree (Pistacia atlantica) is in the churchyard of the medieval Agioi Sergios and Vakhos church. It is a 600 years old tree, 16 meters tall and its trunk has a perimeter of five meters. There's a running stream (the Chapotami river) very close to the church and its cemetery. There is a watermill that is at a good structural state nearby. It is found downstream about 500 meters south west of the village and can be easily accessed from the paved road between Agios Amvrosios and Omodos village.

The small nearby Potamiou village has a good collection of natural and cultural attractions. There's a large number of wineries in the area (e.g. in Vasa, Malia, Pachna), well preserved stone-built villages, ancient trees, chapels, monasteries and more.

Distance (km) : Platres : 15 Limassol : 43 Paphos : 49 Polis : 84 Nicosia : 101 Larnaca: 109 Agia Napa : 150 Protaras : 156

OAK TREE IN MOUTOULLAS

(Map 23 – page 188, 27)

Moutoullas village is in Marathasa valley and immediately south (west) of Kalopanagiotis village. The valley boasts three UNESCO World Heritage Troodos painted churches in close proximity (in Pedoulas, Moutoullas, Kalopanagiotis), a manmade small lake north of Kalopanagiotis, the renovated impressive Kykkos watermill, medieval bridges, walking routes, museums and more. Moutoullas is home to two ancient oak trees (Quercus infectoria subsp. Veneris). One of these (shown in the photo above) is very close to the main road connecting Pedoulas to Kalopanagiotis village, just as one enters Moutoullas, but access is difficult. It is a 350 years old tree, 26 meters tall and its trunk has a perimeter of about four meters. There is another ancient oak tree next to the church of the Transfiguration of the Saviour, about one kilometer east of Moutoullas.

One could easily compose an eleven - km long circular walking route that passes by most of the attractions of Kalopanagiotis and Moutoullas village, including the UNESCO World Heritage Church of Panagia (our Lady) tou Moutoulla. For those who like to explore on bicycles, the narrow paved road between Kykkos monastery – Pedoulas road and Panagia tou Moutoulla chapel is highly recommended for its vistas.

Distance (km) : Platres : 25 Limassol : 65 Polis : 70 Nicosia : 77 Paphos : 85 Larnaca: 131 Agia Napa : 172 Protaras : 178

OAK AND KERMES OAK IN PACHNA

(Map 25 – page 190, 28-29)

Oak

Kermes oak

The picturesque village of Pachna is built at an altitude of 700 meters, about 42 km north west of Limassol. There are two ancient trees in the village, which of course deserve our respect. The oak tree of Pachna is found near the church of St George (please ask the locals for directions). The tree is of the species Quercus infectoria subsp. veneris, it is 300 years old, has a height of 16 meters and a trunk perimeter of a bit over 3.50 meters. The kermes oak tree (Quercus coccifera subsp. calliprinos) of Pachna is found in the old cemetery (please ask the locals for directions). It was referred to as "Pernos" by older villagers I talked to. The tree is 350 years old, has a height of 14 meters and a trunk perimeter of almost three meters.

Vines are a very important agricultural produce of Pachna and the wider area. There's a large number of wineries in the vicinity (e.g. in Pachna, in Malia, in Agios Amvrosios), well preserved stone-built villages, ancient trees, chapels, monasteries, a medieval Venetian bridge (in Potamiou), a well preserved watermill (near Kissousa) and more.

Distance (km) : Platres : 19 Paphos : 38 Limassol : 42 Polis : 73 Nicosia : 105 Larnaca: 108 Agia Napa : 149 Protaras : 155

KERMES OAK IN KALOPANAGIOTIS

(Map 23 – page 188, 30)

Kalopanagiotis village is built at an altitude of about 700 m and is found 27 km north of Platres village. The impressive kermes oak (Quercus coccifera subsp. calliprinos) tree is in the yard of the Panagia Theoskepasti chapel, about 300 meters to the east of Agios Ioannis Lampadistis monastery. The tree is huge, 700 years old, 17 meters tall and has a trunk perimeter of almost four meters. It is used as the chapel's belfry.

There are good possibilities for walks on the dirt road network in the area e.g. east of Kalopanagiotis towards Moutoullas village and its attractions. There are angling possibilities in the small manmade lake north of Kalopanagiotis.

There's also a five km long circular walking route called 'Ariadni' that begins by the paved road near the village of Gerakies to the west of Kalopanagiotis. Ariadni walking route begins about seven km from Kalopanagiotis.

Marathasa valley (where Kalopanagiotis village is found) has some outstanding attractions, especially cultural. There are three UNESCO World Heritage Troodos painted churches in close proximity (in Pedoulas, Moutoullas, Kalopanagiotis), a manmade small lake north of Kalopanagiotis, the renovated impressive Kykkos watermill, two medieval bridges, museums, a few ancient trees and more.

Distance (km): Platres : 27 Limassol : 67 Polis : 72 Nicosia : 75 Paphos : 87 Larnaca: 133 Agia Napa : 174 Protaras : 180

PINE TREE IN CHANDRIA

(Map 19 – page 184, 31)

Chandria village is found about 25 km to the north east of the village of Platres, at an altitude of 1,200 meters. The ancient pine tree (Pinus brutia) lives in the courtyard of the village church. The tree is 350 years old, 16 meters tall and its trunk has a perimeter of 4.5 meters. The tree is used as the chapel's belfry.

Chandria is about four km south of the excellent Madari circular walking route. Other nearby attractions include Panagia tou Araka monastery near Lagoudera and Timios Stavros (Holly Cross) church at Pelendri village, both of which are UNESCO World Heritage Troodos painted churches. In the wider area there are a few well preserved watermills, a partly damaged medieval bridge south of Potamitissa village on Ambelikos river and a hidden medieval Venetian bridge near Xyliatos manmade lake.

Distance (km) : Platres : 25 Limassol : 38 Nicosia : 47 Polis : 84 Paphos : 90 Larnaca: 91 Agia Napa : 127 Protaras : 133

MASTIC TREE IN AGIOS THERAPON

(Map 25 – page 190, 32)

Agios Therapon is a charming village about 26 km south of Platres, at an altitude of 640 meters. The ancient mastic tree (Pistacia atlantica) is in the western outskirt of the village. The tree is 350 years old, ten meters tall and its trunk has a perimeter of three meters.

Besides exploring this traditional village itself, attractions in the area include other nearby beautiful villages (e.g. Lofou, Vouni), local wineries (e.g. in Malia, Vasa, Agios Amvrosios), the watermill near Kissousa, the medieval Venetian bridges near Potamiou and near Koilani, and more.

Distance (km) : Platres : 26 Limassol : 33 Paphos : 41 Polis : 76 Nicosia : 116 Larnaca: 119 Agia Napa : 160 Protaras : 166

PINE, OAK AND TEREBINTH IN AGIOS THEODOROS AGROU

(Map 19 – page 184, 33-35)

Pine

Oak

Terebinth – next to Panagia tis Kivotou church

Agios Theodoros Agrou is a lush small village built at an altitude of 1,000 meters. It is about seven km south east of Agros village, one of the biggest in the Pitsilia area, on the Troodos mountain range, and about 30 km east of Platres village. Agios Theodoros is blessed with having three ancient trees in its grounds. A pine (Pinus brutia) - known as 'Koutsoftas pine', an oak (Quercus infectoria subsp. Veneris) - known as 'Koutsoftas oak' and a terebinth (Pistacia terebinthus). The pine tree is 120 years old, 18 meters tall and its trunk has a perimeter of about 2.5 meters. It is found in a yard in (or above I would say) the center of the village. The oak is very close and to the south of the pine tree. It is 300 years old, 16 meters tall and its trunk has a perimeter of about 3.5 meters. The terebinth is found in the courtyard of a renovated very pretty church further to the south called "Panagia tis Kivotou" (Our Lady of the Ark). The terebinth is 200 years old, six meters tall and its trunk perimeter is almost two meters.

While Agios Theodoros Agrou may be a worthy destination on its own, there are at the same time very important attractions in the vicinity. There's a small waterfall by the village of Agios Ioannis, a partly damaged medieval Venetian bridge near the village of Potamitissa and a watermill at that village. There are three UNESCO World Heritage Troodos Painted churches at a distance of less than 20 km from the village (Metomorfosis tou Sotiros in Palaichori, Timios Stavros in Pelendri, and Panagia tou Araka near Lagoudera). The excellent Madari Circular walking route is less than 20 km away.

For those wanting to explore on bicycles I recommend the route from the junction of the Agros-Palaichori road with the road that leads to the village of Alona, all the way to Alona, (and further to Polystypos, Lagoudera and from there either to Spilia, Kakopetria or to Xyliatos).

Distance (km) : Limassol : 30 Platres : 30 Nicosia : 43 Larnaca: 94 Paphos : 96 Polis : 102 Agia Napa : 135 Protaras : 141

THREE CYPRESSES AND STORAX TREE IN SALAMIOU

(Map 25 – page 190, 36, 37)

The three Cypresses

The Storax

Salamiou is an attractive village at an altitude of 600 meters, almost 30 km south west of Platres, with many restored stone built houses. The three huge ancient cypress trees are inside a small park, half a kilometer in the south west direction from the main village square. There's a children's playground in the plot where the trees live. The ancient storax tree (Styrax officinalis) grows in the yard of the Salamiotissa monastery. It is 150 years old, eight meters tall and its trunk has a perimeter of about two meters. The region has a lot of natural and other attractions. There are many stone built villages in the area, and besides Salamiotissa, another important chapel (the Europa Nostra awarded 'Panagia tou Sinti' monastery – this doesnot function as a monastery for many decades) is quite close, in the Xeros Potamos valley. Both Xeros Potamos valley and Diarizos valley (east of Salamiou) have many watermills still in a good structural state. Paphos Forest and Arminou dam are a few km away.

Distance (km) : Platres : 30 Paphos : 38 Limassol : 65 Polis : 73 Nicosia : 116 Larnaca: 123 Agia Napa : 172 Protaras : 178

OAK TREE IN LAGOUDERA

(Map 19 – page 184, 38)

The huge tree is found next to Panagia tou Araka church, one of the ten UNESCO World Heritage Troodos painted churches. The church is found just west of Lagoudera village which is built at an altitude of 1,000 meters, 33 km north east of Platres. The ancient oak tree (Quercus infectoria subsp. veneris) is 700 years old, 16 meters tall and its trunk has a perimeter of nearly five meters. The area is known on the island for its hazelnut 'forests' (plantations). It is a prime destination for walking and exploration. Specifically Madari Circular walking route is highly recommended. Those interested in walking just a few km can do the three-km long circular Teichia tis Madaris walking route (or maybe a short eight-km version of Madari Circular walk returning to the starting point on the Saranti - Spilia road - part of the road is paved and part of it is a dirt road). The Stavros tou Agiasmati church – Panagia tou Araka church linear walking route is also good; it would need some prearrangement with relation to transportation unless one wants to walk back eight more kilometers on the same walking route.

Distance (km) : Platres : 33 Nicosia : 39 Limassol : 46 Polis : 92 Paphos : 98 Larnaca: 99 Agia Napa : 136 Protaras : 141

ONE CYPRESS AND TWO OAK TREES IN KANNAVIA

(Map 19 – page 184, 39)

Kannavia is a small Troodos village at an altitude of nearly 800 meters, 31 km north east of Platres. The ancient trees (two oaks and a cypress) are found in the area of the community park. As per the erected sign, one of the oak trees is more than 750 years old, with a height of 21 meters and trunk perimeter of nearly four meters. The cypress is in the yard of the nearby church and it is used as belfry. The playground is very pleasant. The village borders Adelfi Forest. There is a five-km walking route from the nearby village of Agia Eirini (Agia Eirini – Limeria) but I would rather recommend the excellent 13-km long Madari Circular walk which is five kilometres south (one can do a shorter eight-km version of Madari Circular walk returning to the starting point on the Saranti - Spilia road).

It makes sense to combine a trip from Nicosia with a stop at Peristerona village to see the renovated 11th century Apostles Varnavas and Ilarionas church (one of two ancient five-domed churches in Cyprus) and with a visit to the amazing Panagia Asinou UNESCO World Heritage Troodos painted church (and/or Panagia tou Araka UNESCO World Heritage Troodos Painted church near Lagoudera).

Distance (km) : Platres : 31 Nicosia : 41 Limassol : 44 Polis : 90 Paphos : 96 Larnaca: 97 Agia Napa : 134 Protaras : 139

CYPRESS IN AGIA EIRINI

(Map 19 – page 184, 40)

Agia Eirini is a small Troodos village at an altitude of nearly 900 meters, about 30 km north east of Platres. The ancient cypress tree is found in the church yard in the south end of the village, by the paved road coming from Spilia village. It is used as belfry.

There is a five-km walking route from here (Agia Eirini – Limeria) but I would rather recommend the excellent 13 km long Madari Circular walk which is four kilometres south (one can do a shorter eight-km version of Madari Circular walk returning to the starting point on the Saranti - Spilia road).

It makes sense to combine a trip from Nicosia with a stop at Peristerona village to see the renovated 11th century Apostles Varnavas and Ilarionas church (one of two ancient five-domed churches in Cyprus) and with a visit to the amazing Panagia Asinou UNESCO World Heritage Troodos painted church (and/or Panagia tou Araka UNESCO World Heritage Troodos Painted church near Lagoudera).

Distance (km) : Platres : 30 Nicosia : 42 Limassol : 43 Polis : 89 Paphos : 95 Larnaca: 96 Agia Napa : 133 Protaras : 138

OAK TREE IN FTERIKOUDI

(Map 18 – page 183, 41)

Fterikoudi is a small village almost 40 km south west of Nicosia, at an altitude of 1,000 meters. It is one of the villages in Pitsilia region where one finds extensive hazelnut plantations. This huge tree is found in the village center, on the right side of the main road from Nicosia. This oak tree (Quercus infectoria subsp. Veneris) is just 200 years old, 16 meters tall and has a trunk perimeter of three meters.

Fterikoudi is just six kilometers north west of the large Palaichori village (in fact there are two connected villages having the same name – Palaichori Morphou and Palaichori Oreinis) where one of the ten UNESCO World Heritage Troodos Painted churches, the church of Metamorfosis tou Sotiros lies.

For those wanting to explore on bicycles I recommend the route between Palaichori to Polystypos as it is relatively flat and short (about 15 km long with an elevation range of just 100 meters), on narrow paved winding roads offering glorious vistas.

There are two more UNESCO World Heritage Troodos painted churches that are quite close, about 15 km away (Panagia tou Araka near Lagoudera and Stavros tou Agiasmati towards the north, off the road to Kato Moni). Nearly five kilometers north of Alona, on the side of the road that leads to Moni village one finds a well preserved watermill.

Distance (km) : Platres : 33 Limassol : 39 Nicosia : 42 Polis : 99 Larnaca: 105 Paphos : 107 Agia Napa : 146 Protaras : 152

WHITE MULBERRY IN TRACHYPEDOULA

(Map 25 – page 190, 43)

The village of Trachypedoula is about 30 km south west of Platres, on the west bank of Diarizos valley. It is built at an altitude of 500 meters, and it is a small stone built, well preserved village. The ancient white mulberry tree (Morus alba) is found in a private house courtyard, in the center of the village, very close to the coffee shops. Explorers need to ask the locals for directions (and inquire about permission to enter the courtyard).

Attractions in the area include many watermills in Diarizos valley. There's a paved road leading to the village of Salamiou, just five km north (east) where the Salamiotissa monastery is found. The area has tourist amenities in the form of small restaurants and some agrotouristic accommodation. There are walking opportunities both in the Diarizos as well as in the Xeros Potamos valley.

Distance (km): Platres : 33 Paphos : 35 Limassol : 60 Polis : 70 Nicosia : 119 Larnaca: 126 Agia Napa : 167 Protaras : 173

OLIVE TREES IN ANOGYRA

(Map 25 – page 190, 44)

The village of Anogyra is built at an altitude of 500 meters, about 38 km north west of Limassol. It is an old village with rich culture and history. Olive, carob and vine play a major role in the economic and social life of its inhabitants. 43 ancient olive trees here have been declared as a natural monument. It was difficult for me to locate these olive trees. A local guided me to a few of them in the south part of the village, of which I include a photo above. Even if explorers do not search for, or even if they fail to find the rest of the trees, they will probably enjoy their visit to this picturesque village, one of the few on the island that are developing using their natural and cultural heritage as an asset. There's a winery, a carob processing plant and an olive press in the village.

The church of the Holy Cross (formerly a monastery), built in the 14th century in an area where ancient ruins (columns, arches, etc) are seen, is an excellent place for a visit and for a photo safari. The monastery is found a km south east of the village center on the road to Avdimou.

The village of Avdimou is just six km south east (and Avdimou coast five more km to the south) while Pachna is just nine km to the north east.

Distance (km): Platres : 35 Paphos : 36 Limassol : 38 Polis : 71 Larnaca: 104 Nicosia : 121 Agia Napa : 145 Protaras : 151

OAK TREE IN KAMPOS

(Map 20 – page 185, 45)

Kampos is a picturesque remote village in the north east part of Paphos Forest, and has a long tradition in the timber industry. It is built at an altitude of 700 meters, about 30 km north of Troodos Square and almost 50 km north west of Platres. This is a very sparsely populated rather pristine area of Cyprus, not frequented by many tourists. The huge oak tree is found in the village center, on the left side of the main road coming from Kykkos monastery. It is 350 years old, 22 meters tall, and its trunk has a perimeter of almost five meters.

Recently a museum of forestry and woodcrafts was developed (found between Kampos and Tsakkistra - not on the main road). One would need to call +357 22942450 to make arrangements to visit the museum.

Kambos can be a good base for people wanting to explore the north east part of the vast Paphos Forest. It offers great possibilities for forest exploration on foot, by bicycle and by car on an extensive network of forest dirt roads (e.g. one may walk on the dirt road from Tsakkistra village to the locality known as "Mavres Sidjies" ie black fig trees). Recently a set of mountain biking routes were developed in the area.

Kykkos monastery, the richest on the island is the main cultural attraction in the vicinity (and a main source of employment for nearby villages).

Distance (km): Platres : 36 Polis : 52 Limassol : 100 Nicosia : 100 Paphos : 100 Larnaca: 166 Agia Napa : 207 Protaras : 213

GOLDEN OAK TREE NEAR TSAKKISTRA (KREMMOS TIS PELLIS)

(Map 20 – page 185, 46)

This atypically large in size golden oak (200 years old, ten meters tall, with a trunk perimeter of five meters) is found deep inside Paphos Forest, some 45 kilometers west of Platres and far from any community. It is by the road that connects Kykkos monastery to Stavros tis Psokas Forest station (and picnic area).

Paphos Forest is just perfect for those looking to explore the forest on foot, by bicycle or by car. There is a good number of pleasant walks in the vicinity (e.g. the ones to Tripylos peak). The network of dirt (or paved) roads is also very suitable for those who like to explore on bicycle. A good, easy, circular and relatively flat cycling route inside the forest could start at Kykkos monastery pass by Kremmos tis Pellis and return to Kykkos monastery via Cedar Valley (the route is 40 km long, on paved road and has an elevation variation of just 200 meters. Probably it makes sense for most of us to bike many of the other routes linearly (e.g. from Kykkos monastery to Stavros tis Psokas to Lysos, or via Agios Merkourios picnic site to Argaka or Gialia, from Kykkos via Cedar Valley to Pano Panagia (maybe even via Agia valley) or even to Pomos village (via Leivadi picnic area and dam) or Kato Pyrgos.

Distance (km): Platres : 45 Polis : 45 Paphos : 95 Limassol : 107 Nicosia : 107 Larnaca: 173 Agia Napa : 214 Protaras : 220

KALIDONIA WATERFALL

(Map 24 – page 189, ⑥)

The waterfall is found about two km north of Platres village. It can be accessed either via a road off the Troodos - Platres village road, or from the two ends of a linear, somewhat difficult nature study walking trail that begins three km south of Troodos Square and ends in Platres village.When there are not many visitors, it is a wonderful, serene environment. There is at least some water all year round. The water falls vertically from a height of twelve meters.

The stream ('Kryos Potamos' which in Greek means 'Cold River') subsequently reaches Myllomeris waterfall, and passes under the medieval Venetian bridge of Milia. It fills up the small Pera Pedi dam, passes under the medieval bridges of Agia Mavri and Koilani and finally ends up at Kouris manmade lake.

Distance (km) : Platres : 2 Limassol : 42 Paphos : 62 Polis : 70 Nicosia : 84
Larnaca: 108 Agia Napa : 149 Protaras : 155

MYLLOMERIS WATERFALL

(Map 24 – page 189, ⑦)

With a height of 15 meters it is the tallest of the Platres waterfalls. It is found about two km from the village. It is relatively easily accessible through a dirt road, but there is a steep stairway (down) to the waterfall. There is also a 1.2 km linear walking route from the village center, with considerable elevation changes (a range of nearly 150 meters).

One could compose a circular walking route from Platres village that is about seven km long, has an elevation range of 200 meters and passes by Myllomeris waterfall, Milia medieval Venetian bridge and Pera Pedi dam.

Distance (km) : Platres : 4 Limassol : 40 Paphos : 64 Polis : 76 Nicosia : 90
Larnaca: 106 Agia Napa : 147 Protaras : 153

CHANTARA WATERFALL

(Map 24 – page 189, ⑧)

It is about three km from Platres village and just over a km from the village of Foini. It can be accessed through a short dirt road (well signed, from Foini). The waterfall is only eight meters high but it is the widest of the four waterfalls in the area. There is a linear walking route (on a dirt road) that passes through here. The walking route's length is just over four km and the elevation variation is 400 meters. It connects the village of Foini to the monastery of Trooditissa. Downstream the water passes under the medieval Venetian bridges of Stavros (inside Foini village) and Piskopos near the village, and Elia before it joins into the Diarizos river, which then passes under the larger Kelefos bridge before it ends in the Arminou manmade lake. One could walk or cycle along the stream. Paphos Forest nearby offers excellent walking and cycling opportunities on an extensive network of forest dirt roads.

Those looking for a relatively extreme outdoors experience can try to climb their way from Chantara waterfall upstream to the picnic site near Trooditissa monastery. There are several small waterfalls and pools on the way and the cliffs may not be very high, but they can be slippery and nearly impassible when the water flow is significant.

The area's other attractions include the atypical watermill at Palaiomylos and two medieval bridges between the villages of Treis Elies and Kaminaria.

Distance (km): Platres : 3 Limassol : 43 Paphos : 58 Polis : 75 Nicosia : 89
Larnaca: 109 Agia Napa : 150 Protaras : 156

MESA POTAMOS WATERFALL

(Map 24 – page 189, (9))

It is about six km from Platres village, and can be reached on dirt (and partly paved) roads from the villages of Saittas, Moniatis, Platres and Kato Amiantos. It is found in a dense forested area, much of which sadly got burnt in the 2007 summer wildfires. There is a picnic area and a monastery nearby. It is a very small waterfall deep inside the forest. The peaceful area around offers very good possibilities to explore on foot and by bicycle.

Attractions in the area, besides the nature walking routes in Troodos and Platres (and other waterfalls), include the dark coloured watermill in Amiantos village (eight km towards the north east) and Trimiklini and Kardaki medieval Venetian bridges (seven and ten kilometers towards the south and the north east respectively).

Distance (km) : Platres : 6 Limassol : 46 Paphos : 66 Polis : 78 Nicosia : 92
Larnaca: 112 Agia Napa : 153 Protaras : 159

MILIA MEDIEVAL BRIDGE (Map 24 – page 189)

STAVROS MEDIEVAL BRIDGE (Map 24 – page 189)

PISKOPOS MEDIEVAL BRIDGE (Map 24 – page 189)

TRIMIKLINI MEDIEVAL BRIDGE (Map 22 – page 187)

AGIA MAVRI MEDIEVAL BRIDGE (Map 22 – page 187)

KOILANI MEDIEVAL BRIDGE (Map 22 – page 187)

KARDAKI MEDIEVAL BRIDGE (Map 24 – page 189)

POTAMIOU MEDIEVAL BRIDGE (Map 25 – page 190)

PELENDRI MEDIEVAL BRIDGE (Map 22 – page 187)

MYLOS MEDIEVAL BRIDGE (Map 21 – page 186)

TREIS ELIES MEDIEVAL BRIDGE

(Map 21 – page 186)

ELIA MEDIEVAL BRIDGE

(Map 21 – page 186)

KELEFOS MEDIEVAL BRIDGE (Map 21 – page 186)

(DAMAGED) POTAMITISSA MEDIEVAL BRIDGE (Map 19 – page 184)

ROUDIAS MEDIEVAL BRIDGE (Map 25 – page 190)

KALOPANAGIOTIS MEDIEVAL BRIDGE (Map 23 – page 188)

ORKONTAS MEDIEVAL BRIDGE (Map 23 – page 188)

WATERMILL IN PERA PEDI (Map 22 – page 187)

WATERMILL IN KATO AMIANTOS (Map 24 – page 189)

WATERMILL NEAR KISSOUSA (Map 25 – page 190)

WATERMILL IN KALOPANAGIOTIS

(Map 23 – page 188)

WATERMILL NEAR PALAIOMYLOS

(Map 24 – page 189)

WATERMILL IN POTAMITISSA (Map 19 – page 184)

WATERMILL NEAR KIDASI (Map 25 – page 190)

WATERMILL NEAR VRETSIA (Map 25 – page 190)

WATERMILL IN KAKOPETRIA (Map 11 – page 109)

A WATERMILL IN GALATA (Map 11 – page 109)

ANOTHER WATERMILL IN GALATA (Map 11 – page 109)

WATERMILL NEAR AGIOS IOANNIS (Map 25 – page 1

WATERMILL AT AGIOS MAMAS CHAPEL (Map 25 – page 190)

WATERMILL AT ARCHANGELOS MICHAIL CHAPEL (Map 25 – page 190)

WATERMILL NEAR GALATARIA (Map 25 – page 190)

WATERMILL IN EVRYCHOU (Map 11 – page 109)

WATERMILL NEAR PENTALIA (Map 25 – page 190)

WATERMILL NEAR SALAMIOU (Map 25 – page 190)

WATERMILL IN FLASOU (Map 11 – page 109)

WATERMILL IN FLASOU (Map 11 – page 109)

WATERMILL IN KATYDATA (Map 11 – page 109)

CHURCH OF TIMIOS STAVROS (HOLY CROSS) (Map 19 – page 184)

CHURCH OF ARCHANGELOS MICHAIL (Map 23 – page 188)

CHURCH OF AGIOS NIKOLAOS TIS STEGIS (ST. NICHOLAS OF THE ROOF)

(Map 11 – page 109)

MONASTERY OF AGIOS IOANNIS (ST JOHN) LAMPADISTIS

(Map 23 – page 188)

CHURCH OF PANAGIA (OUR LADY) TOU MOUTOULLA (Map 23 – page 188)

PANAGIA (OUR LADY) TIS PODITHOU CHURCH (Map 11 – page 109)

THE CHURCH OF THE TRANSFIGURATION OF THE SAVIOUR (Map 18 – page 183)

PANAGIA TOU ARAKA CHURCH (Map 9 – page 107)

TIMIOS STAVROS (OF MESA POTAMOS) MONASTERY (Map 24 – page 189)

TROODITISSA MONASTERY (Map 24 – page 189)

AGIA MAVRI CHAPEL (Map 22 – page 187)

TIMIOS STAVROS MONASTERY (OMODOS) (Map 25 – page 190)

APOSTOLOS PHILIPPOS CHAPEL (Map 25 – page 190)

PANAGIA THEOSKEPASTI CHAPEL (Map 23 – page 188)

PANAGIA SALAMIOTISSA MONASTERY (Map 25 – page 190)

KYKKOS MONASTERY (Map 20 – page 185)

TIMIOS STAVROS CHURCH (ANOGYRA) (Map 25 – page 190)

PANAGIA TOU SINTI MONASTERY (Map 25 – page 190)

AGIOS MNASONAS CHURCH RUINS

(Map 25 – page 190)

PAPHOS

Aphrodite, the Greek goddess of love and beauty was born in the Paphian sea, at the locality known as Aphrodite's Rock, a few km to the east of ancient Palaipaphos. Ancient PalaiPaphos (meaning 'old Paphos' in Greek, a major center of worship of Aphrodite in the ancient Greek world) and Nea Paphos (meaning 'new Paphos' in Greek – as it was founded about 1,000 years later, in the 4th century BC) constitute a UNESCO World Heritage site. The ancient mosaics in Nea Paphos are stunning and not to be missed by any visitor to Cyprus.

In long valleys (Diarizos, Xeros Potamos, Ezousa) and their slopes there's a good number of attractions to be explored on foot, by bicycle or by car, including hard to find watermills, remote medieval chapels, historic monasteries, well preserved traditional settlements and quality wineries in the area. The vine has been with the Paphians since antiquity and until today it is a prime cultivated crop on much of the land.

BEACHES/COASTS	
54	Aphrodite's Rock / Petra tou Romiou
55	Kouklia
56	Mandria
57	Timi
WALKING ROUTES	
34	Petra tou Romiou
WETLANDS	
22	Asprokremmos dam
ANCIENT TREES	
47	Two olives in Nikokleia
WATERMILLS	
43	Nikokleia
44	Souskiou
OTHER CULTURAL ATTRACTIONS	
	Palaipaphos

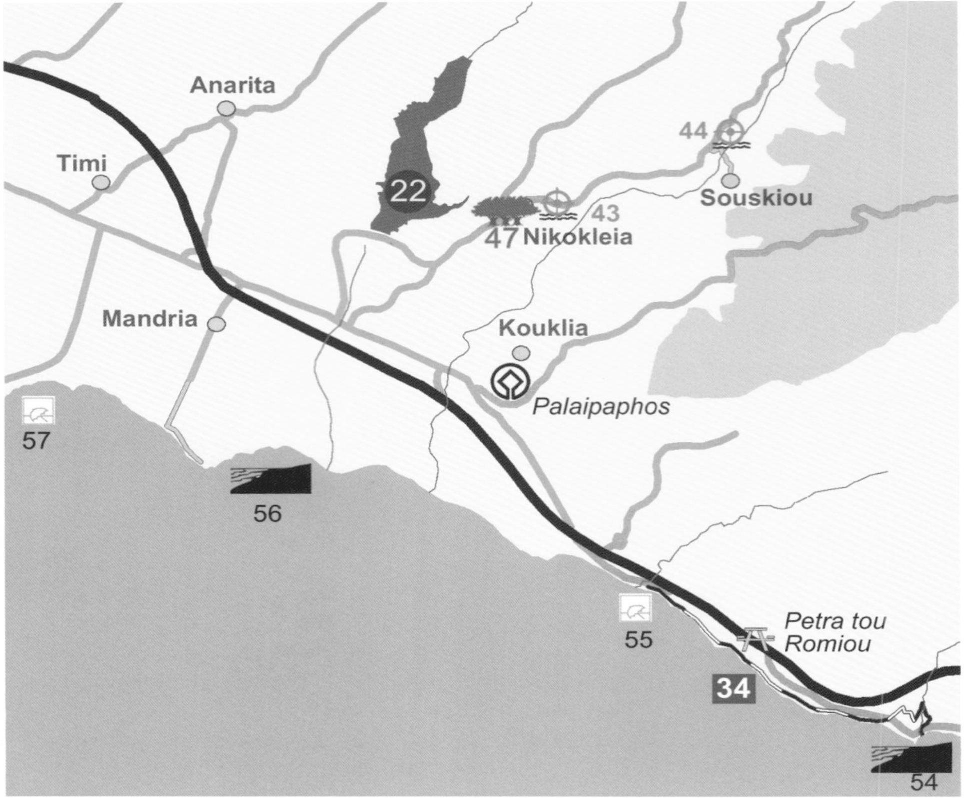

WALKING ROUTES	
35	Episkopi - Choulou

ANCIENT TREES	
48	Oak in Choulou

WATERMILLS	
45	Moronero
46	Moronero
47	Moronero
48	Choulou

CHAPELS AND MONASTERIES
Agios Georgios

OTHER CULTURAL ATTRACTIONS
Agios Theodoros
Agios Ilarionas

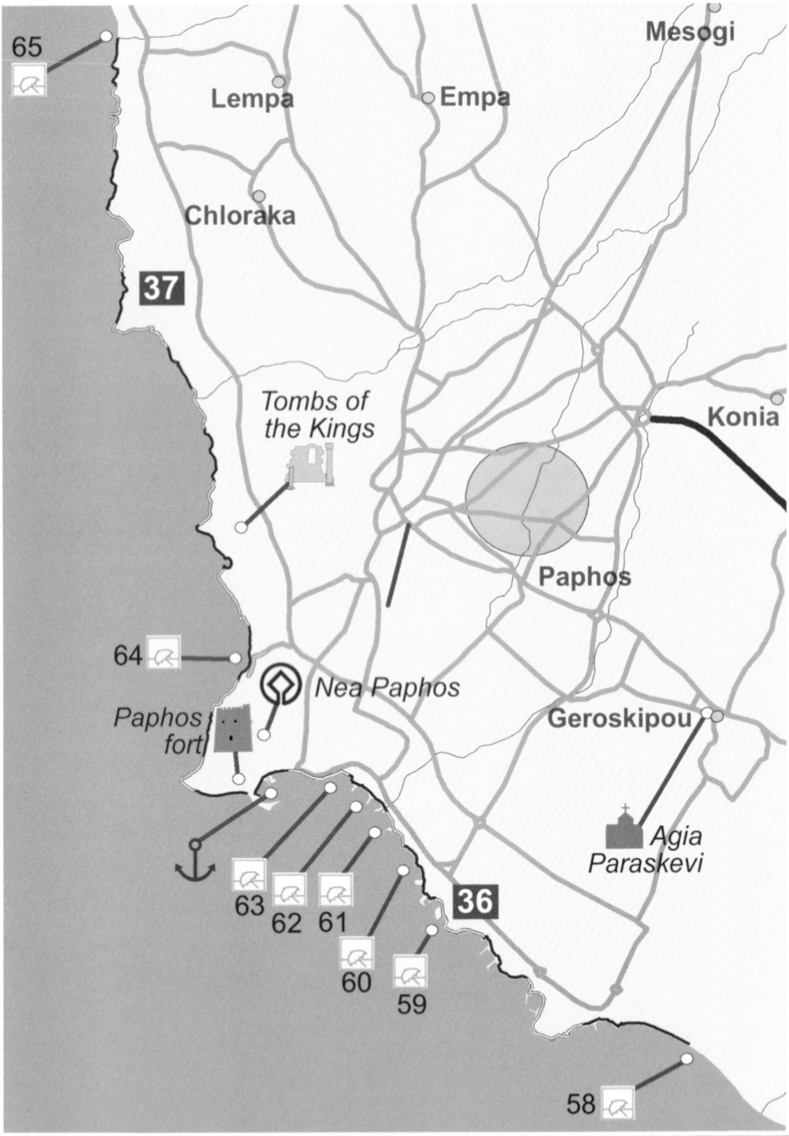

BEACHES/COASTS	
58	Geroskipou
59	Pachyammos
60	Vrisoudia A
61	Vrisoudia B
62	Alykes
63	Municipal Baths
64	Faros
65	Kotchas

WALKING ROUTES	
36	Geroskipou beach – Paphos fort
37	Paphos fort – Kotchas beach

CASTLES AND WATCHTOWERS
Paphos fort

CHAPELS AND MONASTERIES
Agia Paraskevi

OTHER CULTURAL ATTRACTIONS
Nea Paphos
Tombs of the Kings

BEACHES/COASTS	
65	Kotchas
66	Potima
67	Coral Beach
68	Laourou

WALKING ROUTES	
38	Kotchas beach – Potima coast
39	Laourou beach – Agios Georgios tis Pegeias fishing port

WETLANDS	
24	Mavrokolympos dam

OTHER NATURAL ATTRACTIONS	
10	Pegeia Sea Caves B
11	Pegeia Sea Caves (Kontarkastoi)

CHAPELS AND MONASTERIES
Agios Neophytos

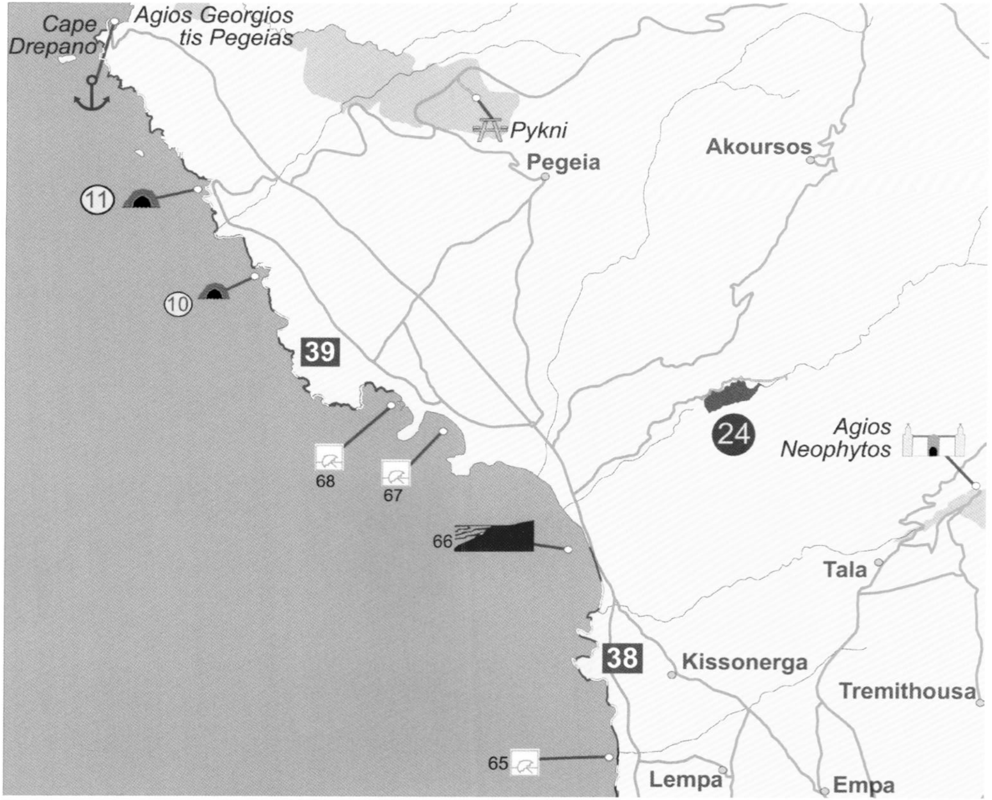

Paphos

WALKING ROUTES	
40	Vouni Panagias
WETLANDS	
23	Kannaviou dam
CHAPELS AND MONASTERIES	
	Agia Moni
	Chrysorrogiatissa

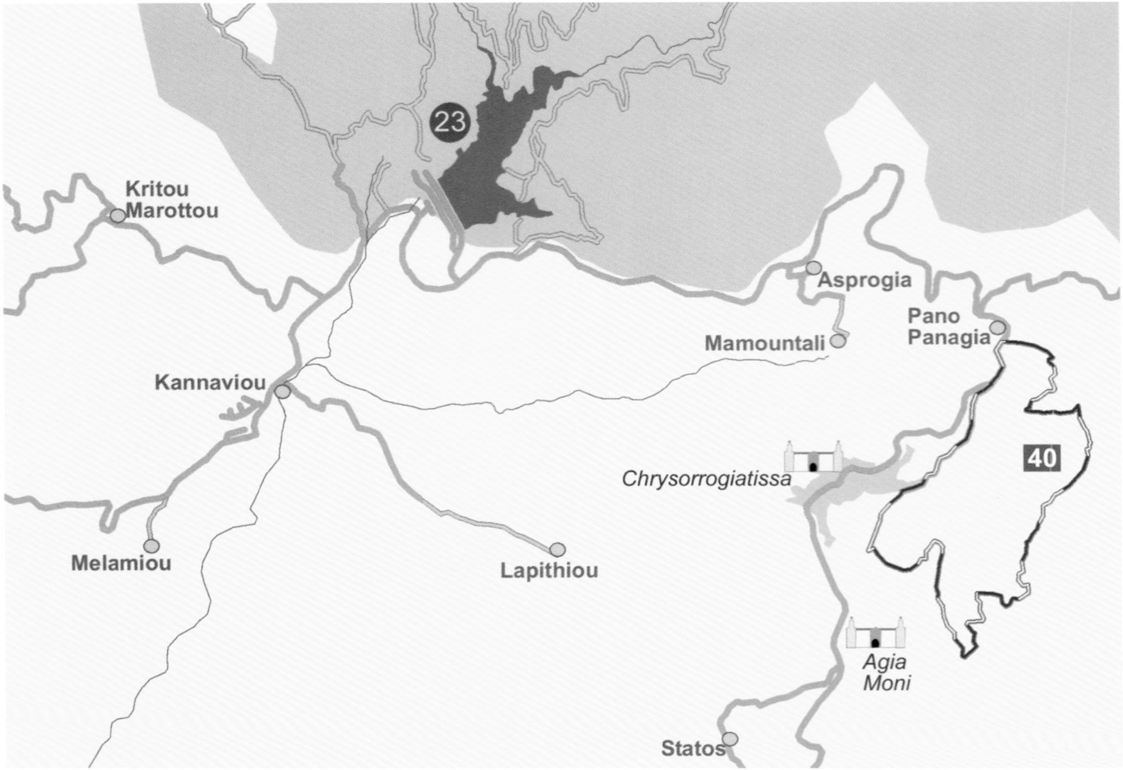

APHRODITE'S ROCK / PETRA TOU ROMIOU COAST

(Map 26 – page 267, 54)

This is a non organised spot on the coast between Limassol and Paphos, some 23 km from the town of Paphos, where according to legend the Greek goddess of love and beauty, Aphrodite was born. The coast has steep slopes over a long stretch (over a six km distance towards Pissouri there are 100 m – 150 m high imposing white cliffs). There are peculiar rocks in the sea, whose composition does not match the geology of the adjacent land. The biggest of the rocks is Aphrodite's Rock, called Petra tou Romiou by the Greek Cypriots, which means "the stone of Romios". Romios is a Byzantine era Cypriot hero, who according to legend threw the rock to a ship that was transporting invaders (or carrying away the woman he loved in another version). The place is scenic and not developed. The beach is mostly pebble on the east side of the Rock and mostly sandy on its west side.

There's frequent public bus connection with the town of Paphos.

A trip here could be combined with a walk on the seven-km long Petra tou Romiou linear coastal walking route towards the west, with a visit to the nearby Aphrodite's sanctuary at Palaipaphos (seven km towards Paphos), Asprokremmos manmade lake (five km west of Palaipaphos), to the ancient city of Kourion and its exquisite mosaics (about thirty km towards Limassol), or with an exploration of nearby Diarizos valley and its many watermills.

Distance (km): Paphos : 23 Limassol : 45 Polis : 58 Platres : 60 Larnaca: 111
Nicosia : 127 Agia Napa : 152 Protaras : 158

Characteristics: -

KOUKLIA BEACH

(Map 26 – page 267, 55)

This is a 300 m long, pebble and sand, organised beach, about three km by car west of Aphrodite's Rock / Petra tou Romiou and 21 km east of Paphos (there is a lifeguard in summer and few amenities). The beach is right to the west of the 50 m high elevation picnic area that is on the Petra tou Romiou, seven km long walking route. The vistas from the picnic area are superb. It is found about five km on the walking route from here to Petra tou Romiou.

Besides walking on the walking route, a trip here could be combined with a visit to Petra tou Romiou (the birthplace of Aphrodite, the Greek goddess of love), the nearby Aphrodite's sanctuary at Palaipaphos (four km towards Paphos) and Asprokremmos dam (five km west of Palaipaphos) as well as exploration of nearby Diarizos or Xeros Potamos valley, or even Ezousa valley.

There's frequent public bus connection with the town of Paphos.

Distance (km) : Paphos : 21 Platres : 38 Limassol : 47 Polis : 56 Larnaca: 113
Nicosia : 129 Agia Napa : 154 Protaras : 160

Characteristics:  *(Jun-Sep)*

MANDRIA COAST

(Map 26 – page 267, 56)

Mandria coast is one km long, near the village of Mandria and some 16 km east of the town of Paphos. The surface is made up of pebble and sand and the coast is not organised. Care is required as there may be currents. During spring, one may find many wild flowers by the coast.

There's frequent public bus connection between the village of Mandria (two km north of the coast) and the town of Paphos.

A trip here could be combined with a visit to nearby Asprokremmos dam (seven km north) and Aphrodite's sanctuary at Palaipaphos (seven km north east) and/or with exploration of nearby valleys such as Xeros Potamos, Diarizos and Ezousa (all have watermills and possibilities for walking or cycling, and picturesque villages except for Xeros Potamos valley which is not inhabited anymore). The deserted Turkish Cypriot village of Foinikas / Finike in Xeros Potamos valley can be an interesting destination on a six-km long linear walk on the west bank of the Asprokremmos manmade lake.

Distance (km): Paphos : 16 Platres : 50 Polis : 51 Limassol : 58 Larnaca: 124
Nicosia : 140 Agia Napa : 165 Protaras : 171

Characteristics:  *(Jun-Sep)*

TIMI BEACH

(Map 26 – page 267, 57)

Timi village has two approved beaches. The biggest one, some 15 km east of the town of Paphos and shown in the photo is called Kathari (which means 'clean' in Greek). Its length is about 500 meters. There is another, smaller beach in the east (almost a km away) called Floria beach. Both beaches have lifeguards in summer.

A trip here could be combined with a visit to nearby Asprokremmos dam (eight km north east) and Aphrodite's sanctuary at Palaipaphos (nine km north east) and/or with exploration of nearby valleys such as Xeros Potamos, Diarizos and Ezousa (all have watermills and possibilities for walking or cycling, and picturesque villages like Episkopi or Choulou, except for Xeros Potamos valley which is not inhabited anymore). The deserted Turkish Cypriot village of Foinikas / Finike in Xeros Potamos valley can be an interesting photo safari destination on a six km long linear walk on the west bank of the Asprokremmos manmade lake (depending on the water's level the walk could involve some off-road walking).

Paphos airport is just a km to the west of Kathari beach.

Distance (km): Paphos : 15 Platres : 50 Polis : 50 Limassol : 58 Larnaca: 124
Nicosia : 140 Agia Napa : 165 Protaras : 171

Characteristics: *(Jun-Aug)*

GEROSKIPOU BEACH

(Map 28 – page 269, 58)

Geroskipou is the most eastern of the beaches of the town of Paphos. It is more than one km long, its surface is predominantly made up of pebble, and has large quantities of sand deposits towards the west, where there is a wave breaker. The beach has been awarded the Blue flag eco-label (www.blueflag.org) and has handicap facilities. There is good road access (and frequent public bus connection) to the beach. A coastal walk from here to the Paphos fort is five km long. Until 2010 the next organised public beach to the west was Pachyammos beach, some 2.5 km away. After 2010 another public beach between Pachyammos beach and Geroskipou beach was organized called Pachyammos 2. It also has been awarded the Blue flag eco-label (www.blueflag.org).

Geroskipou comes from the Greek words for 'Ieros Kipos' meaning 'Holly Garden'. This refers to gardens that existed here in antiquity, related to Aphrodite and the nearby temple at Palaipaphos. The well preserved 11th century, five-domed Byzantine church of Agia Paraskevi is found in the center of the village. There's also a 350 year old, ten meter high mastic tree in the village.

Distance (km): Paphos : 2 Polis : 37 Platres : 60 Limassol : 68 Larnaca: 134
Nicosia : 150 Agia Napa : 175 Protaras : 181

Characteristics: 

(May-Oct)

PACHYAMMOS BEACH

(Map 28 – page 269, 59)

It is a very small cove, and the beach is less than 100 meters long. Pachyammos means "thick sand" in Greek. It is one of the few natural sandy beaches of the south coast of Paphos and has no manmade wave breakers. The beach has been awarded the Blue flag eco-label (www.blueflag.org) and has handicap facilities. The next public organised beach to the west is Vrisoudia A beach (about 400 meters away), and to the east it is the recently organised tiny Pachyammos 2 beach some 400 meters away. The five km long coastal walking route from Geroskipou beach to the Paphos fort passes by here.

The UNESCO World Heritage site of (ancient) Nea Paphos and especially the beautiful, amazingly preserved Roman mosaics are a must see for all Paphos visitors.

Distance (km): Paphos : 0 Polis : 35 Platres : 60 Limassol : 68 Larnaca: 134 Nicosia : 150 Agia Napa : 175 Protaras : 181

Characteristics:  *(Jun-Oct)*

VRISOUDIA A BEACH

(Map 28 – page 269, 60)

The beach is about 1.5 km east of Paphos fort and in front and to the south west of an old winery of Paphos. Vrisoudia means "small springs" in the Greek Cypriot dialect, and apparently there were (are) springs going to the sea here. There are two sandy parts in the beach, the western one is more than 200 meters long and richer in sand, thanks to a wave breaker that was constructed there, while the eastern part is less than 100 meters long. The beach has been awarded the Blue flag eco-label (www.blueflag.org). The next public organised beach to the west is the adjacent Vrisoudia B beach and to the east it is Pachyammos beach, about 400 meters away. The five km long coastal walking route from Geroskipou beach to the Paphos fort passes by here.

The UNESCO World Heritage site of (ancient) Nea Paphos and especially the beautiful, amazingly preserved Roman mosaics are a must see for all Paphos visitors.

Distance (km): Paphos : 0 Polis : 35 Platres : 60 Limassol : 68 Larnaca: 134
Nicosia : 150 Agia Napa : 175 Protaras : 181

Characteristics:  *(Jun-Oct)*

VRISOUDIA B BEACH

(Map 28 – page 269, 61)

The beach is over a km east of the Paphos fort and just to the west of Vrisoudia A beach. Vrisoudia means "small springs" in the Greek Cypriot dialect, and apparently there were (are) springs going to the sea here. The sandy beach is just over 100 meters long, and enriched (with sand) as a result of the construction of wave breakers all around (vertical and parallel to the coast). The beach has been awarded the Blue flag eco-label (www.blueflag.org) and has handicap facilities. The next public organised beach to the west is Alykes beach (just 200 meters away) and to the east it is the adjacent Vrisoudia A beach. The five km long coastal walking route from Geroskipou beach to the Paphos fort passes by here.

The UNESCO World Heritage site of (ancient) Nea Paphos and especially the beautiful, amazingly preserved Roman mosaics are a must see for all Paphos visitors. Ancient Nea Paphos has historical importance also for Christianity as Saul took his Christian name ('Paulus') here where he preached and converted the Roman proconsul Sergius Paulus. About 1,000 meters north west of the beach one can find a stone called St. Paul's Pillar where according to tradition the saint received 39 lashes.

Distance (km): Paphos : 0 Polis : 35 Platres : 60 Limassol : 68 Larnaca: 134
Nicosia : 150 Agia Napa : 175 Protaras : 181

Characteristics: 

(Jun-Oct)

ALYKES BEACH

(Map 28 – page 269, 62)

It is found about one km east of the Paphos fort. Alykes means "salt lakes" in Greek, and presumably salt was harvested from this rocky part of the coast in the past. There are wave breakers by the beach, but still not considerable sand quantities. This is a peculiar beach in relation to most other beaches in Cyprus, as a big part of it is elevated higher up the rocks. Certain construction has been carried out and material brought in, in order to make the coast more comfortable for guests. The beach has been awarded the Blue flag eco-label (www.blueflag.org). It is not apparent exactly where the border with the adjacent Municipal Baths (beach) is, at its west end. The next public organised (sandy) beach towards the east is Vrisoudia B beach (about 200 meters away). The five km long coastal walking route from Geroskipou beach to the Paphos fort passes by here.

The UNESCO World Heritage site of (ancient) Nea Paphos and especially the beautiful, amazingly preserved Roman mosaics are a must see for all Paphos visitors. The Ottoman era Paphos fort is another charming attraction. There used to be two towers in the same complex during Frankish rule but the Ottomans only rebuilt the (north) western tower.

Distance (km) : Paphos : 0 Polis : 35 Platres : 60 Limassol : 68 Larnaca: 134
Nicosia : 150 Agia Napa : 175 Protaras : 181

Characteristics:  *(Jun-Oct)*

MUNICIPAL BATHS BEACH

(Map 28 – page 269, 63)

This is the swimming area on the south coast nearest to Paphos harbour. The Municipal Baths are less than one km to the east of the Paphos fort, and the 'beach' has a length of less than 150 meters. Swimmers enter the sea from the rocks. Construction has been carried out and material brought in to make the area more comfortable for visitors. It is not apparent exactly where the border with the adjacent Alykes beach is at its east end. The beach has been awarded the Blue flag eco-label (www.blueflag.org) and has handicap facilities. The five km long coastal walking route from Geroskipou beach to the Paphos fort passes by here.

The UNESCO World Heritage site of (ancient) Nea Paphos and especially the beautiful, amazingly preserved Roman mosaics are a must see for all Paphos visitors. The Ottoman era Paphos fort is a landmark attraction. For a few evenings every year world class opera houses perform in front of the fort.

Distance (km) : Paphos : 0 Polis : 35 Platres : 60 Limassol : 68 Larnaca: 134
Nicosia : 150 Agia Napa : 175 Protaras : 181

Characteristics:  ***(May-Oct)***

FAROS BEACH

(Map 28 – page 269, 64)

The beach got its name from the Greek word 'Faros' which means lighthouse, as the Paphos lighthouse dominates the background. It is the first beach to be found north (northwest) of the Paphos fort. There is good road access to the beach, but visitors can also walk on the almost two km long walking trail from the fort, on the rocky coast. The area is frequented by birdwatchers. The beach has a large capacity for visitors at a length of almost 300 meters and a depth inland of about 40 meters. It has been awarded the Blue flag eco-label (www.blueflag.org) and has handicap facilities.

Walkers may also like to try the coastal walking route towards the north. It is about seven km to Kotchas beach. The route offers continuous sea views from a higher elevation and passes by a number of luxury hotels and small coves (natural or manmade).

The UNESCO World Heritage site of (ancient) Nea Paphos and especially the beautiful, amazingly preserved Roman mosaics are a must see for all Paphos visitors. The entrance to the necropolis known as 'Tombs of the Kings' which is part of the site, is about 1.5 km to the north of the beach. The Ottoman era Paphos fort in the south is a Paphos landmark.

Distance (km) : Paphos : 0 Polis : 35 Platres : 60 Limassol : 68 Larnaca: 134
Nicosia : 150 Agia Napa : 175 Protaras : 181

Characteristics:  *(May-Oct)*

KOTCHAS BEACH

(Map 29 – page 270, 65)

Kotchas beach is about eight km north by road from the Paphos fort. Visitors can reach it via the coastal road from Paphos to Coral Beach. There is a stream flowing to this sandy beach. The beach is just 150 meters wide, with a rocky coastline on both sides. The environment is rather undeveloped touristically. There is a lifeguard in summer and few amenities at the beach. There's frequent public bus connection with the town of Paphos (the bus stop is about 400 m to the south).

The walks on the coast, either towards the north (three km to Potima coast) or to the south (seven km to Faros beach) are very pleasant. Both routes offer continuous sea views from a higher elevation and pass by a number of luxury hotels and small coves (natural or manmade).

The UNESCO World Heritage site of (ancient) Nea Paphos and especially the beautiful, amazingly preserved Roman mosaics are a must see for all Paphos visitors. Other attractions in the area include ruins (and reconstructions) of a chalcolithic settlement in Lempa (1,300 meters east of the beach), the 12th century church of Panagia Chryseleousa found in Empa village (2.5 km south east) and the historic monastery of Saint Neophytos near Tala (nine km north east).

Distance (km) : Paphos : 8 Polis : 33 Platres : 68 Limassol : 76 Larnaca: 142
Nicosia : 158 Agia Napa : 183 Protaras : 189

Characteristics:  ***(Jun-Sep)***

POTIMA COAST

(Map 29 – page 270, 66)

Potima coast is about 10.5 km north by road from the Paphos fort. It is not organised. The south 800 meters long part is sandy and provides a good environment for playing on the beach or sun bathing. The north part is pebble. There may be currents in the bay. There's frequent public bus connection with the town of Paphos. The popular Coral Beach is located in the north, two km away by car from Potima coast (there's frequent public bus connection).

Visitors can walk on a coastal route towards the south. It is about three km to Kotchas beach. The route offers continuous sea views from a higher elevation and passes by a number of luxury hotels and small coves (natural or manmade). Mavrokolympos dam is quite near (three km northeast) and well worth a visit.

Other attractions in the area include ruins (and reconstructions) of a chalcolithic settlement in Lempa (4.5 km south east of the coast), the 12th century church of Panagia Chryseleousa found in Empa village (six km south east) and the historic monastery of Saint Neophytos near Tala (nine km east).

Distance (km) : Paphos : 11 Polis : 26 Platres : 71 Limassol : 79 Larnaca: 145 Nicosia : 161 Agia Napa : 186 Protaras : 192

Characteristics: -

CORAL BEACH

(Map 29 – page 270, 67)

Coral Beach is the most well known and popular beach on the western coast of Paphos. It is found about 14 km north by road from the Paphos fort. It is well organised and touristically developed, with many hundreds of people visiting daily in summer. The beach has been awarded the Blue flag eco-label (www.blueflag.org) and has handicap facilities. It is about 400 meters long with an average width of more than 30 meters. There's frequent public bus connection with the town of Paphos (and other beaches on the west coast).

The ruins of Maa-Paliokastro bronze age settlement (and small museum) are less than one km (north) west of the beach and may be worth a visit by those really into archaeology. The UNESCO World Heritage site of (ancient) Nea Paphos and especially the beautiful, amazingly preserved Roman mosaics are a must see for all Paphos visitors.

Explorers could walk on a rugged coast route north to Agios Georgios tis Pegeias fishing port (about ten km north west). About 2.5 km south of the fishing port starts a collection of sea caves.

Distance (km): Paphos : 14 Polis : 23 Platres : 74 Limassol : 82 Larnaca: 148
Nicosia : 164 Agia Napa : 189 Protaras : 195

Characteristics:  ***(May-Oct)***

LAOUROU BEACH

(Map 29 – page 270, 68)

This is the last public organised beach to the north of Paphos on the west coast (about 15 km by road from the Paphos fort). It is a 300 meter long sandy beach, which has been enriched through the use of a wave breaker. It looks like material has also been placed on the rocks to expand the beach inland. The beach has been awarded the Blue flag eco-label (www.blueflag.org). There's frequent public bus connection to Paphos town and less frequent to Agios Georgios tis Pegeias fishing port.

For those into walking, the coastal rocky route north to Agios Georgios tis Pegeias fishing port (about nine km long) provides excellent exploration possibilities. About 2.5 km south of the fishing port starts a collection of sea caves.

Distance (km) : Paphos : 14 Polis : 25 Platres : 74 Limassol : 82 Larnaca: 148
Nicosia : 164 Agia Napa : 189 Protaras : 195

Characteristics:  *(May-Oct)*

PETRA TOU ROMIOU WALKING ROUTE

(Map 26 – page 267, 34)

Petra tou Romiou / Aphrodite's Rock is a non organised spot on the coast between Limassol and Paphos, some 23 km from Paphos. It is here that according to legend, Aphrodite (the Greek goddess of love and beauty) was born. The coast is ragged with steep slopes over a long stretch of land. The walking route is seven km long and has elevation between ten and fifty meters offering sea views from above. At about five km from Petra tou Romiou (or two km from the west end of the walking route) it passes by a picnic area and the organised Kouklia beach. There are various points on the walking route from where walkers can come down to the pebble beach and visit a few coves.

One could compose and walk a ten km long walking route between Petra tou Romiou/ Aphrodite's Rock and Aphrodite's temple at Palaipaphos in Kouklia (part of the ancient Paphos UNESCO World Heritage site). Petra tou Romiou walking route would be the main part of the route.

There are relatively frequent public bus connections between the town of Paphos and Petra tou Romiou / Aphrodite's Rock, with stops in Kouklia village and near the west side of the Petra tou Romiou walking route.

Distance (km) : Paphos : 18 Polis : 43 Limassol : 45 Platres : 55 Larnaca: 111 Nicosia : 127 Agia Napa : 152 Protaras : 158

EPISKOPI - CHOULOU WALKING ROUTE

(Map 27 – page 268, 35)

This easy walking route connects the village of Episkopi with the village of Choulou, in Ezousa valley. Ezousa valley is one of a collection of valleys on Troodos mountains that offer outstanding walking opportunities. The suggested walk is twelve km long and relatively flat with an elevation difference of only 200 meters. The walk takes the explorer through orchards and pastures, reed beds and patches of alder trees (Ammati forest is one of these patches). The land is decorated with a large number of wildflowers, hawthorn, oaks and olive trees. It is a very important area for birds and offers quite good birdwatching opportunities. The walk takes the explorer past three watermills. There's a running river in the valley, but the construction of Kannaviou dam upstream decreased the amount of water in the river significantly.

The village of Episkopi is characterized by a huge monolith and the medieval church of Agios Ilarion, now in ruin. There's an Environmental Education center in the village well worth a visit. Choulou is a historic medieval village with both Orthodox and Catholic churches and a mosque. It is the home of Arodafnousa, a beautiful local heroine in a medieval love – hate poem. Both of the villages have accommodation facilities as well as restaurants.

Distance (km) : Paphos : 14 Polis : 38 Platres : 63 Limassol : 65 Larnaca: 131
Nicosia : 147 Agia Napa : 172 Protaras : 178

GEROSKIPOU BEACH – PAPHOS FORT WALKING ROUTE

(Map 28 – page 269, 36)

It is an easy coastal, five km long, walking route that connects the beach of Geroskipou at its east end to the Paphos fort at the west end. The walking route passes by a number of Blue flag eco-label (www.blueflag.org) awarded beaches (Pachyammos B - Pachyammos, Vrisoudia A, Vrisoudia B, Alykes, Municipal Baths) as well as a number of other coves (many a result of wave breaker construction). Those looking for longer walks could combine this one with 'Paphos fort – Kotchas beach' walking route to compose a 13 km long walking route (especially as one doesnot necessarily need to return on foot - there are frequent bus connections between the beaches).

The walk could include exploration of the UNESCO World Heritage site of (ancient) Nea Paphos taking in the beautiful, amazingly preserved Roman mosaics, the ruins of the nearby Byzantine castle known as Saranta Kolones (Forty Columns in English), the ancient theater, St Paul's pillar and more, and the necropolis known as 'Tombs of the Kings' further north (which can be accessed almost one km east of the Paphos fort – Kotchas beach' walking route).

Distance (km): Paphos : 0 Polis : 35 Platres : 60 Limassol : 68 Larnaca: 134 Nicosia : 150 Agia Napa : 175 Protaras : 181

PAPHOS FORT – KOTCHAS BEACH WALKING ROUTE

(Map 28 – page 269, 37)

This is a nine km long coastal walking route from the Paphos fort north to Kotchas beach. Kotchas beach is about eight km by road, north of the Paphos fort. The route passes by the beach of Faros and the adjacent fenced area of the lighthouse, the fenced area of the Tombs of the Kings, and a number of coves. The greatest percentage of the coast is not developed, though there are parts with a considerable amount of construction, especially near Kotchas beach where many luxury hotels are found.

There's frequent public bus connection between a large stretch of the west coast (up north until Laourou beach) and Paphos port. This allows explorers to virtually walk as long as they prefer on the west coastal walking routes. The bus stop closest to Kotchas beach is about 400 m to the south. There's also a less frequent public bus line connecting Laourou beach to Agios Georgios tis Pegeias fishing port, but most of the bus stops are between one and two km inland from the coast.

Distance (km): Paphos : 0 Polis : 33 Platres : 60 Limassol : 68 Larnaca: 134 Nicosia : 150 Agia Napa : 175 Protaras : 181

KOTCHAS BEACH – POTIMA COAST WALKING ROUTE

(Map 29 – page 270, 38)

It is a three km long walking route. Kotchas beach is about eight km by road north of the Paphos fort and Potima coast is about 10.5 km north by road from the fort. The route is on a moderately developed rocky coast. It passes by a few small coves, high rocks and tourist villas.

There's frequent public bus connection between a large stretch of the west coast (up north until Laourou beach) and Paphos port. This allows explorers to virtually walk as long as they prefer on the west coastal walking routes. However the stretch between Potima coast and Laourou beach can realistically only be completed on paved roads. The bus stop closest to Kotchas beach is about 400 m to the south. There are two bus stops along Potima coast. There's also a less frequent public bus line connecting Laourou beach to Agios Georgios tis Pegeias fishing port, but most of the bus stops are between one and two km inland from the coast.

Those looking to enrich the coastal route could walk to (or all around) the nearby Mavrokolympos manmade lake, extending the walk by six to twelve km (the first and last two km of the walk would be on paved road). One can easily walk around the north bank of the lake (staying at a distance of 100 m or closer to the water) but the south bank is more difficult (walkers would be at a distance of 500 m from the water).

Distance (km) : Paphos : 8 Polis : 31 Platres : 68 Limassol : 76 Larnaca: 142 Nicosia : 158 Agia Napa : 183 Protaras : 189

LAOUROU BEACH – AGIOS GEORGIOS TIS PEGEIAS FISHING PORT WALKING ROUTE

(Map 29 – page 270, 39)

This is a nine km long route and probably the best walk on the coast of Paphos. It goes past very unusual rock formations, rocky islets and sea caves in a relatively undeveloped part of the coast. There are two main areas with sea caves, one that is about 3.5 km north of Laourou beach and the one known as the Sea Caves (or 'Kontarkastoi') that are found about 5.5 km north of Laourou beach. From the fishing port (where there is a taverna) one enjoys close views of the Akamas peninsula and Lara coast.

Laourou beach is about 15 km north by road from the Paphos fort. There is frequent public bus connection between Laourou beach and Paphos port, and less frequent public bus connection between Laourou beach and Agios Georgios tis Pegeias fishing port (having a public bus line is very convenient as it means that one can do the walk without worrying too much about a ride back to the start of the walk). For most of the walking route, bus stops are between one and two km inland. At Agios Georgios tis Pegeias there are ruins of an ancient settlement, with a Roman era necropolis, mosaics still standing from 6th century churches and more. Close to the modern Agios Georgios (St. George) church there's a medieval chapel (founded around 1400 AD) in good condition. There are also archaeological finds in Geronisos, the small island about 400 m south west of the port.

This coast is a prime destination for coastal sea exploration (in a sea kayak or similar). Unfortunately the sea here is often rough.

Distance (km) : Paphos : 14 Polis : 23 Platres : 74 Limassol : 82 Larnaca: 148 Nicosia : 164 Agia Napa : 189 Protaras : 195

VOUNI PANAGIAS WALKING ROUTE

(Map 30 – page 271, 40)

I would consider this as a top-ten walk in Cyprus. One could walk it year round and live the change of seasons literally inside vineyards. The vineyards are well kept. On the route there are also many storax trees and red hawthorn (Crataegus monogyna, which is rather rare in Cyprus compared to the widespread yellow fruit Crataegus azarolus species). The route is entirely on dirt roads, at a relatively high elevation, rising 300 meters from the start (usually at Panagia village) to over 1,100 m, and offers cool air for a morning or afternoon walk in summer. In winter it may snow sometimes and be foggy, which adds yet more variety to what the walker sees, hears and feels during the walk. There are unusual rock formations and excellent views both of the Ezousa valley as well as of Paphos Forest. The route passes by the small chapel of Profitis Elias and walkers can take optional longer routes that take them to any of the two monasteries in the area (Chrysorrogiatissa and Agia Moni).

Panagia is a stone-built village found 35 kilometers north east of Paphos, it borders Paphos Forest and it is very close to Kannaviou manmade lake. There are a few local good quality wineries in the vicinity.

Distance (km) : Paphos : 35 Polis : 45 Platres : 72 Limassol : 80 Larnaca: 146
Nicosia : 162 Agia Napa : 187 Protaras : 193

ASPROKREMMOS DAM

(Map 26 – page 267, 22)

It is about 16 km from Paphos and close to the villages of Nikokleia and Anarita. It was built in 1982 on the river Xeros at an altitude of about 50 meters and having a capacity of 53 million cubic meters, it is by far the second biggest dam on the island. The manmade lake has a maximum surface area close to 2.5 sq. km and it is an important birdwatching spot. Fish in the lake include carp, mosquito fish, roach, silver bream, bass, tilapia and catfish. The deserted Turkish Cypriot village of Foinikas / Finike in Xeros Potamos Valley can be an interesting destination on a six-km linear walk on the west bank of the manmade lake (depending on the water's level the walk could involve some off-road walking). Until recently at least, goat herds were kept at the village. Panagia tou Sinti monastery is about 15 km to the north on the west bank of the river. Near the monastery there are watermills and further north on the east side of the river, the vulture "restaurant" is found. There are good mountain biking (and walking) possibilities in the Xeros Potamos Valley.

The UNESCO World Heritage Palaipaphos (Aphrodite's temple) site is just five km south east of the dam. The sea is three km away and the coast of Mandria is seven km south of the dam.

Distance (km) : Paphos : 16 Platres : 44 Polis : 51 Limassol : 52 Larnaca: 118
Nicosia : 130 Agia Napa : 159 Protaras : 165

KANNAVIOU DAM

(Map 30 – page 271, 23)

It is about 25 km from Paphos and can be accessed on the road from Kannaviou village to Panagia village. It was built in 2004 on the Ezousa river at an altitude of about 400 meters and has capacity of 18 million cubic meters. The lake has an irregular shape and a surface area of about 70 hectares. It is not really possible to walk around relatively close to the lake. It borders the vast Paphos Forest. Fish in the lake include bleak, mosquito fish, pumpkinseed sunfish and rainbow trout. . There is a network of dirt roads on its south (east) bank and good walking and cycling possibilities there.

A trip to Kannaviou manmade lake could be combined with exploration of Agia valley through which Ezousa river flows. Agia valley is ten km north east of Kannaviou dam. Another suggestion would be to combine a stay at the manmade lake with visits to nearby wineries and/or monasteries, and walking the very particular Vouni Panagias walking route (from which one enjoys excellent views also of the Kannaviou manmade lake). The walking route is six km north east of the lake and has an elevation range of between 800 and 1,100 m.

Distance (km) : Paphos : 25 Polis : 35 Platres : 82 Limassol : 90 Larnaca: 156
Nicosia : 172 Agia Napa : 197 Protaras : 203

MAVROKOLYMPOS DAM

(Map 29 – page 270, 24)

It is about eleven km from Paphos, not far from Potima coast, and can be easily accessed from the coastal Paphos to Coral Beach road. It was built in 1966 on the Mavrokolympos river at an altitude of about 100 meters and has capacity of 2.2 million cubic meters. It has a regular shape and a surface area of about 13 hectares. Fish in the lake include carp, mosquito fish, roach, bass and silver bream. The lake is a birdwatching spot. The dirt road parallel to the lake is in a bad state. Visitors may see herds of goats around. Explorers can easily walk around the north bank of the lake (staying at a distance of 100 m or closer to the water) but the south bank is more difficult (walkers would be at a distance of 500 m from the water). One could compose a six km circular walk. On the south bank of the manmade lake explorers may be able to spot parts of an old watermill.

There's frequent public bus connection between Paphos port and Coral Beach, with two bus stops along the nearby Potima coast, two km west of the dam.

Distance (km) : Paphos : 11 Polis : 29 Platres : 71 Limassol : 79 Larnaca: 145
Nicosia : 161 Agia Napa : 186 Protaras : 192

TWO OLIVE TREES IN NIKOKLEIA

(Map 26 – page 267, 47)

These two ancient trees live by the road connecting the village of Nikokleia to Paphos. Nikokleia is found 17 km east of Paphos and offers accommodation facilities and a good base for those interested in exploring Diarizos valley on foot, by bicycle and car.

There are many attractions in the vicinity including (at least) six watermills (one by Nikokleia village), picturesque stone built villages (e.g. Trachypedoula), remote chapels and abandonded communities (eg Souskiou/ Susuz, three km north east on a dirt road from Nikokleia), the UNESCO World Heritage site of Palaipaphos in Kouklia (three km on foot on a dirt road south of NIkokleia) and Asprokremmos dam (two km west of Nikokleia). The coast is just five km south (via dirt roads). Nikokleia could also be a convenient base from where to explore the coast between Mandria and legendary Aphrodite's Rock/Petra tou Romiou (thirteen km south east on a walking route on dirt roads and on the Petra tou Romiou walking route).

Distance (km): Paphos : 17 Platres : 43 Limassol : 51 Polis : 52 Larnaca: 117 Nicosia : 129 Agia Napa : 158 Protaras : 164

OAK TREE IN CHOULOU

(Map 27 – page 268, 48)

The ancient oak tree (Quercus infectoria subsp. veneris) lives by the main road in the center of the historic Choulou village. It is 400 years old, 18 meters tall and its trunk perimeter is five meters. This historic medieval village has both Orthodox (including the 12th century Agios Georgios chapel and ruins of Agios Theodoros) and Catholic churches and a mosque. It is the home of Arodafnousa, a beautiful local heroine in a medieval love – hate poem. There is a watermill about one km north west of the village and good walking opportunities by the Ezousa river to Episkopi village towards the south as well as upstream to Kannaviou village. There's a running river in the valley, but the construction of Kannaviou dam upstream decreased the amount of water in the river significantly. Choulou has accommodation facilities as well as restaurants.

There are good quality local wineries nearby (in Lemona village, just one km south and near Statos-Agios Fotios about ten km north east of Choulou).

Distance (km) : Paphos : 23 Polis : 33 Platres : 85 Limassol : 92 Larnaca: 158 Nicosia : 174 Agia Napa : 199 Protaras : 205

PEGEIA SEA CAVES B

(Map 29 – page 270, ⑩)

They are found in a bay about two km south of the set of caves that are known as Pegeia Sea Caves and about 3.5 km north of Laourou beach (Laourou beach is about 15 km north by road from the Paphos fort) and 17.5 km north of the Paphos fort. The geology is quite peculiar. Maybe the best way to visit the caves is on a nine-km long walk from Laourou beach towards the north, finishing at Agios Georgios tis Pegeias fishing port. An even more exciting way of visiting the caves would be on a sea exploration trip (in a sea kayak or other environmentally friendly watercraft). One can visit the caves by car on paved roads. There's also rather frequent public bus connection between Coral Beach and Agios Georgios tis Pegeias fishing port, but the bus stop is about two km inland from the caves.

Distance (km) : Paphos : 18 Polis : 23 Platres : 79 Limassol : 87 Larnaca: 153
Nicosia : 169 Agia Napa : 194 Protaras : 200

PEGEIA SEA CAVES (KONTARKASTOI)

(Map 29 – page 270, (11))

The caves are in a bay shaped like the letter M, and they are found some 5.5 km north of Laourou beach, 3.5 km south of Agios Georgios tis Pegeias fishing port and about 16 km north of the Paphos fort. Maybe the best way to visit the caves is on a nine-km long walk from Laourou beach (15 km north by road from the Paphos fort) towards the north, finishing at Agios Georgios tis Pegeias fishing port. An even more exciting way of visiting the caves would be on a sea exploration trip (in a sea kayak or other environmentally friendly watercraft). One can visit the caves by car on paved roads. There's also rather frequent public bus connection between Coral Beach and Agios Georgios tis Pegeias fishing port, but the bus stop is about 1,300 m inland from the caves. It is believed that in older times, the caves were used by Monachus monachus (Mediterranean monk) seals.

Distance (km) : Paphos : 16 Polis : 21 Platres : 76 Limassol : 84 Larnaca: 150
Nicosia : 166 Agia Napa : 191 Protaras : 197

WATERMILL NEAR MAMONIA (Map 25 – page 190)

WATERMILL IN NIKOKLEIA (Map 26 – page 267)

WATERMILL NEAR SOUSKIOU (Map 26 – page 267)

WATERMILL NEAR MORONERO (Map 27 – page 268)

ANOTHER WATERMILL NEAR MORONERO (Map 27 – page 268)

A THIRD WATERMILL NEAR MORONERO (Map 27 – page 268)

WATERMILL NEAR CHOULOU (Map 27 – page 268)

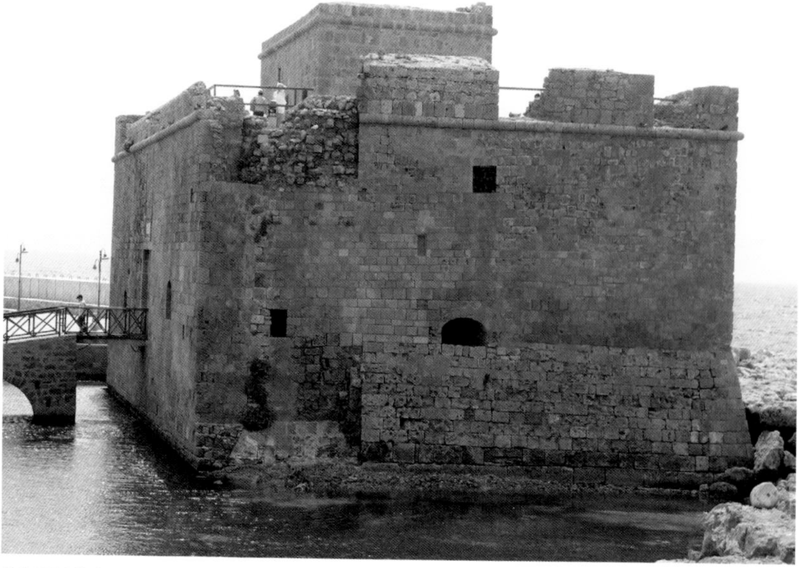

PAPHOS FORT (Map 28 – page 269)

AGIOS GEORGIOS CHAPEL (Map 27 – page 268)

AGIA PARASKEVI CHURCH (Map 28 – page 269)

AGIOS NEOPHYTOS MONASTERY (Map 29 – page 270)

AGIA MONI MONASTERY (Map 30 – page 271)

CHRYSORROGIATISSA MONASTERY (Map 30 – page 271)

PALAIPAPHOS RUINS (Map 26 – page 267)

AGIOS THEODOROS CHAPEL RUINS (Map 27 – page 268)

AGIOS ILARIONAS CHAPEL RUINS (Map 27 – page 268)

NEA PAPHOS (MOSAICS) (Map 28 – page 269)

NEA PAPHOS (TOMBS OF THE KINGS) (Map 28 – page 269)

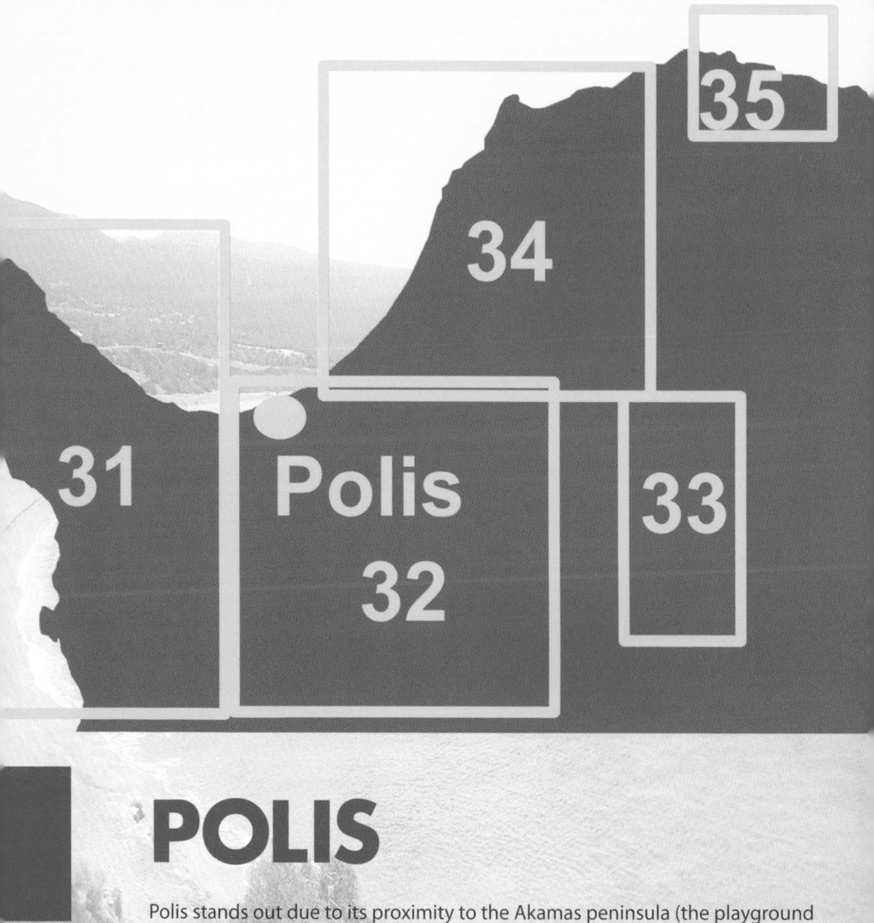

POLIS

Polis stands out due to its proximity to the Akamas peninsula (the playground of Aphrodite, the Greek goddess of love and beauty) and to the huge (by Cyprus standards) Paphos Forest; both pockets of rich biodiversity on the island. The area gets very high marks for walking possibilities, and also generally for outdoor activities focused on nature (exploration by bicycle, coastal sea exploration, birdwatching, nature study, sea turtle and moufflon spotting – occasionally even monk seal spotting). The coast has a number of organised beaches, while for exceptional, blue waters, the hardly accessible Blue Lagoon on the ragged north Akamas coast is highly recommended. The dramatic coastline continues near Pomos and all the way to Kato Pyrgos (and further to Petra tou Limniti). There are at least three pretty manmade lakes in the region (Evretou lake is the most significant), gorges, vineyards and some quality local wineries, carob and citrus orchards as well as ancient trees and survivors of ancient oak forests.

The region's cultural heritage is also rich and (besides Neolithic and ancient ruins) provides a mix of medieval (mostly remote) chapels, watermills, a medieval Venetian bridge, even ruins of ancient monasteries in Paphos Forest and in Akamas, and many pretty villages (e.g. Fyti, Lysos, Kritou Tera).

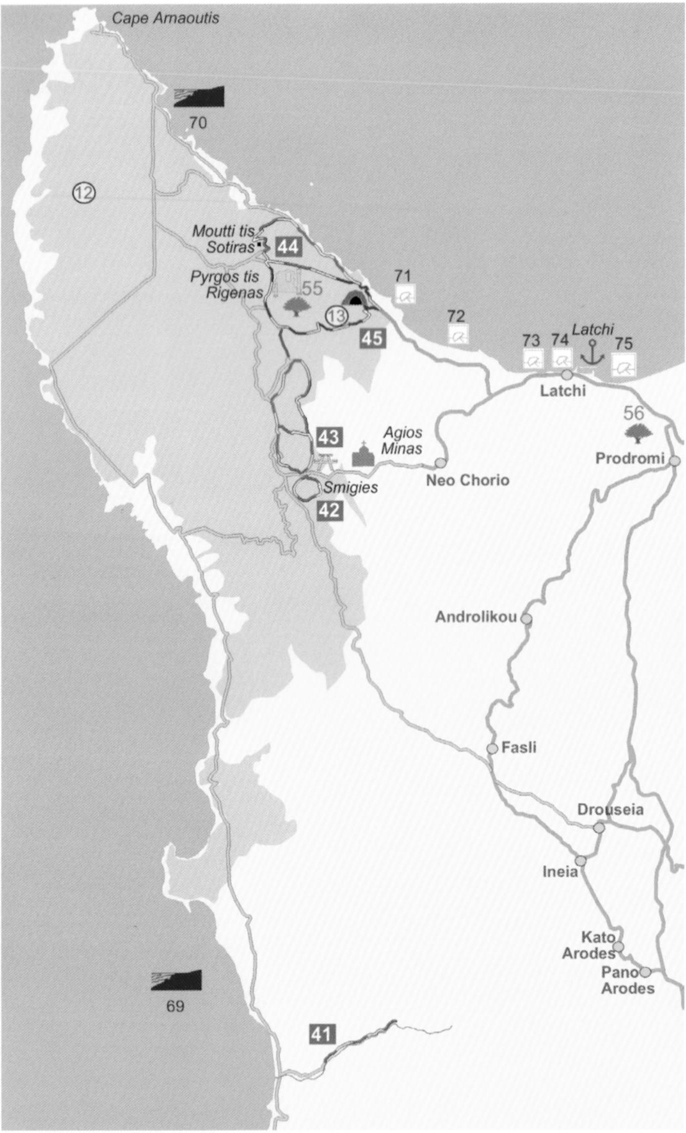

OTHER CULTURAL ATTRACTIONS
Pyrgos tis Rigenas

CHAPELS AND MONASTERIES
Agios Minas

BEACHES/COASTS	
69	Lara coast
70	Blue Lagoon
71	Xistarokampos
72	Halavro
73	Kampos tou Souliou
74	Latchi (or 'Lakki')
75	Municipal beach

ANCIENT TREES	
55	Oak at Pyrgos tis Rigenas (near Neo Chorio)
56	Oak in Prodromi

OTHER NATURAL ATTRACTIONS	
12	Akamas peninsula
13	'Aphrodite's Baths' cave

WALKING ROUTES	
41	Avakas gorge
42	Pissouromoutti
43	Smigies
44	Aphrodite
45	Adonis

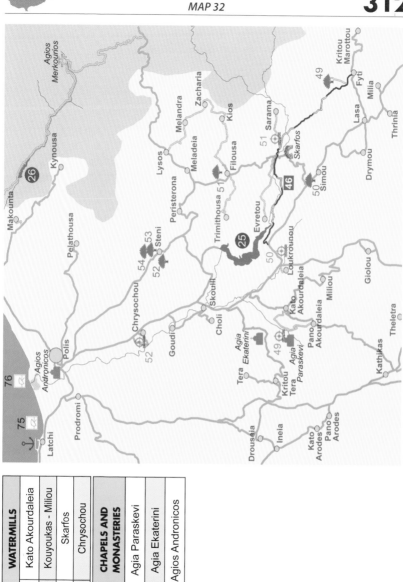

BEACHES/COASTS	
75	Municipal beach
76	Dasoudi (Camping site)

WALKING ROUTES	
46	Fyti village – Evretou dam

WETLANDS	
25	Evretou dam
26	Argaka dam

ANCIENT TREES	
49	Oak in Fyti
50	Mastic in Simou
51	Olive in Filousa
52	White Mulberry in Steni
53	Carob in Steni
54	Olive in Steni

MEDIEVAL BRIDGES
Skarfos

WATERMILLS	
49	Kato Akourdaleia
50	Kouyoukas - Miliou
51	Skarfos
52	Chrysochou

CHAPELS AND MONASTERIES
Agia Paraskevi
Agia Ekaterini
Agios Andronicos

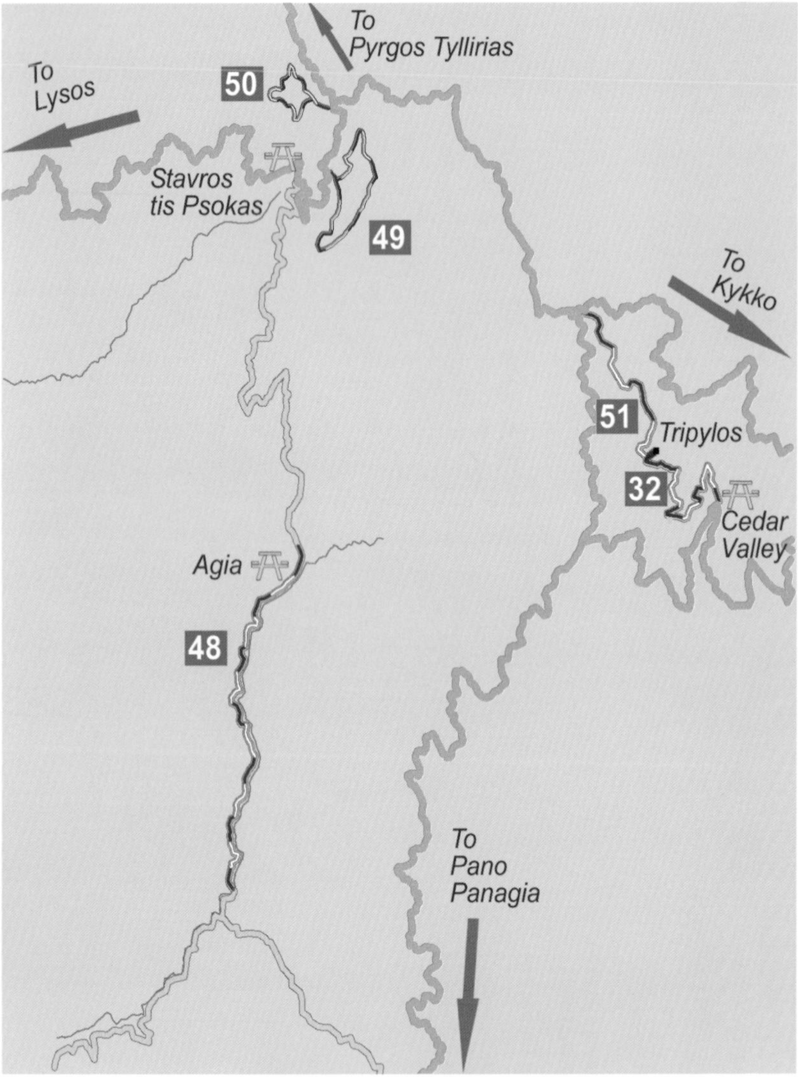

WALKING ROUTES	
32	Cedar Valley – Tripylos peak
48	Agia valley
49	Horteri
50	Moutti tou Stavrou
51	Panagia village junction – Tripylos peak

BEACHES/COASTS	
77	Argaka – Gialia coast
78	Pomos coast
79	Pachyammos

WALKING ROUTES	
47	Pomos valley

WETLANDS	
26	Argaka dam
27	Pomos dam

ANCIENT TREES	
57	Pine at Marotis (near Pomos)

WATERMILLS	
53	Gialia

CHAPELS AND MONASTERIES
Panagia Chrysopateritissa

OTHER CULTURAL ATTRACTIONS
Panagia Chrysogialotissa Georgian monastery

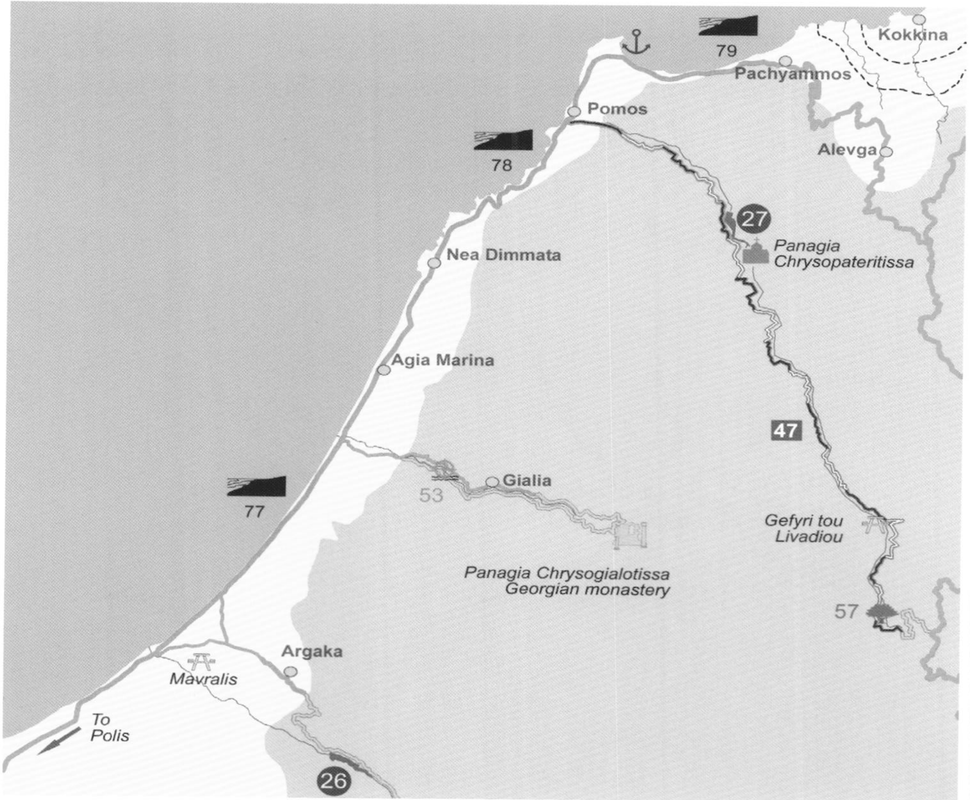

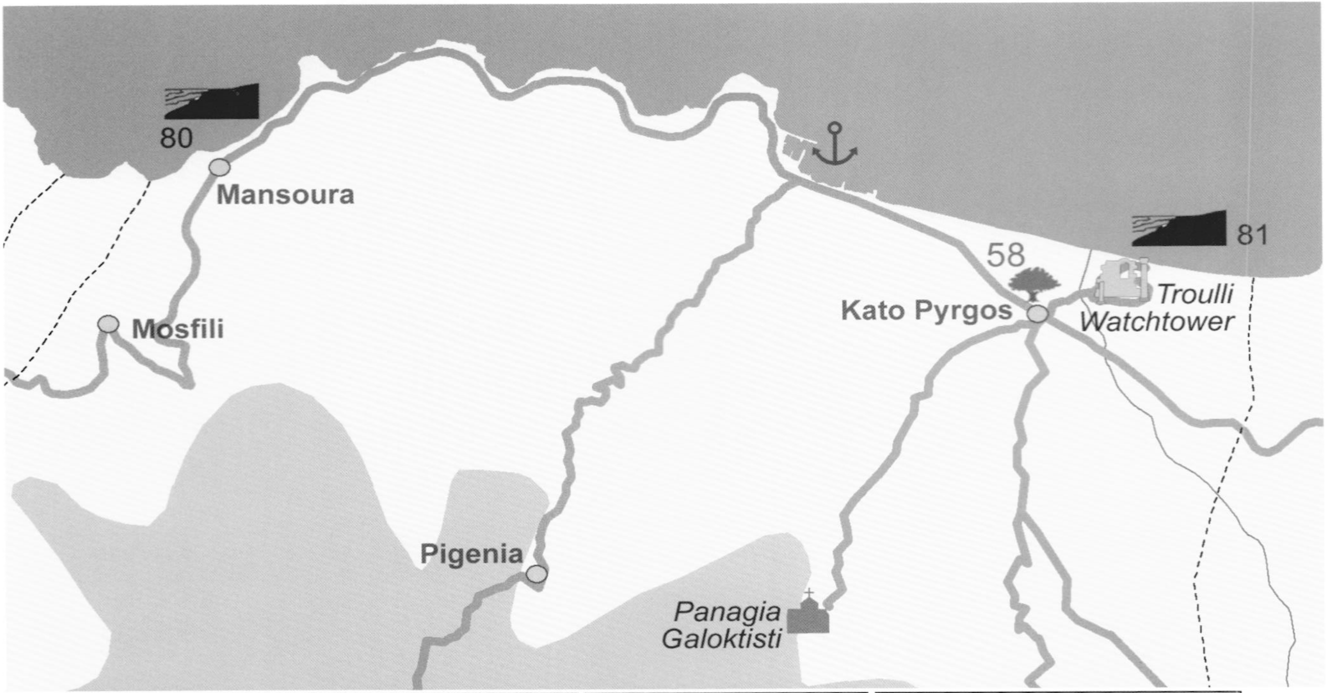

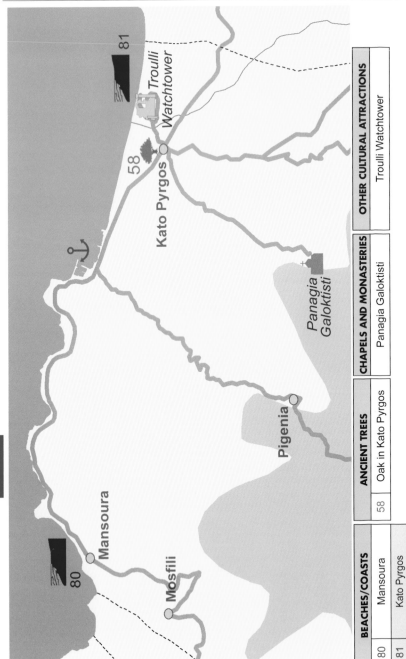

BEACHES/COASTS	
80	Mansoura
81	Kato Pyrgos

ANCIENT TREES	
58	Oak in Kato Pyrgos

CHAPELS AND MONASTERIES
Panagia Galoktisti

OTHER CULTURAL ATTRACTIONS
Troulli Watchtower

LARA COAST

(Map 31 – page 311, 69)

Though there is a beach called Lara beach, probably one should treat the collection of beaches and coves over this vast (by the island's standards) pristine coast as a group. Lara coast extends a couple of tens of km in the western coastline of the Akamas peninsula. The main coastal dirt road is more than 23 km long. There are a few kilometers towards the north end of the coastline that are not covered by the road. For those who want beaches or coves all for themselves, then Lara coast is the place to come. No organised beaches exist. The dirt roads are of a poor quality at a few places, which means that travelling here by car may not be the best option for the explorer. This coast is excellent for those interested in (long) walking or exploration on bicycle. The Cyprus extension of the European long distance E4 walking route passes all along the coastal dirt road. There are a few dirt roads connecting the west coast with the ridge, and then with the north coast and also with the villages at the plateau, i.e. Drouseia, Kathikas, etc, thus providing the possibility of circular trips. However the dirt roads inland as a rule are of a poor quality at places and may give 2-wheel drive cars a hard time. The coast is also a prime destination for coastal sea exploration having sandy coves in between long rocky stretches and islets (though the sea is often rough).

The south end of Lara coast is about 18 km from the town of Paphos and there are relatively frequent public bus connections with Coral Beach (and from there frequent connections with the port of Paphos).

Distance (km) : Paphos : 18 Polis : 15 Platres : 75 Limassol : 83 Larnaca: 149
Nicosia : 165 Agia Napa : 190 Protaras : 196

Characteristics: -

BLUE LAGOON COAST

(Map 31 – page 311, 70)

This cove is found deep inside the Akamas peninsula and some twelve km north west of Polis. The water is simply amazing. There is no real beach (no smooth access to the water and only a bit of sand and pebble to lie on). Blue Lagoon can be accessed with some difficulty by foot. Access by sea is a lot easier, either from the adjacent Fontana Amoroza cove (immediately west) or by watercraft (boat, sea kayak or similar). No tourist infrastructure exists in the vicinity. Towards the south stands the imposing "Moutti tis Sotiras" peak, which at an altitude of 370 m dominates the horizon. The walking routes of Aphrodite and Adonis pass through the peak. There is a coastal dirt road from Aphrodite's Baths cave (passes close to the cove) but it is very difficult even for off road vehicles. The Cyprus extension of the European long distance E4 walking route in fact uses this dirt road (and goes as far as Fontana Amoroza cove before ascending on the slope towards the west coast). There's a small rhombus shaped rocky islet in Blue Lagoon called Chamili (with a surface area of about 300 sq. meters). In summer swimmers will likely share the company of small boats. Lucky snorkelers may swim with sea turtles during the hot season.

There's frequent public bus connection between Baths of Aphrodite Cave and Polis and between Polis and Paphos.

Distance (km): Polis : 12 Paphos : 47 Platres : 84 Limassol : 115 Larnaca: 181 Nicosia : 197 Agia Napa : 222 Protaras : 228

Characteristics: -

XISTAROKAMPOS BEACH

(Map 31 – page 311, 71)

This is a small, 150 meters long beach a few hundred meters east of the Akamas peninsula and nine km west of Polis center. It is a sand and pebble beach with a taverna and a lifeguard in summer.

A trip to this beach can be combined with a visit to Aphrodite's Baths cave (500 meters west of the beach). A swim here can be very refreshing after exploration of the Akamas peninsula on foot (e.g. after a walk on Aphrodite or on Adonis circular walking route or to the north coast from Drouseia or Neo Chorio via Smigies picnic area). Explorers have the option to discover the richness of the peninsula also by bicycle through the extensive network of dirt roads that covers Akamas. The beach can be the perfect starting point for coastal sea exploration of the ragged north Akamas coast in an ecological watercraft (e.g. in a Waterbike or a sea kayak).

There's public bus connection with Polis almost every hour (conveniently timed for those who want to use the Polis-Paphos public bus).

Distance (km) : Polis : 9 Paphos : 44 Platres : 81 Limassol : 112 Nicosia : 175
Larnaca: 178 Agia Napa : 219 Protaras : 225

Characteristics: 

(Jun-Oct)

HALAVRO BEACH

(Map 31 – page 311, 72)

Halavro beach is a one km long sand and pebble beach almost eight km west of Polis center. It is an organised beach with amenities and a lifeguard. There is luxury accommodation by the beach and places to eat. The 150 m long Xistarokampos beach is just to the west of Halavro beach. Akamas is only two km north west of the beach.

A trip to this beach can be combined with a visit to the mythical Aphrodite's Baths cave which is found nearly two km west of the beach. A swim here can be very refreshing after exploration of the Akamas peninsula on foot (e.g. after a walk on Aphrodite circular walking route or from Drouseia or Neo Chorio via Smigies picnic area to the north coast and especially after a walk on Adonis circular walking route which reaches the paved road one km north west of Halavro beach). Alternatively one could explore the peninsula by bicycle through the many dirt roads found there and the peninsula's (north) coastal waters in an ecological watercraft (e.g. in a sea kayak). Snorkeling is also quite nice especially as there are a couple of rocky islets within two km north west of Halavro beach. Snorkelers during the warmer season may be blessed with an encounter with sea turtles in the area (which use many of the beaches here to lay their eggs in summer).

There's public bus connection with Polis almost every hour (conveniently timed for those who want to use the Polis-Paphos public bus).

Distance (km): Polis : 8 Paphos : 43 Platres : 80 Limassol : 111 Nicosia : 154 Larnaca: 177 Agia Napa : 218 Protaras : 224

Characteristics:  *(Jun-Sep)*

KAMPOS TOU SOULIOU BEACH

(Map 31 – page 311, 73)

It is a 250 meters long sand and pebble beach immediately to the west of Latchi (or 'Lakki') beach, and some 4.5 km from the center of Polis. It is an organised beach with amenities and a lifeguard. The next organised beach to its west side is the longer Halavro beach (it is more than one km long and about 2.5 km away by car). The Akamas peninsula is only five km away (to the north west).

Kampos tou Souliou beach could act as a gateway towards picturesque Neo Chorio village (three km south west of the beach) and as a base for exploration of the Akamas peninsula ridge via Smigies picnic area. Similarly to other beaches in the area, snorkelers during the warmer season may be blessed with an encounter with sea turtles (which use many of the beaches here to breed in summer).

There's public bus connection with Polis almost every hour (conveniently timed for those who want to use the Polis-Paphos public bus).

Distance (km) : Polis : 5 Paphos : 40 Platres : 77 Limassol : 108 Nicosia : 151
Larnaca: 174 Agia Napa : 215 Protaras : 221

Characteristics:  *(Jun-Oct)*

LATCHI BEACH

(Map 31 – page 311, 74)

Latchi (or 'Lakki') beach is a 500 meters long sand and pebble beach, immediately to the west of Latchi port, and some four km from the center of Polis. It is an organised beach with amenities including restaurants and cafes and a lifeguard. To its west it borders the smaller 'Kampos tou Souliou' beach. The Akamas peninsula is only six km away to the north west.

A stay here could make a relaxing break during a trip to the mythical 'Aphrodite's Baths' cave (nearly six km towards the north west). Beachgoers at Latchi beach enjoy excellent views of imposing Moutti tis Sotiras peak. As in the case of other beaches in the area, snorkelers during the warmer season may be blessed with an encounter with sea turtles (which use many of the beaches here to breed in summer). Latchi fishing port is immediately to the east of the beach. Explorers can take a minicruise along the north Akamas coast or explore the beautiful ragged coastline in a rented boat.

There's a convenient bus stop just east of Latchi beach. A frequent public bus line connects the beach with Aphrodite's Baths cave and with Polis (the bus to Polis is conveniently timed for those who want to use public transportation to Paphos).

Distance (km) : Polis : 4 Paphos : 39 Platres : 76 Limassol : 107 Nicosia : 150
Larnaca: 173 Agia Napa : 214 Protaras : 220

Characteristics:  ***(May-Oct)***

POLIS MUNICIPAL BEACH

(Map 31 – page 311, 75)

This is the second organised beach very near Polis. It is about 1.5 km long and extends from Dasoudi beach on its eastern end close to Latchi fishing port on its western end. The beach has been awarded the Blue flag eco-label (www.blueflag.org) and has handicap facilities. It is a sand and pebble beach. The Akamas peninsula is only seven km away (to the north west). Along the beach there's a walking route all the way to Dasoudi beach towards the east. By the side of the walking route there are many restaurants, cafes and shops. Explorers can find accommodation nearby. As in the case of other beaches in the area, snorkelers during the warmer season may be blessed with an encounter with sea turtles (which use many of the beaches here to breed in summer). Explorers can take a minicruise along the north Akamas coast or explore the beautiful ragged coastline in a rented boat.

There's a convenient bus stop at the west end of Polis municipal beach. Frequent public buses connect the beach both with the mythical Aphrodite's Baths cave and with Polis (the bus to Polis is conveniently timed for those who want to use public transportation to Paphos).

The huge ancient oak tree in Prodromi village is 2.5 km south east on the road to Polis. Polis is further 500 meters east. It provides a comfortable base, especially during winter when tourism is low and many shops and relevant amenities may be closed elsewhere. It has a number of attractions like the frescoed 16th century Agios Andronicos church and the nearby ancient 1,100 year old mastic tree.

Distance (km): Polis : 0 Paphos : 35 Platres : 72 Limassol : 103 Nicosia : 146 Larnaca: 169 Agia Napa : 210 Protaras : 216

Characteristics:  *(May-Oct)*

DASOUDI (CAMPING SITE) BEACH

(Map 32 – page 312, 76)

It is about 400 meters long and a bit over one km to the north of Polis. The beach takes its name after the eucalyptus forest ("Dasoudi" means small forest in the Greek Cypriot dialect) found immediately behind the beach (the forest is a camping site). It is a very popular place for campers and has a more relaxed and liberal atmosphere than most of the other organised beaches in Cyprus. Dasoudi beach has been awarded the Blue flag eco-label (www.blueflag.org) and has handicap facilities. On its surface it has sand mixed with pebble. Dasoudi beach to the west borders Polis Municipal Beach (they are connected by a walking path), whereas on its eastern side the coast is not developed.

Polis (the bus stop is nearly 1.5 km south east of Dasoudi) has frequent public bus connection with Baths of Aphrodite's cave, with Paphos and with many villages in the vicinity. It provides a comfortable base, especially during winter when tourism is low and many shops and relevant amenities may be closed elsewhere. Polis has interesting attractions like the frescoed 16th century Agios Andronicos church, the nearby ancient 1,100 year old mastic tree, pretty Agios Nicolaos church at the pedestrian traditional center, and more. There's a preserved watermill just four km south, at the Turkish Cypriot village of Chrysochou.

Distance (km): Polis : 1 Paphos : 36 Platres : 73 Limassol : 104 Larnaca: 170 Nicosia : 186 Agia Napa : 211 Protaras : 217

Characteristics:  *(May-Oct)*

ARGAKA – GIALIA COAST

(Map 34 – page 314, 77)

This is an eight km long sand and pebble stretch from the west of the village of Argaka towards the east and up to the village of Gialia. In its eastern part the coast becomes very rocky yet flat for about 2.5 km, before it becomes ragged, with dramatic rock formations, cliffs and small coves in between the rocks. At the west end of the Argaka - Gialia coast there is a jetty of a nearby mine (at a place called Limni, which means "lake" in Greek - the mine is no longer operating) almost four km from Polis center. Near the jetty explorers may observe (yellow) sulphur deposits by the sea. East of the jetty there is the picnic area of Mavralis. The coast is not organised, not congested and great for those seeking tranquility and those who like long strolls by the sea.

Nearby attractions include scenic Argaka manmade lake (found just inside Paphos Forest), a renovated watermill in Gialia village (there's another damaged one in the village) and the ruins of Panagia Chrysogialotissa Georgian monastery deep inside Paphos Forest. Huge Paphos Forest provides excellent opportunities for exploration by foot or bicycle on its extensive network of dirt roads. There are good possibilities for moufflon spotting in the forest and chances for sea turtle spotting in the water during the hot season. Coastal sea exploration of nearby ragged Pomos coast (on an environmentally friendly watercraft) is highly recommended.

There's limited public bus access to the coast from Polis (and from Pachyammos).

Distance (km): Polis : 5 Paphos : 40 Platres : 77 Limassol : 108 Larnaca: 174 Nicosia : 190 Agia Napa : 225 Protaras : 231

Characteristics:

POMOS COAST

(Map 34 – page 314, 78)

The village of Pomos is about twenty km north east of Polis center. Pomos coast is a ragged coastline (near the village) almost ten km long, with steep slopes, strange rock formations and small coves between the rocks. The coast is dramatic, very particular and atypical of Cyprus. The best way to explore it is from inside the sea, on an environmentally friendly watercraft such as a sea kayak or similar. There is a small port on the east part of the coastline, and further east, a cave called "Spilia tou Drakou" whose English translation would be "Dragon's cave". The vistas along the coastline are superb. Those preferring bigger coves can try Pachyammos coast towards the east (four km from Pomos port).

Other attractions in the area include the scenic Pomos manmade lake (five km south east of the village) and the adjacent peculiar 15th century Panagia Chrysopateritissa chapel. Both can be reached on the dirt road through Paphos Forest to Stavros tis Psokas station. Gefyri tou Livadiou picnic area is a few km further south east on the dirt road. The valley of Pomos in particular, through which Livadi river flows, and Paphos Forest in general present excellent opportunities for exploration by foot or bicycle on an extensive network of dirt roads and good possibilities for moufflon spotting.

There's limited public bus access to the coast from Polis (and from Pachyammos).

Distance (km): Polis : 20 Paphos : 55 Platres : 92 Limassol : 143 Nicosia : 166 Larnaca: 209 Agia Napa : 250 Protaras : 256

Characteristics:  ***(Jul-Aug for part of the coast)***

PACHYAMMOS COAST

(Map 34 – page 314, 79)

This is the 750 meter long coast of the village of Pachyammos (which literally means "thick sand" in Greek). It is about 24 km north east of Polis and just four km east of Pomos port. Entrance to the east of the coast is strictly forbidden as it leads to an area occupied by Turkish troops. This is a non organised pebble and sand coastal spot. The cove is surrounded by high hills and Paphos Forest. Though the last decade has seen some tourist development in the form of holiday villas, this is still a very remote, uncongested stretch of Cyprus coastline.

The village of Pachyammos can be a good base for exploration of the ragged Pomos coast and of the north (east) part of huge Paphos Forest. Nearby attractions include the scenic Pomos manmade lake (five km south east of Pomos village) and the adjacent peculiar 15th century Panagia Chrysopateritissa chapel. Both can be reached on the dirt road through Paphos Forest to Stavros tis Psokas station. Paphos Forest presents excellent opportunities for exploration by foot or bicycle on an extensive network of dirt roads and good possibilities for moufflon spotting. Snorkelers in the area have good chances of swimming in the company of sea turtles in summer.

There's limited public bus connection to Polis and to Tilliria region (Kato Pyrgos village).

Distance (km): Polis : 24 Paphos : 59 Platres : 96 Limassol : 127 Larnaca: 193
Nicosia : 194 Agia Napa : 234 Protaras : 240

Characteristics: -

MANSOURA COAST

(Map 35 – page 315, 80)

This is the 1.1 km long coast just north east of Kokkina enclave, about 45 km north east of Polis and 25 km north east of Pomos port. Entrance to the west of the coast is strictly forbidden as it leads to the enclave, an area occupied by Turkish troops. Mansoura coast is a non organised pebble and sand coastal stretch. It combines easy access via the paved road from Pomos to Kato Pyrgos (Kato Pyrgos is four km east of the beach), and the presence of some amenities in the form of a local restaurant with a very low density of beach goers. In 2010 a checkpoint was opened between Kato Pyrgos and Limnitis/Yeşilırmak, making a trip to the area from Nicosia significantly shorter (around 75 mınutes by car – 80 km).

Kato Pyrgos has good tourist infrastructure, including accommodation and restaurants. There are good paved road connections with Stavros tis Psokas forest station and with Kykkos monastery (via Kampos village) and limited public bus connection to Polis and to Kato Pyrgos village (and from there to Nicosia).

A visit to Mansoura coast could be combined with exploration of the wider area including the extremely remote north east part of the huge Paphos Forest (whose extensive network of forest dirt roads provides outstanding walking, cycling and moufflon spotting possibilities). The ancient city kingdom of Soloi and the ancient palace at Vouni, in the north part of Cyprus on the coastal road are just 21 km and 17 km away respectively.

Distance (km): Polis : 45 Paphos : 80 Nicosia : 86 Platres : 86 Limassol : 117
Larnaca: 183 Agia Napa : 224 Protaras : 230

Characteristics:

KATO PYRGOS COAST

(Map 35 – page 315, 81)

This is the 1.7 km long east coastal stretch of Kato Pyrgos, the least organised and probably the most attractive of the beaches of Kato Pyrgos. There are few amenities including a restaurant and hardly any houses close to the coast. Towards the east it ends up at a hill by the buffer zone (it is forbidden to enter the buffer zone). The other smaller beach (called Omega) is to the west of the fishing port, 400 meters long and organized (including lifeguards). The coast is about 50 km north east of Polis and 30 km north east of Pomos port. In 2010 a checkpoint was opened between Kato Pyrgos and Limnitis/ Yeşilırmak making a trip to the area from Nicosia significantly shorter (around 75 minutes by car – 80 km). Kato Pyrgos has good tourist infrastructure, including accommodation and restaurants. Other attractions include the ruins of Troulli medieval watchtower (with panoramic views), the very particular Panagia Galoktisti chapel (Galoktisti literally means 'built using milk'), and the ancient oak tree at the center of the village.

The extremely remote north east part of the huge Paphos Forest (with an extensive network of forest dirt roads) provides excellent walking, cycling and moufflon spotting possibilities. The ancient city kingdom of Soloi and the ancient palace at Vouni, in the north part of Cyprus on the coastal road are just 17 km and 13 km away respectively.

There are good paved road connections with Stavros tis Psokas forest station and with Kykkos monastery (via Kampos village) and limited public bus connection to Polis and to Nicosia.

Distance (km): Polis : 51 Nicosia : 80 Paphos : 86 Platres : 92 Limassol : 123 Larnaca: 189 Agia Napa : 230 Protaras : 236

Characteristics:  *(Jul-Sep)*

AVAKAS GORGE WALKING ROUTE IN AKAMAS PENINSULA

(Map 31 – page 311, 41)

This spectacular gorge is in the western part of the Akamas peninsula close to Lara coast (Lara coast has many remote coves), about 20 km from Paphos and can be accessed through the dirt coastal road from Agios Georgios tis Pegeias to Lara coast. The walking route is linear 2.5 km long and has signs naming some of the plant species in the gorge. The gorge is two km long, with steep rocks on both sides going up 80 meters. At its narrowest point it is just three meters wide. Walkers may hear and see various bird species and probably meet goats and other tourists. The walk is not very tiring, but caution is required as the flowing water makes many rocks in the gorge quite slippery (also at times some rocks may fall from the top).

The walking route lies four km north east of the closest bus stop of the rather frequent public bus line that connects Coral Beach and Agios Georgios tis Pegeias fishing port. At Agios Georgios tis Pegeias there are ruins of an ancient settlement, with a Roman era necropolis, mosaics still standing from 6th century churches and more. Close to the modern Agios Georgios (St. George) church there's a medieval chapel (founded around 1400 AD) in good condition.

Explorers could incorporate a walk in Avakas gorge into very pleasant 20-25 km long circular walking routes (that the explorers compose) that start and finish at one of the picturesque Laona villages (e.g. Drouseia, Kathikas). If they prefer a shorter walk they could compose a linear walking route and use public transportation to return to their starting point.

Distance (km) : Polis : 18 Paphos : 20 Platres : 80 Limassol : 88 Larnaca: 154
Nicosia : 170 Agia Napa : 195 Protaras : 201

PISSOUROMOUTTI WALKING ROUTE IN AKAMAS PENINSULA

(Map 31 – page 311, 42)

It is a three km long circular walking route near the picnic area of Smigies, in the Akamas peninsula, three km west of Neo Chorio village. The easiest way to reach it is on a dirt road leading west from the village of Neo Chorio (Neo Chorio is at an altitude of about 150 meters just to the east of the Akamas peninsula). It is easy to identify Pissouromitti peak and the adjacent Piana peak (just north west of Smigies picnic area) at least from as far as Latchi. Both are about 400 m high. Pissouromoutti peak offers glorious views of the west coast of Akamas (in other words of Lara coast) as well as of the coast to the north east, and also of the south towards Drouseia village. The scenery is rocky, forest like or bushy at places.

Agios Minas is a 16th century stone built chapel just 700 east of the walking route (by the dirt road to Neo Chorio). Unfortunately the frescoes did not survive. The trip can be combined with other walks in the area. Besides the official walking routes (e.g. the nearby Smigies circular walking route - short 2.5 km or longer nearly seven km) walkers can compose their own route in the peninsula in a number of directions, e.g. to the lighthouse in the north and/or to the north coast, to Lara coast in the west, or towards Drouseia in the south. The Cyprus extension of the E4 European long distance walking route traverses most of the peninsula ridge.

Distance (km) : Polis : 12 Paphos : 47 Platres : 84 Limassol : 115 Nicosia : 158
Larnaca: 181 Agia Napa : 222 Protaras : 228

SMIGIES WALKING ROUTE IN AKAMAS PENINSULA

(Map 31 – page 311, 43)

It is a circular seven km long (there is also a shorter 2.5 km route) walking route in the Akamas peninsula that starts at the Smigies picnic area, three km west from Neo Chorio village. The easiest way to reach it is on a dirt road leading west from the village of Neo Chorio. The village is at an altitude of about 150 meters just to the east of the Akamas peninsula. It is easy to identify Piana peak (just north west of Smigies picnic area) and the adjacent Pissouromitti peak at least from as far as Latchi. Both are about 400 m high.

The walking route is ascending and steep for the first 500 meters or so (clockwise) as the elevation rises 100 meters. After that it is relatively easy. Walkers enjoy fantastic views of the west coast (Lara) as well as the east coast (Latchi up to Pomos village). The vegetation is dominated by junipers, lentisc, thorny broom and pine trees. In spring visitors may see blooming rockrose and gladiolus. The route has certain stretches on dirt road. Walkers need to be careful to follow the arrows for the right direction. There is a restored kiln on the walking route. At its northern end (after a short 600 m walk further north) one reaches Adonis walking route; one could follow it to reach the north coast (possibly combining them with Aphrodite walking route). The circular Pissouromoutti walking route also starts near Smigies picnic area.

Distance (km): Polis : 12 Paphos : 47 Platres : 84 Limassol : 115 Nicosia : 158
Larnaca: 181 Agia Napa : 222 Protaras : 228

APHRODITE WALKING ROUTE IN AKAMAS PENINSULA

(Map 31 – page 311, 44)

It is a circular 7.5 km long walking route in the Akamas peninsula that starts at 'Aphrodite's Baths' cave. Walking on the walking route clockwise, it shares the first third of the route with Adonis walking route. The highlight of the route is the 370 m 'Moutti tis Sotiras' peak, which from a distance of just half a km from the sea offers amazing panoramic views of the north west coast. The scenery is rocky or bushy (many junipers mainly at the peak, the vegetation is very low throughout) and the route gives the opportunity to study the local flora. The descent needs care and the whole trip can be tiring because of the significant elevation difference (330 m). The last part of the trip is on the coastal dirt road. For many of us it would make sense to extend the walk towards the north west up to the superb Blue Lagoon (and possibly include a refreshing swim during warmer weather); the walk would be extended by seven-eight km but it would be either descending or flat.

Moutti tis Sotiras can also be accessed from Smigies picnic area on a mountain bike or on a long walk (also by an off road car). Two hundred meters to the south east walkers may see Pyrgos tis Rigenas (Queen's castle) believed to have been part of a medieval monastery and a huge ancient oak tree next to it. These are right on Adonis walking route.

Distance (km) : Polis : 10 Paphos : 45 Platres : 82 Limassol : 113 Larnaca: 179
Nicosia : 195 Agia Napa : 220 Protaras : 226

ADONIS WALKING ROUTE IN AKAMAS PENINSULA

(Map 31 – page 311, 45)

It is a circular 7.5 km long walking route in the Akamas peninsula that starts at 'Aphrodite's Baths' cave. It shares the first third of the route with Aphrodite walking route. The highlight of the route is the 370 m 'Moutti tis Sotiras' peak, from where one has amazing panoramic views of the north west coast. The scenery is rocky or bushy (many junipers) and the route gives the opportunity to study the local flora. Moutti tis Sotiras can also be accessed from Smigies picnic area on a mountain bike or on a long walk (also by an off road car). The walking route passes by the ruins of Pyrgos tis Rigenas (Queen's castle) believed to have been part of a medieval monastery and a huge ancient oak tree next to it. One needs to be careful not to lose the walking route as it goes south from Pyrgos (and not east). There's another 100 meter elevation ascent south of Pyrgos before a largely smooth descent that meets the Polis – Aphrodite's Baths cave road, at a distance of one km south east of the cave. On their descent walkers enjoy glorious views of Chrysochou bay all the way to Pomos port, 25 km towards the north east.

It is relatively easy to compose walking routes mostly on dirt roads from Drouseia (around 20 km long) or from Neo Chorio (around 15 km long) that pass through Smigies picnic area and reach the splendid north Akamas coast via Adonis (and Aphrodite) walking routes.

Distance (km) : Polis : 10 Paphos : 45 Platres : 82 Limassol : 113 Larnaca: 179
Nicosia : 195 Agia Napa : 220 Protaras : 226

FYTI VILLAGE - EVRETOU DAM WALKING ROUTE

(Map 32 – page 312, 46)

It is an excellent, easy, linear ten km-long route on dirt roads in the Evretou valley and around Evretou manmade lake. The route starts at the picturesque Fyti village, which is 20 km south west of Polis at an elevation of nearly 700 meters and descends to an elevation of about 200 meters. On the way walkers enjoy glorious vistas all the way to Troodos mountains, the Evretou valley and Evretou manmade lake and even Chrysochou bay. The vegetation is dominated by large oak trees some of which (a group between Lasa and Fyti village for example) are ancient. The route passes near Fyti ancient oak tree (a short detour is needed to visit it), crosses the Stavros tis Psokas river a couple of times, and passes by a well preserved watermill (there are a few others very near but they are in a bad state). Opposite the watermill at a distance of just 100 meters Skarfos medieval bridge stands proud. In order to visit it walkers need to walk an additional kilometer (in total). It is worthwhile to do so. On the north side of the lake stands the deserted Turkish Cypriot village of Evretou. When the dam is full the last stretch of the route becomes submerged and walkers would need to ascend to the paved road a lot earlier.

Evretou (or Stavros tis Psokas) valley is home to a number of deserted Turkish Cypriot villages (e.g. Sarama, Zacharia, Kios).

Distance (km): Polis : 20 Paphos : 40 Platres : 60 Limassol : 108 Nicosia : 185
Larnaca: 188 Agia Napa : 229 Protaras : 235

POMOS VALLEY WALKING ROUTE

(Map 34 – page 314, 47)

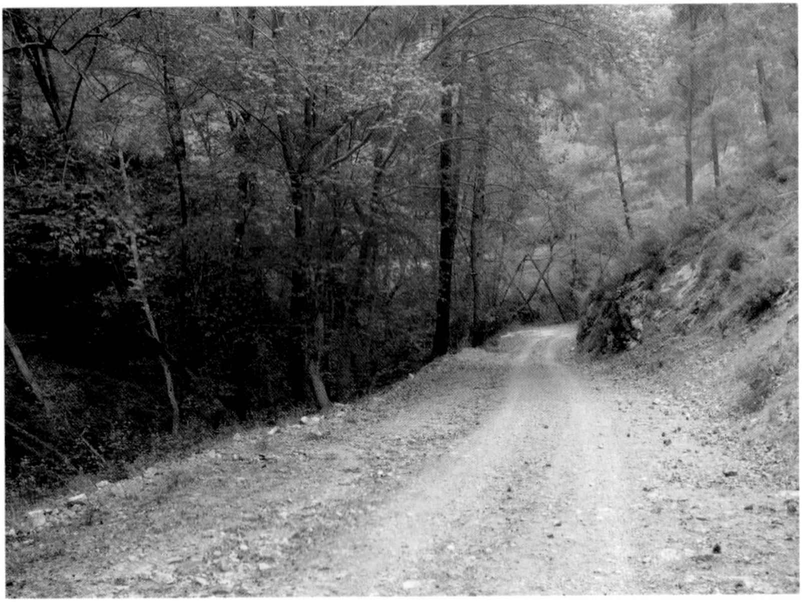

It is about 30 km from Polis. One can access Pomos valley from Pomos village, driving to the direction of the scenic Pomos manmade lake and the adjacent peculiar 15th century Panagia Chrysopateritissa chapel (both of which are worth a visit) and then towards Stavros tis Psokas forest station. Alternatively, one can access Pomos valley from high up in Paphos Forest by descending the paved road from Stavros tis Psokas forest station to Kato Pyrgos village and about three km downhill on the paved road turning north east on the dirt road to Pomos village. I would especially recommend the part of the valley upstream from the manmade lake for walking, as it is found inside Paphos Forest rather than in farmland. Walking takes place on a dirt road that goes parallel to the stream in the valley. The dirt road is steeper than that of Platy valley (100 m more of an elevation drop over the same distance of about ten km). In the valley about seven km south east of Pomos manmade lake one finds the picnic site of Gefyri tou Livadiou. Explorers may spot moufflon early in the morning or late in the afternoon in the valley. The lower part of the valley is greener and the route is easier and more interesting. There's at least one ancient tree (one is declared a natural monument and is described in the Book) in the valley.

Exploring the valley downhill on a bicycle (e.g. starting from Cedar Valley) is also highly recommended as the route is either on paved roads or on good quality dirt roads, the distance is rather short at 40 km and the elevation drops gradually by 1,200 m.

Distance (km): Polis : 30 Platres : 45 Paphos : 65 Limassol : 85 Nicosia : 119 Larnaca: 131 Agia Napa : 192 Protaras : 198

AGIA VALLEY WALKING ROUTE

(Map 33 – page 313, 48)

Agia valley is in the huge Paphos Forest and about 30 km from Polis. The Ezousa river runs through it. It is a pleasant valley, with good walking and mountain biking (and photo safari) possibilities. There is also an organised picnic area. Agia valley can be reached via a (good) dirt road from Stavros tis Psokas forest station, Kannaviou dam or Panagia village. Usually there are no cars around. The recommended walking route is in the lower part of the valley, has a length of about ten km and a relatively flat elevation profile as the range is just 150 m. Like in other parts of huge Paphos Forest, explorers (in the absence of loud noise, e.g. car or motorcycle engines which scare animals away) have good possibilities of spotting moufflon. Those who would prefer a longer walk could start from Stavros tis Psokas forest station and reach Kannaviou dam via Agia valley (20 km long, elevation descent of 500 m). Those who want to explore by bicycle could start at Cedar Valley and cycle towards Stavros tis Psokas and then Agia to Kannaviou manmade lake (a distance of nearly 40 km), or even start at Kykkos monastery and cycle to Cedar Valley first (an extra distance of 16 km). A GPS navigation device would be highly recommended for those exploring the dirt road network of Paphos Forest.

It makes sense to end the trip at Kannaviou manmade lake and also possibly visit a couple of the good quality local wineries (and/or monasteries) in the area.

Distance (km): Polis : 30 Paphos : 35 Platres : 45 Limassol : 103
Nicosia : 155 Larnaca: 169 Agia Napa : 210 Protaras : 215

HORTERI WALKING ROUTE

(Map 33 – page 313, 49)

Horteri (or Chorteri) is a five km long circular nature walking trail deep inside Paphos Forest, nearly two km to the east of Stavros tis Psokas forest station. It starts right on the road linking Kykkos monastery to Stavros tis Psokas forest station. It can be tiring as there is significant elevation change (more than 300 m). The vegetation is dominated by pine trees and golden oak. By the walking route one can see many other plant species found in Paphos Forest, including strawberry trees, plane, maple, sumach, myrtle, bramble and rock rose.

The Cyprus extension of E4, one of the European long distance paths passes from here connecting Kykkos monastery to Stavros tis Psokas forest station (26 km long – it may be too long for most of us).

At Stavros tis Psokas there are facilities for explorers including a restaurant, accommodation and a picnic site. Those who are not lucky enough to spot moufflon in the wild in Paphos Forest could see these animals in captivity in an enclosure at Stavros tis Psokas forest station.

Distance (km) : Polis : 34 Platres : 38 Paphos : 55 Limassol : 98 Nicosia : 118
Larnaca: 142 Agia Napa : 207 Protaras : 213

MOUTTI TOU STAVROU WALKING ROUTE

(Map 33 – page 313, 50)

It is a rather flat (elevation range is no more than 100 meters) three km long circular walking trail, almost 35 km from Polis, deep inside huge Paphos Forest. It is found three km north of Stavros tis Psokas forest station, at the point where the road from Stavros tis Psokas forest station to Kykkos monastery meets the road to Kato Pyrgos village. The vegetation is dominated by pine trees. There are nice views of the huge Paphos Forest. To the west and the north west walkers enjoy views towards Chrysochou bay and the Akamas peninsula. The walking route can be combined with other walks, for example one of the walks through the cedar forest to Tripylos peak.

At Stavros tis Psokas there are facilities for explorers including a restaurant, accommodation and a picnic site. Those who are not lucky enough to spot moufflon in the wild in Paphos Forest could see these animals in captivity in an enclosure at Stavros tis Psokas forest station. The ancient golden oak at Kremmos tis Pellis is nine km south east on the road to Kykkos monastery. The extraordinary Cedar Valley (home to Cyprus population of 130,000 cedar trees) is 14 km to the south east.

Distance (km) : Platres : 36 Polis : 36 Paphos : 53 Limassol : 105 Nicosia : 110
Larnaca: 139 Agia Napa : 212 Protaras : 218

PANAGIA VILLAGE JUNCTION – TRIPYLOS PEAK WALKING ROUTE

(Map 33 – page 313, 51)

It is found about 35 km from Platres. The walk starts at the junction where the Kykkos monastery to Stavros tis Psokas forest station road meets the road from Panagia village at an elevation of 1,150 m. The linear route is three km long on a forest dirt road that leads to the Tripylos forest fire lookout station (elevation 1,400 m). From Tripylos peak one can have a panoramic view of the north coast, all the way from the Akamas peninsula to Morphou bay and beyond. The walk is through the cedar forest of Cyprus which has about 130,000 cedar trees. The fauna includes many jay (and other species) birds. Early in the morning or late in the afternoon walkers have good chances to spot some of the elusive moufflon of Cyprus.

One can combine this route with the Cedar Valley to Tripylos peak route for a good six km long combined linear walk. There's paved road access to both ends of this route. The route is part of the Cyprus extension of E4, one of the European long distance paths, which connects Kykkos monastery to Stavros tis Psokas forest station (26 km long – it may be too long for most of us).

Distance (km) : Polis : 34 Platres : 38 Paphos : 55 Limassol : 78 Nicosia : 112
Larnaca: 154 Agia Napa : 185 Protaras : 191

EVRETOU DAM

(Map 32 – page 312, 25)

The dam (construction) is about eight km from Polis and can be accessed from the road from Skoulli that meets the road from Polis to Peristerona village. It was built in 1986 on the Stavros tis Psokas river at an altitude of about 200 meters and has capacity of 24 million cubic meters. The manmade lake has a crescent-like shape and a surface area of about 100 hectares. Fish in the lake include carp, mosquito fish, roach, pikeperch, bass and catfish. There are birdwatching possibilities here.

Walking on the dirt road along the south bank of the manmade lake (at a distance from the water of no more than 200 m and at an elevation difference of about 50 m) is excellent and offers glorious views of the lake (and at points also of Troodos mountains and Chrysochou bay). The abandoned Turkish Cypriot village of Evretou on the eastern end of the north bank of the lake offers good photo safari opportunities. One could approach the east end of the lake on a paved road that connects the village of Simou in the south of the lake to the village of Filousa in the north side of the lake. There are ancient trees in both villages. The Skarfos medieval Venetian bridge is on Stavros tis Psokas river three km upstream from the lake and can be accessed via well-signed roads. There's a preserved watermill just 100 meters north of the bridge, however one needs to travel a km to get to it from the bridge.

Distance (km) : Polis : 8 Paphos : 31 Platres : 70 Limassol : 99 Nicosia : 144
Larnaca: 165 Agia Napa : 206 Protaras : 212

ARGAKA DAM

(Map 32 – page 312, 26)

It is about 12.5 km east of Polis and the easiest way to access it is on a dirt road from Argaka village (which functions also as a walking route). It was built in 1964 on the Makounta river at an altitude of about 100 meters and has capacity of one million cubic meters. The scenic manmade lake at the boundary of Paphos Forest has a regular narrow-triangle shape and a surface area of about 10 he. Fish in the lake include carp, mosquito fish, roach, bleak, bass and catfish. There are birdwatching possibilities here.

The network of dirt roads nearby provides outstanding opportunities for exploration on bicycle (it is quite possible to spot moufflon on the way). Agios Merkourios picnic place is nearly seven kilometers away, deep inside Paphos Forest towards the south east and a great place for a break. Visits to the Panagia Chrysogialotissa Georgian monastery (inside Paphos Forest – about 15 km away) and the watermill in Gialia village are recommended. The coast is just five km away by road.

Distance (km): Polis : 13 Paphos : 48 Platres : 85 Limassol : 116 Larnaca: 182
Nicosia : 198 Agia Napa : 233 Protaras : 239

POMOS DAM

(Map 34 – page 314, 27)

The village of Pomos is about 20 km north east of Polis center. Explorers can reach the scenic Pomos manmade lake (five km south east) on the dirt road from the village, through Paphos Forest that leads to Stavros tis Psokas forest station. The dam was built in 1966 on the Livadi river, at an altitude of about 200 meters and has capacity of 860,000 cubic meters. The manmade like is surrounded by the forest with pine trees reaching its banks, it has a regular long triangular shape and surface area of nearly ten hectares. Fish in the lake include carp, mosquito fish, roach, bleak and bass.

The adjacent 15th century Panagia Chrysopateritissa chapel is is a peculiar composite construction. A visit to Pomos manmade lake could be combined with the exploration of Pomos valley in Paphos Forest (in the valley about seven km south east from the lake one finds the picnic site of Gefyri tou Livadiou) and/or of the ragged coastline of Pomos, almost ten km long, with high cliffs, strange rock formations and small coves between the rocks.

Distance (km): Polis : 20 Paphos : 55 Platres : 92 Limassol : 143
Nicosia :166 Larnaca: 209 Agia Napa : 250 Protaras : 256

OAK TREE IN FYTI

(Map 32 – page 312, 49)

It is a large 800 year old oak tree (Quercus infectoria subsp. veneris) with a height of twenty meters and a trunk perimeter of nearly ten meters. It is found about a kilometer north of the village of Fyti and 21 km south east of Polis. There are road signs to the tree (and a small construction around it). The Evretou valley is home to a large number of oak trees, remnants of Cyprus ancient oak forests. There's a group of 25 ancient oaks and one ancient kermes oak between Lasa and Fyti (they are hard to locate, as there are no signs).

The area around Evretou valley is home to many picturesque stone built villages (e.g. Fyti, Lasa, Filousa), a number of abandoned Turkish Cypriot villages (e.g. Evretou, Sarama, Zacharia, Kios), ancient trees, watermills and the pretty Evretou manmade lake. The dirt road network in much of the valley is good for cars when it is dry. The valley is a good area to explore on a bicycle (especially if one starts in Paphos Forest going downhill, in which case a GPS navigation device is a good idea), but I would recommend a walk, especially the linear ten-km long Fyti – Evretou dam walk. It makes sense to combine the walk with exploration of the village of Fyti. Walking to the ancient oak tree and back to the walking route would add just a bit over one km to the walk.

Distance (km) : Polis : 21 Paphos : 41 Platres : 61 Limassol : 109 Nicosia : 186 Larnaca: 189 Agia Napa : 230 Protaras : 236

MASTIC TREE IN SIMOU

(Map 32 – page 312, 50)

The mastic tree (Pistacia atlantica) is found south of the main road that passes through Simou, in the renovated village square close to the church. The tree is 1,000 years old, 16 meters tall, with a trunk perimeter a bit over six meters. The village is pleasant and the tree provides a good excuse for a Cyprus coffee break. Until recently another ancient mastic tree lived in the village, but sadly it perished. Simou is 15 kilometers south east of Polis.

A stop in Simou can be combined with exploration of the valley of Evretou. There's a paved road starting about half a km on the main road towards Polis, that descends Evretou valley and then ascends to the village of Filousa and the main road from Lysos to Polis. The descent offers splendid views of the valley and the Evretou manmade lake. Skarfos medieval Venetian bridge isthree km down the valley via the paved road. The abandoned Turkish Cypriot village of Evretou (good subject for a photo safari) is three km west from the point where the paved road from Simou reaches the river bed. There are a few dirt roads descending from the village to the (Stavros tis Psokas) river bed.

There's a watermill that has been developed into a tourist project, 100 meters south of the junction of the road from Simou with the Polis-Paphos highway.

Distance (km) : Polis : 15 Paphos : 36 Platres : 65 Limassol : 104 Larnaca: 184 Nicosia : 190 Agia Napa : 225 Protaras : 231

OLIVE TREE IN FILOUSA

(Map 32 – page 312, 51)

Filousa is a small village on the north slope of Evretou valley 13 km south east of Polis. Until recently three ancient trees lived there, but the ancient carob tree perished. The ancient olive tree (Olea europaea) is 600 years old, seven meters tall with a trunk perimeter a bit over seven meters. It is found in the village center, in a private plot (tens of meters) to the north of the main road from Lysos. There is also an ancient oak tree north of the village. It is 250 years old, twelve meters tall with a trunk perimeter of nearly three meters. Access to the tree is difficult. There are very few people living in Filousa and no tourist infrastructure. There's a paved road from Filousa that descends Evretou valley and then ascends the south slope meeting the Polis – Simou road about half a km north west of Simou.

A visit to Filousa can be combined with exploration of the wider area (e.g. of the abandoned Turkish Cypriot village of Evretou, the Evretou manmade lake, the Skarfos watermills and the Skarfos medieval Venetian bridge). Exploration on foot in the valley is recommended.

Distance (km) : Polis : 13 Paphos : 38 Platres : 67 Limassol : 106 Larnaca: 186 Nicosia : 192 Agia Napa : 227 Protaras : 233

WHITE MULBERRY, CAROB AND OLIVE TREE IN STENI

(Map 32 – page 312, 52, 53 & 54)

The white mulberry tree

The carob tree

The olive tree

Steni is a small picturesque village six km south east of Polis, built at an elevation of nearly 200 meters. There are three ancient trees living here. The white mulberry (Morus alba) in the west side of the village is 150 years old, nine meters tall with a peculiar trunk whose perimeter is three meters. The carob (Ceratonia siliqua) and the olive tree (Olea europaea) are in the north part of the village. They are both 200 years old with a trunk perimeter of about five meters. The carob is 16 meters tall and the olive just four. There's a museum of 'village life' in Steni, as well as a large part of a medieval watermill that became an attraction of a restaurant that operates there. There's a one km gorge towards the south east of Steni going east, parallel to the village of Peristerona. Steni is a good place for a pause on one's way from Polis toward Paphos Forest (or Evretou valley).

Distance (km) : Polis : 6 Paphos : 33 Platres : 66 Limassol : 101 Nicosia : 140 Larnaca: 167 Agia Napa : 208 Protaras : 214

OAK TREE AT PYRGOS TIS RIGENAS (NEAR NEO CHORIO)

(Map 31 – page 311, 55)

This very large oak tree (Quercus infectoria subsp. Veneris) is found next to the ruins of Pyrgos tis Rigenas medieval monastery in Akamas peninsula, about 13 km north west of Polis. It is 500 years old, 18 meters tall and its trunk perimeter is almost 5.5 meters. Explorers could access the ruins and the ancient oak tree by car or bicycle (or on foot) on the dirt road from Smigies picnic area (a distance of about six km). Even better, the ruins and the ancient oak tree lie on Adonis circular nature walking trail, which is 7.5 km long and starts at 'Aphrodite's Baths' cave and just 200 m south east of Aphrodite circular nature walking trail (Aphrodite and Adonis share a common path initially) thus enriching the experience of the walker.

Moutti tis Sotiras peak (with its awesome vistas) is 800 meters towards the north east. Ascending the peak for a view is not to be missed by any visitor in the area. For those looking for longer walks I would highly recommend the route from Neo Chorio or even from Drouseia via Smigies towards Adonis walking trail and the last stretch of Aphrodite walking trail.

Distance (km) : Polis : 13 Paphos : 48 Platres : 85 Limassol : 116 Nicosia : 159 Larnaca: 182 Agia Napa : 223 Protaras : 229

OAK TREE IN PRODROMI

(Map 31 – page 311, 56)

It is a huge ancient oak tree (Quercus infectoria subsp. veneris) found in the village of Prodromi, on the north side of the main road from Polis to Latchi port, less than one km from Polis center. It is a "young" tree, at only 150 years old. Its height reaches 26 meters and its trunk perimeter is almost four meters. The nearest bus-stop of the frequent Polis – Aphrodite's Baths' cave public bus line is 100 meters to the west of the tree.

Explorers can stop here on their way towards the port of Latchi, to one of the beaches to the west of Polis, to Aphrodite's Baths cave and to the Akamas peninsula.

Distance (km) : Polis : 1 Paphos : 36 Platres : 73 Limassol : 104 Nicosia : 147 Larnaca: 170 Agia Napa : 211 Protaras : 217

PINE TREE AT MAROTIS (NEAR POMOS)

(Map 34 – page 314, 57)

The imposing pine tree (Pinus brutia) at a height of 36 meters and trunk perimeter of nearly four meters is relatively young (250 years old). It is well marked, found by the side of the dirt road that connects Pomos to the paved Kato Pyrgos– Stavros tis Psokas road, in the Marotis locality, at an elevation of 650 meters, 17 kilometers south east of Pomos and about 40 km east of Polis. While one could explore the area by car, doing the route between Cedar Valley and Pomos on a bicycle is easy (downhill) and highly recommended. Quite possibly one will spot moufflon on the way.

Distance (km) : Polis : 40 Platres : 45 Paphos : 55 Limassol : 107 Nicosia : 119 Larnaca: 141 Agia Napa : 214 Protaras : 220

OAK TREE IN KATO PYRGOS

(Map 35 – page 315, 58)

This massive oak tree (Quercus infectoria subsp. veneris) is found by the main road from Polis, in the center of the village, about 50 km north east of Polis. It is a young tree, at only 100 years old, twenty meters tall, with trunk perimeter of four meters.

Kato Pyrgos has good tourist infrastructure and a collection of natural and cultural attractions (including an atypical medieval church and ruins of a medieval watchtower). It is a remote quiet coastal resort a few kilometers away from the huge Paphos Forest . While it can be accessed on scenic coastal roads either from Pomos or from Limnitis / Yeşilırmak checkpoint (from Nicosia via Limnitis to Kato Pyrgos takes about 75 minutes by car), there are also paved roads through the massive Paphos Forest, providing the traveller with yet more exploration opportunities. The ancient city kingdom of Soloi and the ancient palace at Vouni, in the north part of Cyprus on the coastal road are just 17 km and 13 km away respectively.

Distance (km) : Polis : 51 Nicosia : 80 Paphos : 86 Platres : 92 Limassol : 123 Larnaca: 189 Agia Napa : 230 Protaras : 236

AKAMAS PENINSULA

(Map 31 – page 311, (12))

The peninsula was the playground of Aphrodite, the Greek goddess of love and beauty and it is one of the jewels of Cyprus nature, a nature lovers' paradise. There are more than 200 square kilometers for walking, exploration on bicycles, bird watching, nature study and photography, and a ragged 40 km long coast that is excellent for coastal sea exploration (e.g. on a sea kayak or on a Waterbike), for swimming, snorkeling and occasionally for sea turtle spotting (even at times for spotting Mediterranean monk seals). There are four official nature walking trails (Aphrodite, Adonis, Smigies, Pissouromoutti) offering breathtaking views of the coast, as well as the extraordinary walking route in the Avakas gorge. One could compose many walking routes in the peninsula, such as a linear one along the Lara coast and one from Drouseia to the north coast (stretches of these are parts of the Cyprus extension of the European long distance E4 walking route). Both on the Lara coast as well as on the north Akamas coast there are breeding 'beaches' for sea turtles and it is not very rare to spot one while snorkeling in summer. The cave of Aphrodite's Baths is a myth-related spot to visit. It is a caved pool where the goddess regularly took her bath according to legend, while Blue Lagoon offers fantastic blue waters for swimming. The Lara coast in the west offers a big collection of coves over more than 20 km, where one can have the sea all to herself. Caution is needed as usually the sea off the west coast is rough. Parts of the peninsula can be accessed on easy dirt roads, but other parts (bad state dirt road stretches) give a hard time even to off-road vehicles. Smigies is a lovely picnic area in the woods near Neo Chorio village, quite near to Agios Minas, a pretty 16th century stone built chapel.

One could spend many days exploring the peninsula, and a visit of at least three-four days is perfect.

Distance (km): Polis : 10 Paphos : 18 Platres : 82 Limassol : 89 Larnaca: 152 Nicosia : 168 Agia Napa : 194 Protaras : 200

APHRODITE'S BATHS CAVE

(Map 31 – page 311, ⑬)

This is a small cave with spring water at the coastal entrance of the Akamas peninsula, some nine km north west of Polis. The cave may seem unimpressive, but it is mythical, as Aphrodite the Greek goddess of love and beauty who used Akamas as her playground, used to take her bath at this small cave. One will probably see hordes of other visitors in summer here. There's frequent public bus to Polis from here.

A visit to the mythical cave is a must for visitors who are going to enter or leave Akamas from its north east coastal entry point (e.g. for those who plan to walk on the Adonis or Aphrodite circular nature walking trails). It's a worthwhile attraction even for those visitors to the wider Polis area who choose not to explore beautiful Akamas.

Distance (km) : Polis : 10 Paphos : 45 Platres : 82 Limassol : 113 Nicosia : 176
Larnaca: 179 Agia Napa : 220 Protaras : 226

SKARFOS MEDIEVAL BRIDGE (Map 32 – page 312)

WATERMILL NEAR KATO AKOURDALEIA (Map 32 – page 312)

WATERMILL IN GIALIA (Map 34 – page 314)

AGIOS MINAS CHAPEL (Map 31 – page 311)

AGIA PARASKEVI CHAPEL (Map 32 – page 312)

AGIA EKATERINI CHAPEL (Map 32 – page 312)

AGIOS ANDRONICOS CHAPEL (Map 32 – page 312)

PANAGIA CHRYSOPATERITISSA CHAPEL (Map 34 – page 314)

PANAGIA GALOKTISTI CHAPEL (Map 35 – page 315)

PYRGOS TIS RIGENAS RUINS (Map 31 – page 311)

PANAGIA CHRYSOGIALOTISSA RUINS (Map 34 – page 314)

TROULLI WATCHTOWER (Map 35 – page 315)

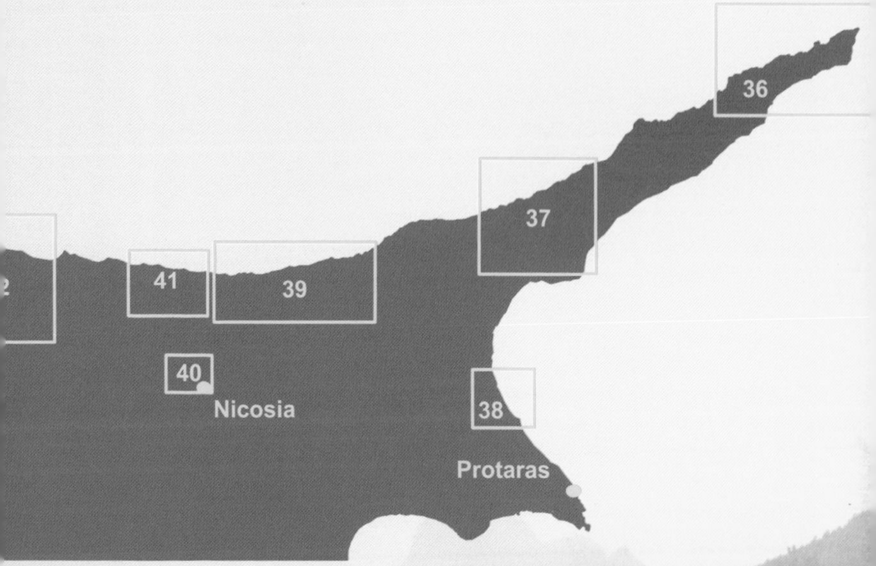

NORTH PART OF CYPRUS

The north part of Cyprus, occupied by Turkish troops, offers many excellent attractions for the traveller. Karpasia in the north east is a jewel and has world-class golden beaches, ruins of ancient churches and of medieval cities, catacombs, and superb walks. The long Keryneia mountain range (also known as Pentadactylos range), which is an extension of the Alps, stretches for more than 100 km and offers glorious panoramic vistas and quite good walking routes. Gothic BellaPais abbey, frescoed Antiphonitis church and at least one of the three fairytale Pentadactylos castles should not be missed. Walled Famagusta, which during the 13th century AD was one of the richest cities in the world is yet another awesome destination. Presently there are seven checkpoints providing access across the buffer zone, from Kato Pyrgos-Limnitis/ Yeşilırmak to Nicosia to Strovilia near Famagusta.

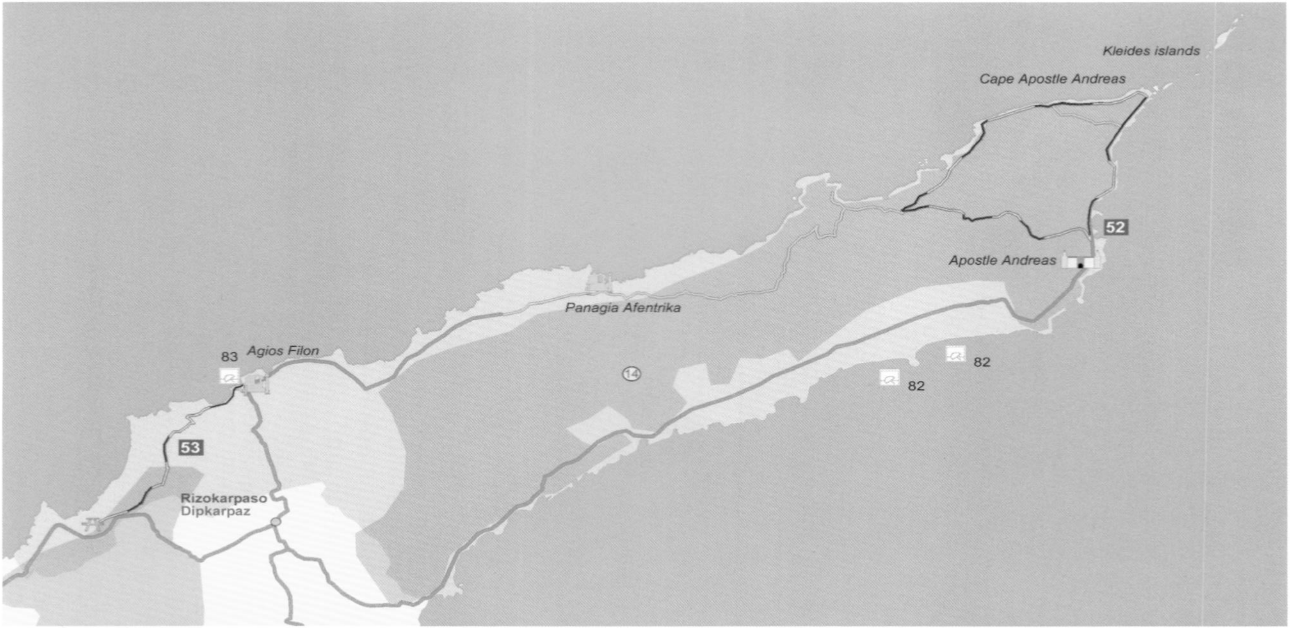

BEACHES/COASTS	
82	Pachyammos/Golden beach
83	Agios Filon
WALKING ROUTES	
52	Apostle Andreas circular
53	Panagia Eleousa picnic - Agios Filon church

OTHER NATURAL ATTRACTIONS	
14	Karpasia/Karpaz

CHAPELS AND MONASTERIES
Apostle Antreas
OTHER CULTURAL ATTRACTIONS
Panagia Afentrika
Agios Filon

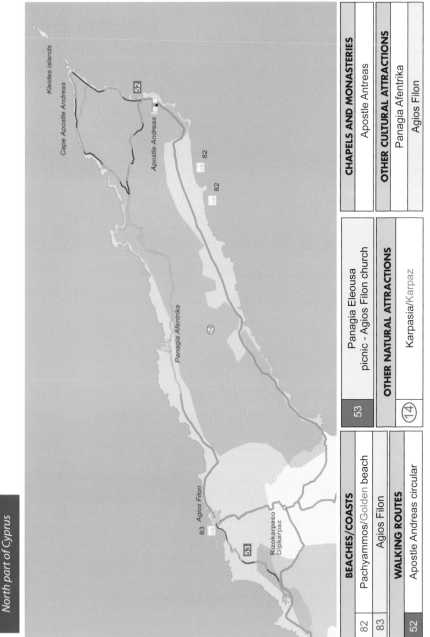

BEACHES/COASTS	
84	Vokolida/Bafra (No description)
85	Davlos/Kaplıca

WALKING ROUTES	
54	Kantara - Komi Kebir

WETLANDS	
28	Galateia/Mehmetçik wetland
29	Ovgoros/Ergazi dam

CASTLES AND WATCHTOWERS
Kantara

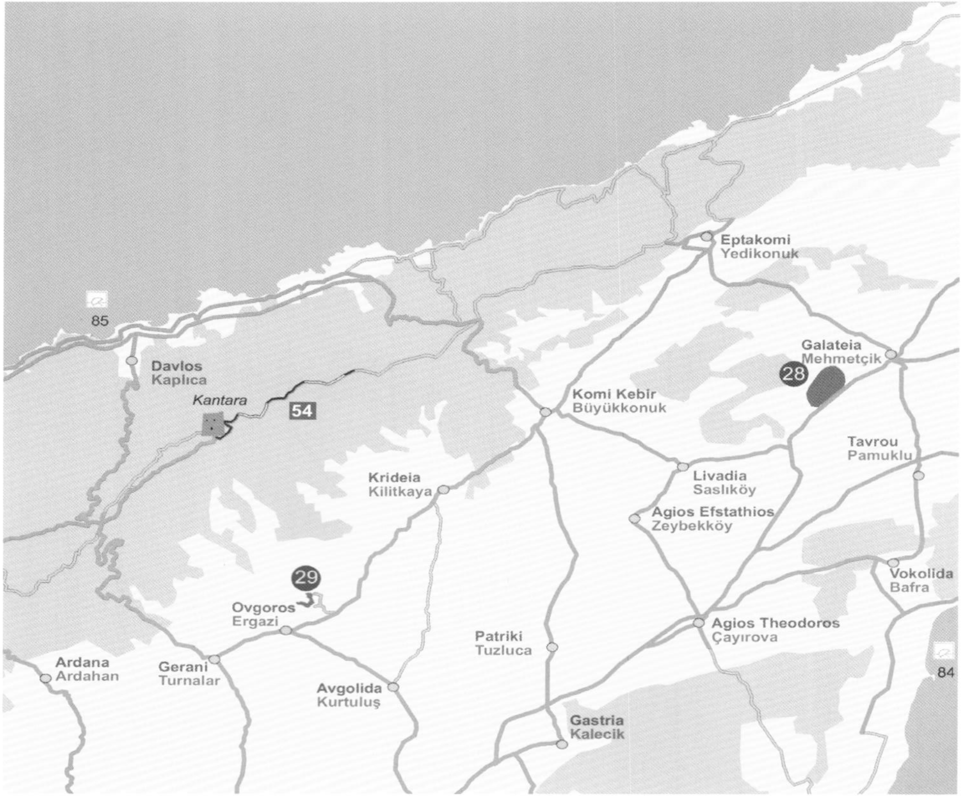

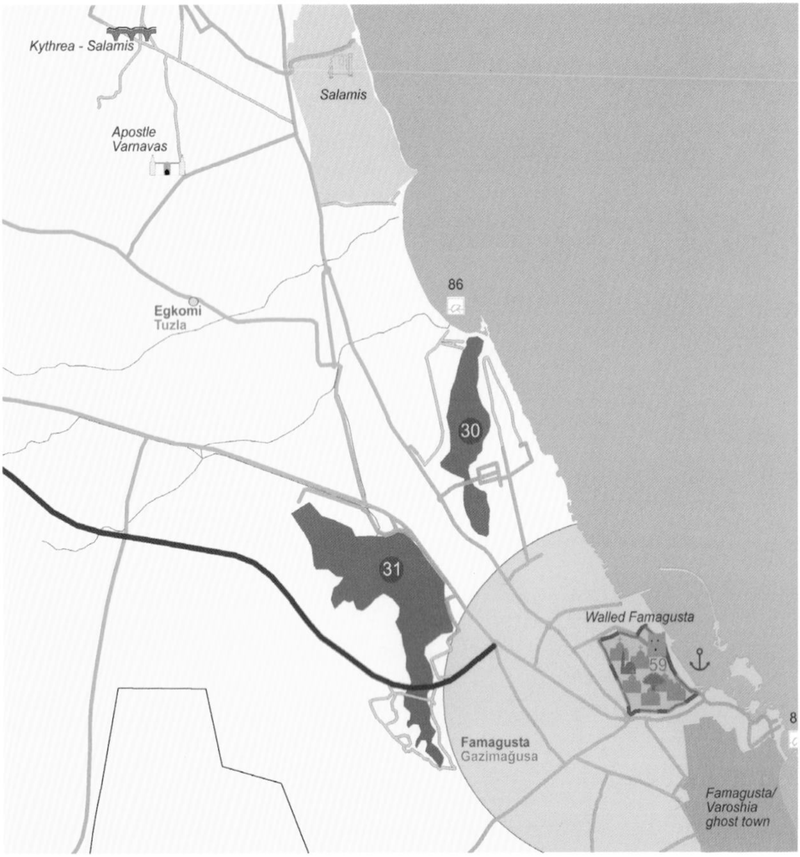

BEACHES/COASTS	
86	Klapsides/Glapsides
87	Varosi

WETLANDS	
30	Karaolos/Gülseren
31	Ais Loukas

ANCIENT TREES	
59	Sycamore in Walled Famagusta

CASTLES AND WATCHTOWERS
Walls and Bastions of Famagusta

AQUEDUCTS
Kythrea-Salamis

CHAPELS AND MONASTERIES
Apostle Varnavas
Walled Famagusta churches

OTHER CULTURAL ATTRACTIONS
Salamis

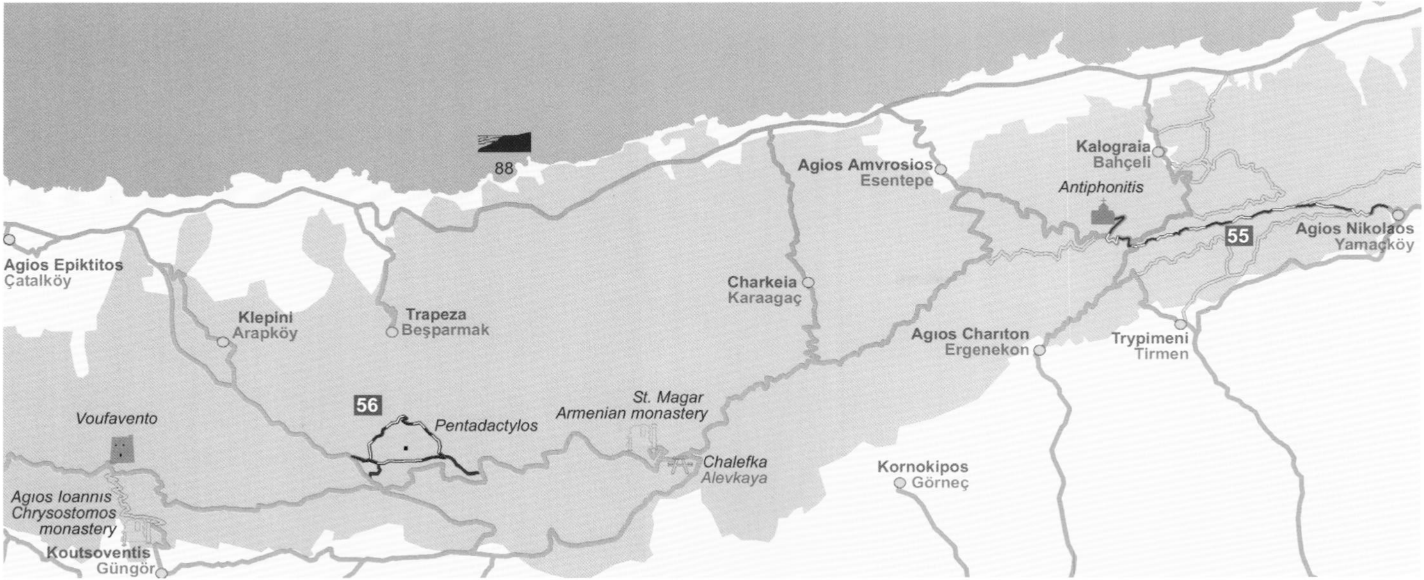

BEACHES/COASTS	
88	Alakati/Alagadi

WALKING ROUTES	
55	Agios Nicolaos/Yamaçköy - Antiphonitis church
56	Pentadactylos peak

CASTLES AND WATCHTOWERS
Voufavento

CHAPELS AND MONASTERIES
Antiphonitis

OTHER CULTURAL ATTRACTIONS
Saint. Magar Armenian monastery
Agios Ioannis Chrysostomos monastery

MAP 40

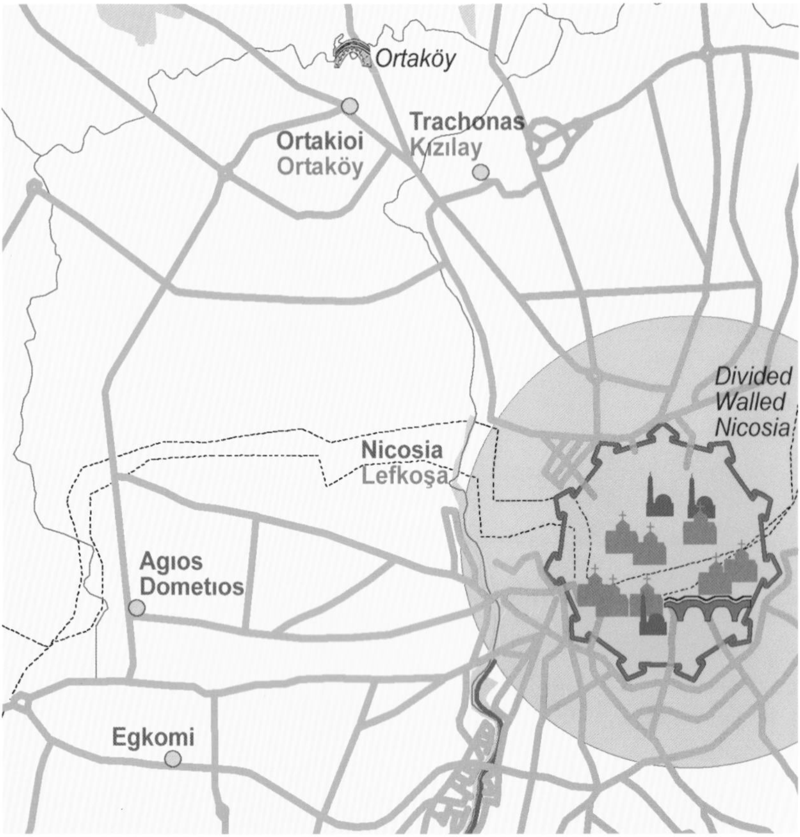

MEDIEVAL BRIDGES
Ortakioi/Ortaköy

AQUEDUCTS
Nicosia/Silihtar

CASTLES AND WATCHTOWERS
Walls and bastions of Nicosia

CHAPELS AND MONASTERIES
Walled Nicosia churches

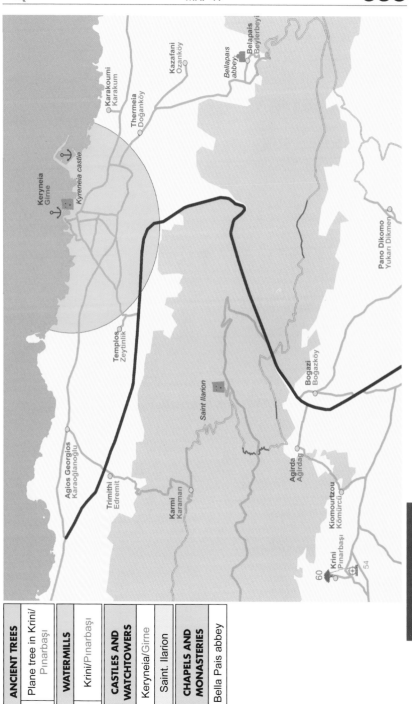

ANCIENT TREES	
60	Plane tree in Krini/ Pınarbaşı
WATERMILLS	
54	Krini/Pınarbaşı
CASTLES AND WATCHTOWERS	
	Keryneia/Girne
	Saint. Ilarion
CHAPELS AND MONASTERIES	
	Bella Pais abbey

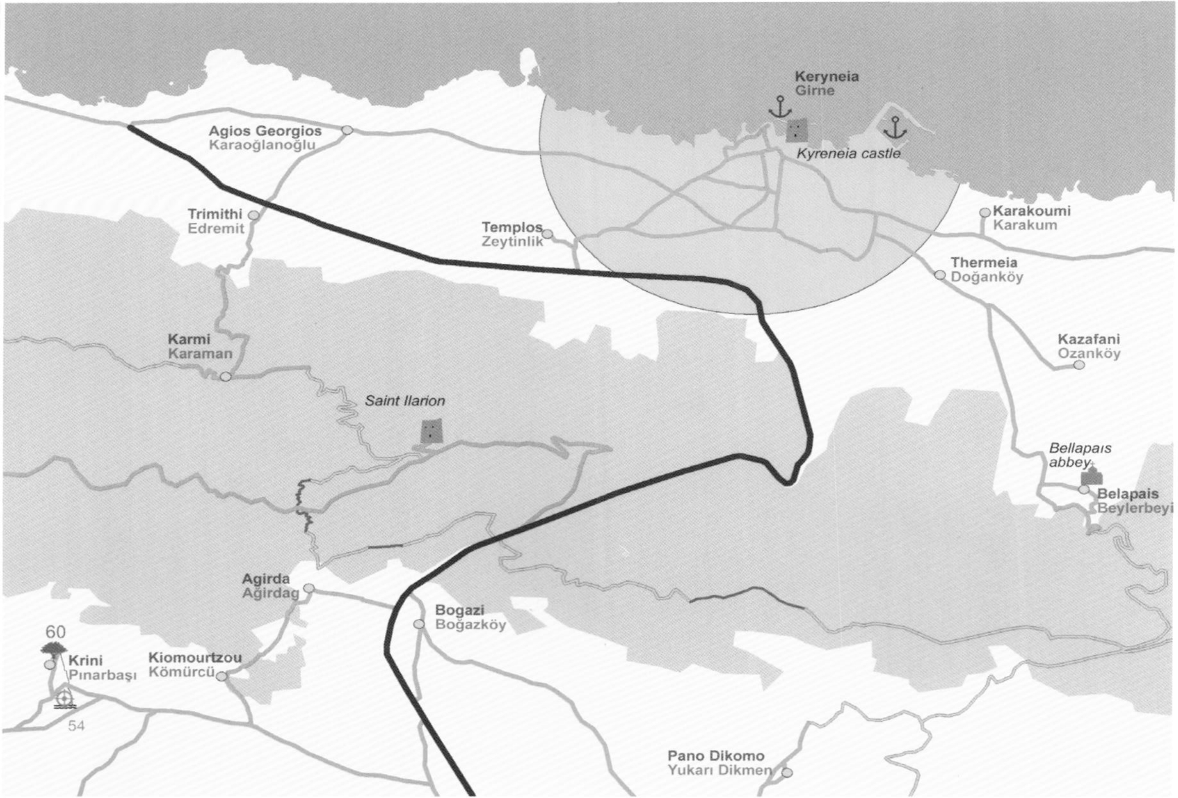

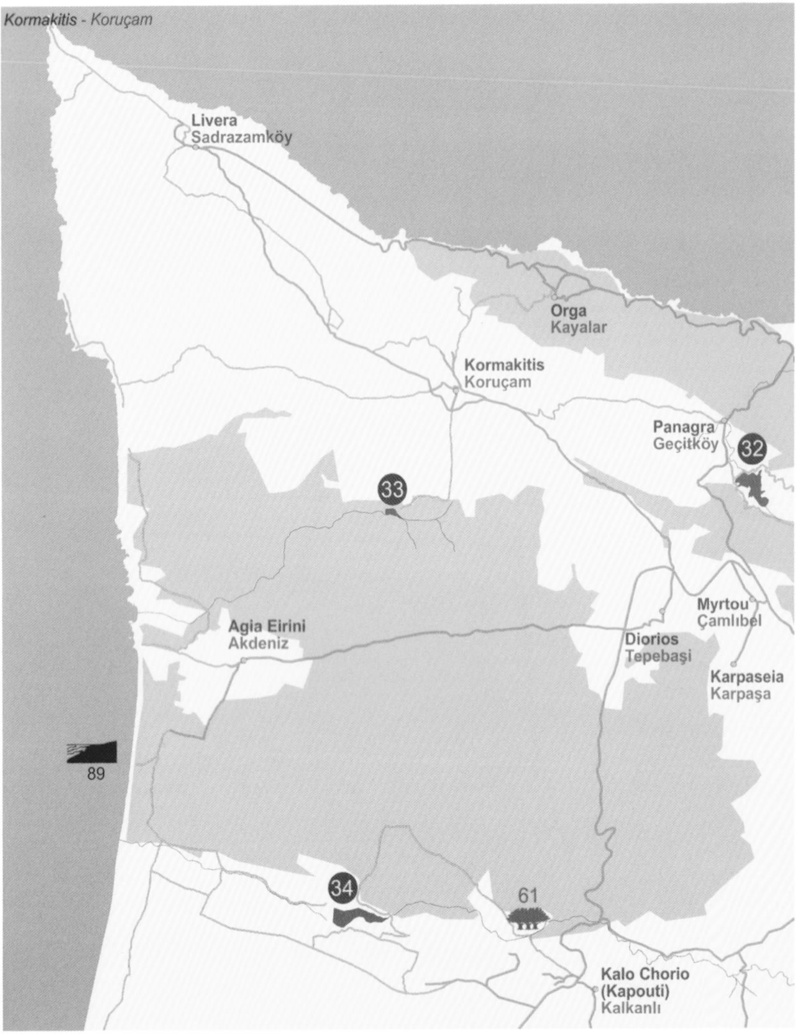

BEACHES/COASTS	
89	Agia Eirini/Akdeniz

WETLANDS	
32	Panagra/Geçitköy
33	Agia Eirini/Akdeniz
34	Kalo Chorio (Kapouti)/Kalkanlı

ANCIENT TREES	
61	Olive trees in Kalo Chorio (Kapouti)/Kalkanlı

PACHYAMMOS/GOLDEN BEACH

(Map 36 – page 361, 82)

The original Greek name ('Pachyammos') of this beach means 'thick sand' and it is indeed a very appropriate name. For many this four km long golden sand, remote beach is the best on the island. It is found inside Karpasia nature park, about 130 km north east of Protaras (assume a one-way drive of at least two hours) and just three km south west of the historic Apostle Andreas monastery. The beach has good road access, yet because of its remoteness and huge length it never feels congested. There are a few huts for rent as well as restaurants and beach bed rental services, but no lifeguards here (or indeed on other public beaches in the north part of Cyprus). A long pause here is worthwhile on its own. At the same time it could be the perfect ending to a day's walk on the Apostle Andreas circular walking route at the north east tip of Cyprus (or to exploration by bicycle in the area).

Distance (km) : Protaras : 131 Agia Napa : 134 Nicosia : 150 Larnaca: 163 Limassol : 229 Platres : 238 Polis : 272 Paphos : 300

Characteristics: 

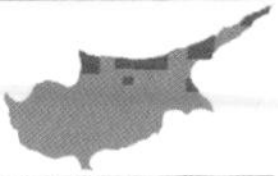

AGIOS FILON BEACH

(Map 36 – page 361, 83)

This is another lovely beach in Karpasia peninsula. This golden beach is 700 meters long, four hundred meters south west of the ruins of Agios Filon church, and four km north of Rizokarpaso/Dipkarpaz village (one of a couple of villages in the north where enclaved Greek Cypriots are still allowed to live). It is nearly 120 km north east of Protaras and one should assume a one-way drive of about two hours. The beach has good road access and beach bed rental services, but no lifeguards (they don't operate on public beaches in the north part of Cyprus). By the church ruins there is accommodation and a restaurant. The beach is right on the 5.5 km long walking route from Panagia Eleousa picnic area to Agios Filon church.

Besides the walk and the visit to the ruins of the 4th-5th century church of Agios Filon, one could combine this trip with exploration on foot, by bicycle or car on the coastal dirt road towards the east where the medieval (ancient) city of Ourania once stood. The ruins of three medieval churches (Panagia Afentrika, Agios Georgios and Asomatoi) are found in close proximity to each other, seven kilometers east of Agios Filon.

Distance (km): Protaras : 116 Agia Napa : 118 Nicosia : 135 Larnaca: 148 Limassol : 214 Platres : 223 Polis : 257 Paphos : 285

Characteristics:  

DAVLOS/KAPLICA BEACH

(Map 37 – page 362, 85)

This golden sand beach is about 700 meters long, and nearly 80 km to the north of Protaras. There are accommodation facilities and a restaurant as a well as a caravan park by the beach. There is access to the beach via the coastal paved road and no lifeguards (they don't operate on public beaches in the north part of Cyprus).

It's a good place to relax by the sea before or after a visit to the nearby Kantara castle (twelve km to the south of this beach, built at an elevation of nearly 600 m). The short walking route from Kantara is also recommended. For bird lovers there are two small wetlands in the area (Ovgoros/Ergazi dam and Galateia/Mehmetçik wetland).

Distance (km) : Protaras : 76 Agia Napa : 78 Nicosia : 95 Larnaca: 108 Limassol : 174 Platres : 183 Polis :215 Paphos : 245

ıaracteristics: 

KLAPSIDES/ GLAPSIDES BEACH

(Map 38 – page 363, 86)

This is a two km long sandy beach 35 km north west of Protaras (and about eight kilometers from Walled Famagusta). The beach is shallow and thus good for young families. There are a few private clubs and restaurants by the beach and a wetland behind it. Nearby there is an area that is fenced off by the Turkish army. Like on all public beaches in the north part of Cyprus, there are no lifeguards on the beach.

The ruins of the city of Salamis, one of two dominant cities in ancient Cyprus (Paphos was the other one) are a couple of kilometers to the north. The historic St. Barnabas monastery which functioned until the 1974 war is now operated by the Turkish authorities as a museum. It is found less than ten kilometers away towards the (north) west. Close to the monastery one can also find ruins of another ancient city, Engomi as well as a few arches of the 50 km long aqueduct which in antiquity was used to transport water from the area of Kythrea to Salamis.

Distance (km) : Protaras : 35 Agia Napa : 37 Nicosia : 65 Larnaca: 67 Limassol : 133 Platres : 163 Polis :187 Paphos : 215

Characteristics:  

VAROSI BEACH

(Map 38 – page 363, 87)

This is part of the most popular beach in Cyprus until the 1974 war. The biggest part of the beach is now fenced off by the Turkish army in what is known as 'the ghost city of Famagusta'. The accessible stretch is about 400 meters long. There's a hotel and restaurant there as well as beach bed rental services. The north three km stretch out of the nearly seven kilometers of the beach was developed before the war. A small stretch of the fenced beach is used for recreation by the Turkish troops. The beach is excellent and the view of the ghost city makes the experience of swimming here strange and unforgettable. Snorkeling here can sometimes offer the excitement of spotting sea turtles. Even though geographically the beach is only ten or so kilometers north of Protaras, because of the buffer zone and the checkpoint the actual route is more than 30 km long. A visit to this beach is a unique experience. It combines perfectly with a long visit to the Walled city of Famagusta, just two kilometers to the north west.

Distance (km): Protaras : 31 Agia Napa : 33 Larnaca: 63 Nicosia : 69 Limassol : 130
Platres : 167 Polis :191 Paphos : 219

Characteristics: 

ALAKATI/ALAGADI BEACH

(Map 39 – page 364, 88)

This fabulous golden sand beach is 16 km east of Keryneia/Girne. It is one kilometer long, with access by road to the two ends and the middle, where there is a restaurant. It is one of the beaches in Cyprus where there are serious efforts to protect sea turtles. Each night during the egg laying (summer) season there are patrols to monitor and look after sea turtles laying eggs. Beachgoers are likely to see special mesh enclosures protecting nests here. Separated by a short rocky stretch, there's another 600 meters long golden sand beach just to the east of Alagati/Alagadi. There are no lifeguards on these beaches. The whole area is not very developed touristically. In the background one gets to see the glorious Keryneia mountains and Pentadactylos (which means 'five fingered' in Greek) peak. The only thing that spoils the scenery is the power plant chimneys a couple of km west of the beach.

One can combine a trip to Alagati/Alagadi with a visit to Keryneia harbor and castle, a visit to exquisite Bellapais abbey, Antiphonitis church, Voufavento castle and a walk on any of the two nearby suggested (or on other) walking routes on Keryneia mountains.

Distance (km): Nicosia : 42 Larnaca: 86 Protaras : 94 Agia Napa : 96 Limassol : 122 Platres : 128 Polis : 166 Paphos : 192

Characteristics:  

AGIA EIRINI/AKDENIZ COAST

(Map 42 – page 367, 89)

The flat coast to the west and north west of Morphou/Güzelyurt extends for more than 15 kilometers. It is mainly composed of dark sand and pebble and luckily it is still quite undeveloped. The coast of Agia Eirini/ Akdeniz is the north part of this coastal stretch, about three to four km long. Behind much of the coast there is a thick acacia forest. Agia Eirini/ Akdeniz coast is part of a bigger area that is being protected as a nature reserve. The coast is more suited to those interested in sports like kite surfing, as it gets quite often very windy and the sea gets rough. There are no amenities and a restaurant that operated before was closed in 2013. The coast can provide good walking opportunities. A stop here can be combined with other attractions in the area, including a few wetlands, the medieval olive orchard at Kalo Chorio (Kapouti)/Kalkanlı and exploration of the enclaved Maronite (Catholics, member of the Greek Cypriot community whose ancestors came to Cyprus from Lebanon many centuries ago) village of Kormakitis/ Koruçam, nearly twenty km to the north east (on paved road).

Distance (km): Nicosia : 51 Platres : 90 Larnaca: 95 Polis : 112 Limassol : 130
Agia Napa : 131 Protaras :137 Paphos : 147

Characteristics: -

APOSTLE ANDREAS CIRCULAR WALKING ROUTE

(Map 36 – page 361, 52)

This 16 km long circular route makes for one of the top nature walks on the island. It combines beautiful surroundings, an undeveloped rocky coast with intermittent sandy coves, hills offering panoramic views and a lush carpet of juniper bushes. Adding to this the location, walking at the most remote east north of the island, and a visit to the nearby historic (but sadly dilapidated) Greek Orthodox monastery of Apostle Andreas and this makes for an unforgettable day. The monastery is some 135 km north east of Protaras and travelling here by car will likely take more than two hours each way. The elevation rises only to 100 meters, so the walk, which takes place on dirt roads is rather flat and easy. Explorers will likely meet some of the feral donkeys living in the Karpasia park. There are no sandy beaches near the north part of the route but there are some in the eastern stretch, one of which is touristically developed. The ruins of the ancient city of Ourania are nearly ten km west of the most western point in this circular walking route. At the Cape Apostle Andreas ruins of the ancient settlement of Kastros were discovered just before the 1974 war but sadly in the last decade these were replaced by a military construction. A stop at the nearby splendid beach of Pachyammos/Golden beach would make for the perfect ending to a perfect day.

Distance (km) : Protaras : 136 Agia Napa : 139 Nicosia : 156 Larnaca: 169 Limassol : 235 Platres : 244 Polis : 278 Paphos : 306

PANAGIA ELEOUSA PICNIC – AGIOS FILON CHURCH WALKING ROUTE

(Map 36 – page 361, 53)

The walk starts at a picnic area by the main road leading to Rizokarpaso/Dipkarpaz village about 17 km east of Gialousa/Yeni Erenköy village. Nearly two km on the south west narrow road from the picnic area stands in a bad state the 15th century chapel of Panagia Eleousa (which is the church of one of four annexes/monasteries on the island of Agia Ekaterini of Sinai monastery). The linear walk is just over five km long, on dirt roads and ends at Agios Filon ancient church. It crosses a couple of streams and passes both through low vegetation, uncultivated land as well as by fields. The ruins of a medieval bridge still stand on one of the streams. At some point the route reaches and passes by Agios Filon beach. Some may prefer to start the walk nearly two km further west, before the main road turns south east (as one comes from Gialousa/ Yeni Erenköy) and thus walk along the excellent three km long Ronnas (or Panagia Eleousa) beach before continuing to Agios Filon beach and the ancient church (this new starting point would not add much to the length of the walk).

For more exploration one could drive (or even better, cycle or walk) seven kilometers east on the dirt road to a collection of three ancient churches (Panagia Afentrika, Agios Georgios and Asomatoi) found at the site of the ancient and medieval city of Ourania.

Distance (km) : Protaras : 107 Agia Napa : 111 Nicosia : 128 Larnaca: 141 Limassol : 207 Platres : 215 Polis : 250 Paphos : 278

KANTARA - KOMI KEBIR WALKING ROUTE

(Map 37 – page 362, 54)

The suggested walking route is linear and five km long, extending from (near) Kantara castle on the mountain ridge towards the east, on a dirt road that meets the paved road that connects the north coast to the south coast (near the village of Komi Kebir/Büyükkonuk). The dirt road starts about 300 meters south west of the imposing Kantara castle (the name of the castle is thought to derive from an Arabic word that means 'small bridge'). The walker slowly descends from an elevation of more than 550 m near Kantara to an elevation of 350 m near the finish point. On stretches of the route there are forest trees (pines or cypresses) on both sides of the road while on other stretches walkers have unobstructed views of the area, including the coast and ragged mountain peaks. I advise that walkers end the linear route as soon as they spot the quarry (which is nearly one km from the end of the suggested linear walking route). If walkers do not mind the view of quarries they can easily walk past two quarry complexes as far as the main road, turn south to the village of Komi Kebir/Büyükkonuk (ten km from the start of the walking route) or even go straight to the village of Eptakomi / Yedikonuk (13 km from the start).

In Komi Kebir/Büyükkonuk there is traditional accommodation for rent as well as restaurants. Maybe a good way to finish a trip here when the weather is warm is with a swim at Davlos/Kaplıca coast; otherwise, with a visit to one of the wetlands in the area with the hope of good birdwatching.

Distance (km) : Protaras : 72 Agia Napa : 74 Nicosia : 91 Larnaca: 104 Limassol : 170 Platres : 179 Polis : 211 Paphos : 241

AGIOS NICOLAOS/YAMAÇKÖY – ANTIPHONITIS CHURCH WALKING ROUTE

(Map 39 – page 364, 55)

This linear nearly eight km long walk begins at the tiny village of Agios Nicolaos/Yamaçköy, about 60 km north east of Nicosia. It is an easy walk and offers glorious views of Keryneia mountain range peaks, the north coast east of Keryneia and the Mesaoria plain. The walk is on dirt roads (the last one and a half km is on paved roads) and ascends from an elevation of 300 meters to 450 meters before descending to 350 meters at Antiphonitis church.
The walking route is found on the mountain ridge and mostly inside the pine forest. The local flora includes also many rockrose bushes, strawberry trees and wild olives trees. The forest is denser on the north slope. The nearest coastal stretch so far largely escaped the overdevelopment that was witnessed by the coast further west, from Agios Epiktitos/Çatalköy, about ten km east of Keryneia to Vasileia/Karşıyaka, about twenty km to the west of Keryneia. There is a steep 450 m long walking route finishing at the church that could replace the last 1,000 meters of paved road in the route, but the walking route may be hard to locate.

After the 1974 war Antiphonitis church suffered looting and destruction. Fortunately now it is protected and functions as a museum (there is a small entry fee). It is a 12th century church that was part of a monastery. Architecturally the building is atypical in Cyprus and has 12th to 15th century frescoes, which although damaged, still offer glimpses of their past glory. The walking route can be easily extended by 13 km west to Chalefka/Alevkaya forest station and picnic area. There are also other worthy walking routes in the area including a circular seven km long walk from Chalefka to the crumbling Armenian monastery of St. Magar.

It is suggested that the walk is combined at least with a visit to the closest of the three Pentadactylos castles, that of Voufavento (30 km west of Antiphonitis church), whose name comes from Italian and means 'Defier of the Winds'. The 1,200 meters long ascent from the parking place to the castle is very steep (an elevation difference of 170 meters). There is no entry fee, not much left of the castle but the vistas from an elevation of 870 meters are breathtaking.

Distance (km) : Protaras : 59 Agia Napa : 61 Nicosia : 62 Larnaca: 91 Limassol : 143
Platres : 151 Polis : 184 Paphos : 212

PENTADACTYLOS PEAK CIRCULAR WALKING ROUTE

(Map 39 – page 364, 56)

The Keryneia or Pentadactylos mountain range is the most south extension of the Alps (the Alps in fact extend to Turkey and Iran). Keryneia mountains are composed of limestone and have many ragged peaks as well as many caves, most of which have not as yet been explored. This nearly five km long circular walk starts by the road that connects Nicosia via Kythrea/Değirmenlik to Keryneia, 34 km north east of Nicosia at an elevation of 430 meters. The lowest point on this dirt road walking route is 340 meters towards the north east and the highest is 530 meters in the south stretch of the route. The walk is all round its major attraction, i.e. Pentadactylos peak. Pentadactylos means 'five fingered' in Greek and the shape of the peak certainly resembles five fingers (at least from certain angles and distance). The name came from a legend according to which Byzantine hero Digenis Akritas touched the peak with his hand and made an imprint in an effort to cross the mountain range while pursuing an invader. The slopes are a lot steeper in the south side of the peak, while in the north there are many pine trees that seem to grow out of the palm of the 'fivefingered' peak. In the north part of the route one also has unobstructed views of a stretch of the north coast that luckily is not overdeveloped, while in the east and the west walkers see a collection of ragged mountain peaks. In the south part of the route the nearby hills block the view to Mesaoria plain. This may in fact be a good thing as the nearby south slope of Keryneia mountain range is scattered with ugly quarries.

It is suggested that the walk is combined at least with a visit to the closest of the three Pentadactylos castles, that of Voufavento (twelve km west of the starting point of this walk), whose name comes from Italian and means 'Defier of the Winds'. The 1,200 meters long ascent from the parking place to the castle is very steep (about 170 meters elevation difference). There is no entry fee, not much left of the castle but the vistas from an elevation of 870 meters are breathtaking.

The excellent Alakati/Alagadi beach where a major effort is carried out to protect sea turtles is just 14 km to the north and is also recommended for a visit.

Distance (km): Nicosia : 34 Larnaca: 78 Protaras : 89 Agia Napa : 91 Platres : 123 Limassol : 126 Polis : 156 Paphos : 184

GALATEIA/MEHMETÇIK WETLAND

(Map 37 – page 362, 28)

This is a place to visit if one is into birdwatching. As this is the most eastern (furthest from the main part of Cyprus and closest to Asia) wetland of a significant size inside Karpasia, it is quite important for migratory birds and a good birdwatching destination in spring and autumn (in the years when it has water). This natural wetland covers an area of under a third of a square kilometer, it is found in a flat area with very low vegetation, at an elevation of nearly 100 meters, 40 km north east of Famagusta and 70 km north of Protaras. Galateia/Mehmetçik wetland does not have water every year (besides the fact that like most wetlands in the north part of Cyprus it gets completely dry in summer). The nearby Ovgoros/Ergazi manmade lake, 18 km west via paved roads is more likely to have water. Galateia/Mehmetçik wetland is just five kilometers off the main road to Karpasia peninsula so for birdwatchers it can be a good break on the way to the attractions further east.

The best nearby beach is the golden sand beach of Vokolida/Bafra village, twelve km south of the wetland, which unfortunately witnessed the construction of big tourist resorts over the recent decade. 15 km south west of the wetland at the village of Gastria/Kalecik around 1200 AD the Templar Knights constructed one of their castles in Cyprus. Some ruins of the castle are still visible. The imposing Kantara castle is about 35 km north west (on paved road).

Distance (km) : Protaras : 70 Agia Napa : 73 Nicosia : 89 Larnaca: 102 Limassol : 168 Platres :177 Polis : 211 Paphos : 239

OVGOROS/ERGAZI DAM

(Map 37 – page 362, 29)

This is a birdwatching destination at the entrance of Karpasia peninsula. It is a small earthfill dam 100 meters long and just a few meters high on the Kastros river (torrent) covering an area of about two hectares. It is found 35 km north east of Famagusta and 65 km north of Protaras. There are reed beds and other low vegetation around its sides as well as various small hills. Keryneia Mountains are less than ten km to the north and a number of ragged peaks (including Kantara) can be seen in the background north of the manmade lake. As one of the few eastern (furthest from the main part of Cyprus and closest to Asia) wetlands of a significant size inside Karpasia, it is quite important for migratory birds and a good birdwatching destination in spring and autumn (especially in the years when the nearby Galateia/Mehmetçik wetland which is 18 km east on paved roads, is dry). To reach the wetland, going (north) east on the paved road from the village of Ovgoros/Ergazi to the village of Krideia/Kilitkaya one needs to turn north after one km. The dam is 0.5 km north on the dirt road. Kantara castle with its breathtaking views is 15 km north on the paved road.

Distance (km) : Protaras : 64 Agia Napa : 67 Nicosia : 84 Larnaca: 97 Limassol : 163 Platres :175 Polis : 209 Paphos : 237

KARAOLOS/GÜLSEREN WETLAND

(Map 38 – page 363, 30)

This is part of the most important group of wetlands in the north part of Cyprus just north of Famagusta, known collectively as Famagusta wetlands. They cover a few square kilometers and border the ruins of the ancient city-state of Salamis in the north, the village of Egkomi/ Tuzla in the west and the outskirts of Famagusta in the south. More than fourty bird species are recorded here annually. The area hosts a significant population of Greater Flamingos every winter. Usually at least a part of the wetlands has some water in summer providing a refuge to waterbirds and an interesting attraction to summer visitors. There are parts of the wetlands that are fenced off by the Turkish military and not accessible to the public. There are various paved and dirt roads that give access to the wetlands.

The wider area has important cultural attractions. Besides Walled Famagusta, the ruins of Salamis, which together with Paphos comprised the two most important ancient city kingdoms in Cyprus, lie here. Other nearby attractions include the historic St. Barnabas monastery (now operated as a museum), the ruins of the ancient city of Egkomi and a few arches of the ancient aqueduct (near the village of Agios Sergios/ Yeni Boğaziçi) brining water to Salamis from Kythrea, 50 km to the north west.

Distance (km) : Protaras : 32 Agia Napa : 34 Larnaca: 64 Nicosia : 67 Limassol : 130 Platres : 166 Polis : 189 Paphos : 217

AIS LOUKAS DAM

(Map 38 – page 363, 31)

This is another wetland in the north part of Cyprus that is a good birdwatching destination as more than thirty bird species are recorded here annually. It covers an area of nearly two square kilometers and it is cut into two by (one branch of) the road connecting Famagusta to Nicosia. There is paved road access to the east of the wetland while in the north west it borders the premises of a university. It is found less than one kilometer south west of Karaolos/ Gülseren wetland. A dam (reservoir) was constructed here in the 60s that has a capacity of 4.5 million cubic meters of water. There is dense vegetation around and inside the wetland of reed beds, eucalyptus, taramix and acacia trees (and others).

The extraordinary Famagusta walled city, with its superb collection of different denomination medieval churches is less than two km to the south east of the wetland and should not be missed in any trip to the area.

Distance (km) : Protaras : 29 Agia Napa : 31 Larnaca: 61 Nicosia : 67 Limassol : 128 Platres : 165 Polis : 189 Paphos : 217

PANAGRA/GEÇITKÖY DAM

(Map 42 – page 367, 32)

This dam with a capacity of nearly two million cubic meters of water and a surface area of about 15 hectares was constructed in 1989. It is found at an elevation of 60 meters, in Kormakitis/ Koruçam peninsula, at the west edge of Keryneia mountain range, at a distance of 40 km north west of Nicosia. The scenery is quite pretty as the manmade lake is nearly surrounded by high hills and a pine forest. Usually it retains water also in summer and is an important refuge for birds. There are walking routes passing by connecting the peninsula to the mountains. There is easy access to the dam on the paved road from Myrtou / Çamlıbel towards the north coast and the village of Vasileia/ Karşıyaka. This dam is part of a project to transport water to the north part of Cyprus from Turkey through a pipeline. Recently a major construction (enlargement) was carried out.

There are various other attractions in the area including walking routes, other wetlands, the enclaved Maronite (Catholics, member of the Greek Cypriot community whose ancestors came to Cyprus from Lebanon many centuries ago) village of Kormakitis/ Koruçam about eleven km north west on paved roads (seven km on dirt roads), and the north west coast from Vasileia/ Karşıyaka all the way to Cape Kormakitis.

Distance (km) : Nicosia : 40 Larnaca: 84 Platres : 86 Polis : 108 Agia Napa : 120 Protaras : 126 Limassol : 126 Paphos : 143

AGIA EIRINI/AKDENIZ DAM

(Map 42 – page 367, 33)

This is a small wetland between the villages of Kormakitis/ Koruçam and Agia Eirini/ Akdeniz. Probably the easiest way to reach the wetland is on a dirt road from Kormakitis/ Koruçam (about three km to the north east – one cannot spot the wetland from the road). This small wetland (with an area of less than three hectares) is found inside a pine forest nearly 50 km north west of Nicosia. The dam, about 100 meters wide is built at an elevation of 100 meters. There are many walking routes one could compose in the area passing through the forest and by fields going all the way west (and north) to the coast or east to Keryneia mountains. The area around Kormakitis/ Koruçam village is one of the few on the island where the endemic Cyprus tulip flourishes. It can be seen in the fields in bloom during early spring. Because of its position as the last significantly sized wetland near Cape Kormakitis, Agia Eirini/Akdeniz wetland is important for birds and a birdwatchers' destination.

There are a few other wetlands in the area, as well as the enclaved Maronite (Catholics, member of the Greek Cypriot community whose ancestors came to Cyprus from Lebanon many centuries ago) village of Kormakitis/ Koruçam. Until recently, Maronites in Cyprus were bilingual speaking both Greek as well as the local dialect of Aramaic, the language widely spoken in the Holly Land at the time of Christ. There are still people in the enclave who speak this language (and an effort is being made to conserve the language).

Distance (km): Nicosia : 51 Platres : 90 Larnaca: 95 Polis : 112 Limassol : 130
Agia Napa : 131 Protaras : 137 Paphos : 147

KALO CHORIO (KAPOUTI)/KALKANLI DAM

(Map 42 – page 367, 34)

This dam is 300 meters long, built at an altitude of 50 meters, nearly 60 km north west of Nicosia. The wetland covers an area of about ten hectares and it is a good birdwatching destination in the area, which is relatively flat. On the south west there is farmland (and a landfill a couple of km away with burning garbage – don't go there, it is not pleasant) whereas in the north and north west there's a pine forest. The western peaks of Pentadactylos can be seen in the background towards the north east and the Morphou/ Güzelyurt bay towards the west. There are low hills surrounding this manmade wetland, which is a good birdwatching destination with more than 30 bird species recorded here every year.

There are many dirt roads in the area and one can compose a pleasant easy three to four km long circular walk around the wetland. There's a university (called 'METU') campus a couple of kilometers east of the wetland. The easiest way to access the lake is on the dirt road immediately before the campus. (The paved way to the campus is via the roundabout about five km from Morphou, on the road that connects Morphou / Güzelyurt to Kalo Chorio (Kapouti)/Kalkanlı village). The dam is about five km on the dirt road.

A trip here can be combined with a visit to the medieval olive grove in the village and possibly with a visit to the historic Agios Mamas church in Morphou/ Güzelyurt which dates back to the 16th century.

Distance (km) : Nicosia : 56 Platres : 76 Polis : 98 Larnaca: 100 Limassol : 117 Paphos : 134 Agia Napa : 136 Protaras : 142

SYCAMORE IN WALLED FAMAGUSTA

(Map 38 – page 363, 59)

This ancient tree (Ficus sycomorus) is of the same species as the sycamores found just outside (south) of Agia Napa monastery in Agia Napa village. It is a massive tree in a unique location inside Walled Famagusta, next to Agios Nicolaos cathedral where in medieval times the kings of Cyprus were crowned kings of Jerusalem and of Armenia. The tree is thought to be at least 600 years old, it has a height of roughly twelve meters and a trunk perimeter of about five meters. In summer it bears sweet fruit. Having a pause here is a good break in one's exploration of the historic city.

Walled Famagusta, found about 30 km north west of Protaras (via the checkpoint), is one of the jewels of Cyprus cultural heritage. It was one of the richest cities in the world during medieval times and despite its decline during Genoese, Ottoman and British rule (when a lot of material was removed and used in the construction of the Suez Canal) one can still see many of the tens of churches constructed during the middle ages. The churches belong to different denominations and sects (e.g. Greek Orthodox, the Templar Knights, the Nestorians, the Armenians etc) and have a variety or architectural styles. They are in urgent need of conservatior and restoration. The walls of the city with a perimeter of nearly four kilometers (and with a moat are impressive. A visit to the (Varosi) beach of the ghost fenced city of Famagusta is a must for those interested to take a glimpse at today's political problems on the island.

Distance (km) : Protaras : 30 Agia Napa : 32 Larnaca: 62 Nicosia : 68 Limassol : 129
Platres : 166 Polis : 190 Paphos : 218

PLANE TREE IN KRINI/PINARBAŞI

(Map 41 – page 366, 60)

This Platanus orientalis tree is found about 26 km north west of Nicosia, in the village of Krini / Pınarbaşı. There is a spring by the tree, still bringing water from inside Keryneia Mountains and watering the tree. Though not as huge as the plane tree of Agia Mavri church, it is still very large with a height of more than 20 meters and a trunk perimeter of about four meters. There are a few other big plane trees in the same yard, creating natural shade for the clients of the local restaurant that operates there.

Downstream from the plane tree, at a distance of 600 meters (there is easy, two-km long access on a paved road) one finds what is probably the best preserved watermill in the north part of Cyprus. Unlike the watermills in the south and west part of the island, the watermills in the north (on Keryneia mountains) were powered by natural springs, the most famous of which were in Kythrea/ Değirmenlik (in antiquity the ancient city of Chytroi stood here). Out of the tens of watermills that operated here, a few can still be seen today, but the structures have deteriorated.

The plane tree and the watermill are a good detour for those planning to visit the impressive Saint Ilarion castle, which is easily accessed from the highway connecting Nicosia with Keryneia (the castle is four kilometers off the highway while the ancient tree is seven kilometers off the highway and 14 kilometers from the castle).

Distance (km) : Nicosia : 26 Larnaca: 70 Protaras : 112 Agia Napa : 106 Limassol : 108 Platres : 112 Polis : 148 Paphos : 183

OLIVE TREES IN KALO CHORIO (KAPOUTI)/KALKANLI

(Map 42 – page 367, 61)

The ancient olives are inside an olive grove that dates back to Lusignan (Frankish) rule of Cyprus. The grove covers an area of about twenty hectares and includes olive (and other) trees, caves, chapel ruins and an irrigation pool. Upton 400 olive trees here are thought to be at least 500 years old. Fortunately the orchard is being protected. One can easily compose a walking route on existing paths that is three-four km long. The orchard is found nearly 50 km north west of Nicosia. There is easy road access about 2.5 km from the village of Kalo Chorio (Kapouti) / Kalkanlı on the paved road to Diorios / Tepebaşi village.

A visit to the ancient olives can be combined well with stops at other nearby attractions such as the wetland of Kalo Chorio (Kapouti) / Kalkanlı and at the historic Agios Mamas church in Morphou / Güzelyurt.

Distance (km): Nicosia : 50 Platres : 74 Polis : 96 Larnaca: 96 Limassol : 115 Paphos : 132 Agia Napa : 132 Protaras : 138

KARPASIA/KARPAZ PENINSULA

(Map 36 – page 361, (14))

Karpasia/Karpaz peninsula is the most remote corner of Cyprus as its tip is more than 150 km from Nicosia (in a straight line more or less). It has the nickname 'panhandle' as it resembles just that, the handle of a pan (alternatively it is thought of resembling a finger).

It has been inhabited for thousands of years (the most well known ancient cities are Achaion Akti, Karpasia and Ourania) and still has relics of Cyprus cultural heritage. It is perfect for the modern explorer looking for ancient ruins in the middle of nowhere (the three churches at Panagia Afentrika, the church of Agios Filon, and the rock-cut tomb chambers near Galinoporni/Kaleburnu and near Koroveia/Kuruova are good examples of such finds). On the other hand there are other places in Cyprus that boast excellent (better) examples of Cyprus rich cultural heritage (e.g. Troodos painted churches, ancient Paphos, Walled Nicosia, Walled Famagusta, etc).

What makes Karpasia/Karpaz peninsula special is its nature. The peninsula has a surface area of about 500 square km and its coastline stretches about 200 km. Much of its coastline is rocky but at the same time it boasts probably the best golden sand beaches on the island. The east third is a park, with no modern villages (and hardly any tourist development), nowadays inhabited by feral donkeys, visited frequently by sea turtles and occasionally by monk seals. Karpasia/ Karpaz peninsula (including Kleides islands at its north east tip) is a very important area for birds (including some raptor and seabird species under threat). It's one of the jewels of Cyprus nature not to be missed by nature lovers.

Distance (km): Protaras : 104 Agia Napa : 108 Nicosia : 125 Larnaca: 138
Limassol : 204 Platres : 212 Polis : 247 Paphos : 275

Characteristics: 

(Jun-Oct)

ORTAKÖY MEDIEVAL BRIDGE (Map 40 – page 365)

WATERMILL NEAR KRINI/PINARBAŞI (Map 41 – page 366)

KANTARA CASTLE (Map 37 – page 362)

WALLS AND BASTIONS OF FAMAGUSTA (Map 38 – page 363)

VOUFAVENTO CASTLE (Map 39 – page 364)

WALLS AND BASTIONS OF NICOSIA (Map 40 – page 365)

KERYNEIA CASTLE (Map 41 – page 366)

SAINT ILARION CASTLE (Map 41 – page 366)

KYTHREA – SALAMIS AQUEDUCT (Map 38 – page 363)

APOSTLE ANTREAS MONASTERY (Map 36 – page 361)

APOSTLE VARNAVAS MONASTERY (Map 38 – page 363)

WALLED FAMAGUSTA CHURCHES (Map 38 – page 363)

ANTIPHONITIS CHAPEL (Map 39 – page 364)

WALLED NICOSIA CHURCHES (Map 40 – page 365)

BELLAPAIS ABBEY (Map 41 – page 366)

PANAGIA AFENTRIKA CHURCH RUINS (Map 36 – page 361)

AGIOS FILON CHURCH RUINS (Map 36 – page 361)

SALAMIS ANCIENT KINGDOM (Map 38 – page 363)

LIST OF BEACHES AND COASTS OF CYPRUS – 1 - 22										
No.	Nearest town / resort	Distance (km) + Direction	Name	Surface						Map No.
1	Protaras	6 N	Kapparis (MAAD)	Golden sand	✓	✓	Public	×	Apr - Oct 09:30-17:15	1
2	Protaras	5 N	Malama (Scoutari)	Golden sand	×	✓	Private	×	×	1
3	Protaras	4 N	Agia Triada	Golden sand	✓	✓	Public	×	Apr - Oct 09:30-17:15	1
4	Protaras	1 N	Vrisoudia	Golden sand & soil	×	✓	Private	×	×	1
5	Protaras	0	Louma	Golden sand	✓	✓	Public	✓	Apr - Oct 09:30-17:15	1
6	Protaras	0	Pernera	Golden sand	✓	✓	Public	✓	Apr - Oct 09:30-17:15	1
7	Protaras	0	Potami	Golden sand	×	✓	Private	×	×	1
8	Protaras	0	Vrisi	Golden sand	✓	✓	Public	✓	Apr - Oct 09:30-17:15	1
9	Protaras	0	Protaras bay	Golden sand	✓	✓	Public	✓✓	Apr - Oct 09:30-17:15	1
10	Protaras	0	Loumbardi	Golden sand	✓	✓	Public	×	Apr - Oct 09:30-17:15	1
11	Protaras	0	Nissia	Golden sand	×	✓	Private	×	×	1
12	Protaras	3 S	Konnos	Golden sand	✓	✓	Public	×	Apr - Oct 09:30-17:15	1
13	Agia Napa	3 E	Kermia	Golden sand	✓	✓	Public	×	Apr - Oct 10:00-18:00	2
14	Agia Napa	1 E	Ammos tou Kampouri	Golden sand	✓	✓	Public	×	Apr - Oct 09:00-18:00	2
15	Agia Napa	0	Glyki Nero	White sand	✓	✓	Public	×	Apr - Oct 09:00-18:00	2
16	Agia Napa	0	Pantahou	Golden sand	✓	✓	Public	×	Apr - Oct 09:00-18:00	2
17	Agia Napa	0	Loukos tou Mandi	Rocks/Golden sand	✓	✓	Public	×	Apr - Oct 09:00-18:00	2
18	Agia Napa	0	Katsarka	Rocks/White sand	✓	✓	Public	×	Apr - Oct 09:00-18:00	2
19	Agia Napa	0	Pernera	Golden sand	✓	✓	Public	×	Apr - Oct 09:00-18:00	2
20	Agia Napa	0	Vathia Gonia	White sand	✓	✓	Public	✓	Apr - Oct 09:00-18:00	2
21	Agia Napa	0	Nissi	White sand	✓	✓	Public	✓	Apr - Oct 09:00-18:00	2
22	Agia Napa	0	Latchi	White sand	×	✓	Private	×	×	2

LIST OF BEACHES AND COASTS OF CYPRUS – 23 - 46										
No.	**Nearest town / resort**	**Distance (km) + Direction**	**Name**	**Surface**						**Map No.**
23	Agia Napa	1 W	Landa	White sand	✓	✓	Public	✓✓	Apr - Oct 09:00-18:00	2
24	Agia Napa	2 W	Makronissos	White sand	✓	✓	Public	×	Apr - Oct 09:00-18:00	2
25	Agia Napa	6 W	Agia Thekla	Golden sand	✓	✓	Public	×	Apr - Oct 09:00-18:00	2
26	Larnaca	5 E	Pyla	Dark sand/Pebble	×	✓	Public	×	15 Jul - Aug 10:30 - 18:00	4
27	Larnaca	2 E	Voroklini (or Yanathes)	Dark sand/Pebble	✓	✓	Public	✓	11:00 - 17:00	4
28	Larnaca	0	Phinikoudes	Dark sand	✓	✓	Public	✓✓	10:00 - 17:00	5
29	Larnaca	0	Kastella	Dark sand	✓	✓	Public	✓	09:00 - 17:00	5
30	Larnaca	0	Mckenzie	Dark sand	✓	✓	Public	✓	10:00 - 17:00	5
31	Larnaca	13 S	Spyros	Dark sand	×	×	×	✓	15 Jul - Aug 10:30 - 18:00	5
32	Larnaca	13 SW	Faros	Dark sand	✓	✓	Public	✓	Jun - Sep 11:00-17:00	5
33	Larnaca	20 SW	Mazotos	Dark sand/Pebble	×	×	×	×	×	6
34	Larnaca	22 SW	Alaminos	Dark sand	×	✓	Private	×	15 Jul - Aug 10:30 - 18:00	6
35	Limassol	24 E	Zygi coast	Large Pebble	×	×	Private	×	×	13
36	Limassol	16 E	Governor's beach	Dark sand/ white rock	✓	✓	Public	✓	10:00 - 17:00	13
37	Limassol	18 E	Latchi (Agios Georgios Alamanos)	Pebble/ white rock	×	×	Private	×	×	13
38	Limassol	1 E	Aoratoi	Dark sand	✓	✓	Public	✓	May – Aug 10:00 - 17:00	14
39	Limassol	1 E	Pareklishia	Dark sand	✓	✓	Public	✓	May – Aug 10:00 - 17:00	14
40	Limassol	0	Santa Barbara	Dark sand/Pebble	✓	✓	Public	×	May – Aug 10:00 - 17:00	14
41	Limassol	0	Loures	Dark sand	✓	✓	Public	×	May – Aug 10:00 - 17:00	14
42	Limassol	0	Vouppa	Dark sand	✓	✓	Public	✓	Apr – Nov 10:00 - 17:00	14
43	Limassol	0	Aphrodite	Dark sand	✓	✓	Public	✓✓	Apr – Nov 10:00 - 17:00	14
44	Limassol	0	Armonia	Dark sand	✓	✓	Public	×	Apr – Nov 10:00 - 17:00	14
45	Limassol	0	Onisilos	Dark sand	✓	✓	Public	✓	Apr – Nov 10:00 - 17:00	14
46	Limassol	0	Kastella	Dark sand	✓	✓	Public	✓	Apr – Nov 10:00 - 17:00	14

LIST OF BEACHES AND COASTS OF CYPRUS – 47 - 69										
No.	Nearest town / resort	Distance (km) + Direction	Name	Surface						Map No.
47	Limassol	0	Dasoudi	Dark sand	×	✓	Public	✓	Apr – Nov 10:00 - 17:00	14
48	Limassol	0	Akti Olympion	Dark sand	✓	✓	Public	✓✓	Apr – Nov 10:00 - 17:00	14
49	Limassol	2 W	Lady's mile	Dark sand	×	✓	Private	×	Jul-Aug 10:00 - 17:00	16
50	Limassol	20 W	Episkopi (Curium)	Dark sand/Pebble	✓	✓	Public	✓	May-Nov 10:00 - 17:00	17
51	Limassol	25 W	Paramali	Dark sand	×	×	×	×	×	17
52	Limassol	30 W	Avdimou	Dark sand/Pebble	×	×	Private	×	Jul – Aug 10:00 - 17:00	17
53	Limassol	30 W	Pissouri	Dark sand/Pebble	✓	✓	Public	✓	Jul – Aug 10:00 - 17:00	17
54	Paphos	23 E	Aphrodite's Rock / Petra tou Romioui	Pebble/Dark sand	×	×	×	×	×	26
55	Paphos	21 E	Kouklia	Pebble/Dark sand	×	×	Public	×	Jun – Sep 11:00 - 17:30	26
56	Paphos	16 E	Mandria	Pebble/Dark sand	×	×	×	×	Jun – Sep 11:00 - 17:30	26
57	Paphos	15 E	Timi	Pebble/Dark sand	×	✓	Private	×	Jun – Aug 11:00 - 17:30	26
58	Paphos	2 E	Geroskipou	Pebble/Dark sand	✓	✓	Public	✓	May – Oct 11:00 - 17:30	28
59	Paphos	0	Pachyam-mos	Golden sand	✓	✓	Public	✓	Jun – Oct 11:00 - 17:30	28
60	Paphos	0	Vrisoudia A	Golden sand	✓	✓	Public	×	Jun – Oct 11:00 - 17:30	28
61	Paphos	0	Vrisoudia B	Golden sand	✓	✓	Public	✓	Jun – Oct 11:00 - 17:30	28
62	Paphos	0	Alykes	Rocks /Golden sand	✓	✓	Public	×	Jun – Oct 11:00 - 17:30	28
63	Paphos	0	Municipal Baths	Rocks /Golden sand	✓	✓	Public	✓	May – Oct 11:00 - 17:30	28
64	Paphos	0	Faros	Golden sand/Rocks	✓	✓	Public	✓	May – Oct 11:00 - 17:30	28
65	Paphos	8 N	Kotchas	Golden sand	×	✓	Public	×	Jun – Sep 11:00 - 17:30	28
66	Paphos	11 N	Potima	Pebble/ Dark sand	×	×	×	×	×	29
67	Paphos	14 N	Coral Beach	Golden sand	✓	✓	Public	✓	May – Oct 11:00 - 17:30	29
68	Paphos	14 N	Laourou	Golden sand	✓	✓	Public	×	May – Oct 11:00 - 17:30	29
69	Paphos	15 SW	Lara coast	Sand/ Pebble	×	×	×	×	×	31

LIST OF BEACHES AND COASTS OF CYPRUS – 70 - 89										
No.	Nearest town / resort	Distance (km) + Direction	Name	Surface						Map No.
70	Polis	12 W	Blue Lagoon	Rocks /sand	×	×	×	×	×	31
71	Polis	9 W	Xistarokampos	Dark sand/Pebble	×	✓	Private	×	Jun – Oct 11:00 - 17:30	31
72	Polis	8 W	Halavro	Dark sand/Pebble	×	✓	Private	×	Jun – Sep 11:00 - 17:30	31
73	Polis	5 W	Kampos tou Souliou	Dark sand/Pebble	×	✓	Private	×	Jun – Oct 11:00 - 17:30	31
74	Polis	4 W	Latchi (or 'Lakki')	Dark sand/Pebble	×	✓	Private	×	May – Oct 11:00 - 17:30	31
75	Polis	0	Municipal Beach	Dark sand/Pebble	✓	✓	Public	✓✓	May – Oct 11:00 - 17:30	32
76	Polis	0	Dasoudi (camping site)	Dark sand/Pebble	✓	✓	Public	✓	May – Oct 11:00 - 17:30	32
77	Polis	5 E	Argaka – Gialia coast	Dark sand/Pebble	×	×	Private	×	×	34
78	Polis	20 E	Pomos coast	Pebble	×	×	×	×	Jul – Aug 11:00 - 17:30	34
79	Polis	24 E	Pachyammos coast	Dark sand/Pebble	×	×	×	×	×	34
80	Polis	44 NE	Mansoura	Dark sand	×	×	Private	×	×	35
81	Polis	50 NE	Kato Pyrgos	Dark sand	×	×	Private	×	Jul – Sep 10:00 - 18:00	35
82	Protaras	131 NE	Pachyammos/ Golden beach	Golden sand	×	✓	Private	×	×	36
83	Protaras	116 NE	Agios Filon	Golden sand	×	✓	Private	×	×	36
84	Protaras	69 N	Vokolida/ Bafra	Golden sand	×	✓	Private	×	×	37
85	Protaras	76 N	Davlos/ Kaplıca	Golden sand	×	✓	Private	×	×	37
86	Protaras	35 NW	Klapsides/ Glapsides	Golden sand	×	✓	Private	×	×	38
87	Protaras	31 NW	Varosi	Golden sand	×	✓	Private	×	×	38
88	Nicosia	42 NE	Alakati/ Alagadi	Golden sand	×	✓	Private	×	×	39
89	Nicosia	51 NW	Agia Eirini/ Akdeniz	Dark sand/Pebble	×	×	×	×	×	42

Note: ✓ under means that there is wheelchair access to the beach whereas ✓✓ means that there is wheelchair access also to the sea.

LIST OF WALKING ROUTES IN CYPRUS - 1 - 22								
No.	Nearest town / resort	Distance (km) + Direction	Name	Length (km)	Altitude differ. (m)	Circular	Difficulty Grade	Map No.
1	Protaras	4 – 7 N	Agia Triada beach – Buffer Zone	3	20		Easy	1
2	Protaras	4 – 2 N	Agia Triada beach – Louma beach	2.5	10		Easy	1
3	Protaras	0 – 2 N	Pernera beach – Protaras bay beach	3	10		Easy	1
4	Protaras	0 - 0	Protaras bay beach – Loumbardi beach	1.5	10		Medium	1
5	Protaras	0 – 2 S	Loumbardi beach – Cyclop's Cave	2	10		Medium	1
6	Protaras	3 S	Konnos beach – Cyclop's Cave	2.4	30	YES	Easy	1
7	Protaras	3 – 4.5 S	Konnos beach – Agioi Anargyroi church	1.4	30		Easy	2
8	Agia Napa	5 E	Aphrodite	3	30	YES	Easy	2
9	Agia Napa	0 – 5 E	Agia Napa Sea Caves – Cape Greko Sea Caves	4.5	20		Easy	2
10	Agia Napa	0 - 0	Pantahou beach – Vathia Gonia beach	2.5	5		Easy	2
11	Agia Napa	0 – 2 W	Vathia Gonia beach – Makronissos beach	3	10		Easy	2
12	Agia Napa	2 – 8 W	Makronissos beach – Potamos tou Liopetriou fishing port	6	5		Easy	2
13	Larnaca	0 - 0	Salt lake - Kamares aqueduct	4	5		Easy	5
14	Larnaca	12 – 22 W	Pervolia coast – Alaminos beach	13	10		Easy	6
15	Nicosia	28 – 28 S	Lefkothea	1.3	200		Medium	7
16	Nicosia	34 – 38 SW	Kionia picnic site – Profitis Elias church	7	650		Tough	7
17	Nicosia	45 – 54 SW	Stavros tou Agiasmati church – Panagia tou Araka church	7.5	300		Medium	9
18	Limassol	16 – 18 E	Governor's beach – Latchi coast	4	20		Easy	13
19	Limassol	0 – 1 E	Moni coast – Limassol pier	14	5		Easy	14
20	Platres	0 -1 S	Myllomeris waterfall	1.2	100		Medium	24
21	Platres	0 – 3 N	Kalidonia waterfall	3	300		Medium	24
22	Platres	6 N	Atalanti	14	50	YES	Easy	24

LIST OF WALKING ROUTES IN CYPRUS - 23 - 47								
No.	Nearest town / resort	Distance (km) + Direction	Name	Length (km)	Altitude differ. (m)	Circular	Difficulty Grade	Map No.
23	Platres	6 N	Persephone	3	100		Easy	24
24	Platres	8 N	Artemis	7	50	YES	Easy	24
25	Platres	14 – 17 W	Platy valley - Kelefos bridge	16.5	450		Easy	21
26	Platres	22 NE	Teichia tis Madaris	3	150	YES	Medium	19
27	Platres	22 NE	Madari Circular (No.28 – 31)	13	350	YES	Tough	19
28	Platres	20 - 22 NE	Madari – Doxa si o Theos	4	200		Medium	19
29	Platres	20 – 22 NE	Doxa si o Theos – Moutti tis Choras	1.6	200		Easy	19
30	Platres	20 – 23 NE	Moutti tis Choras – Selladi tou Karamanli	4	100		Easy	19
31	Platres	22-23 NE	Madari – Selladi tou Karamanli	3.6	300		Tough	19
32	Platres	30 – 33 NW	Cedar Valley – Tripylos peak	2.5	200		Medium	20
33	Platres	34 SW - 25 W	Panagia tou Sinti - Roudias medieval bridge	10	120		Medium	25
34	Paphos	23 – 18 E	Petra tou Romiou	7	50		Easy	26
35	Paphos	14 E - 23 NE	Episkopi - Choulou	12	180		Medium	27
36	Paphos	0 – 2 E	Geroskipou beach – Paphos fort	5	10		Easy	28
37	Paphos	0 – 8 NW	Paphos fort – Kotchas beach	9	30		Easy	28
38	Paphos	8 – 10.5 NW	Kotchas beach – Potima coast	3	30		Easy	29
39	Paphos	15 – 21 NW	Laourou beach – Agios Georgios tis Pegeias fishing port	9	50	YES	Easy	29
40	Paphos	35 NE	Vouni Panagias	8	300	YES	Medium	30
41	Polis	18–21.5 SW	Avakas gorge	2.5	50		Medium	31
42	Polis	12 SW	Pissouromoutti	3	150	YES	Medium	31
43	Polis	12 SW	Smigies	7	100	YES	Medium	31
44	Polis	10 W	Aphrodite	7.5	200	YES	Medium	31
45	Polis	10 W	Adonis	7.5	200	YES	Medium	31
46	Polis	12 - 20 SE	Fyti village - Evretou dam	9.5	500		Easy	32
47	Polis	30 – 36 NE	Pomos valley	6	200		Medium	34

LIST OF WALKING ROUTES IN CYPRUS - 48 - 56								
No.	Nearest town / resort	Distance (km) + Direction	Name	Length (km)	Altitude differ. (m)	Circular	Difficulty Grade	Map No.
48	Polis	30 – 38 SE	Agia valley	10	200		Medium	33
49	Polis	34 E	Horteri	5	250	YES	Medium	33
50	Polis	35 E	Moutti tou Stavrou	3	100	YES	Easy	33
51	Polis	34 – 39 SE	Panagia village junction – Tripylos peak	3	250		Medium	33
52	Protaras	136 NE	Apostle Andreas circular	16	100	YES	Easy	36
53	Protaras	107 - 116 NE	Panagia Eleousa picnic to Agios Filon church	5.5	40		Easy	36
54	Protaras	71 - 76 NE	Kantara - Komi Kebir	5	200		Easy	37
55	Nicosia	49 - 62 NE	Agios Nicolaos/Yamaçköy - Antiphonitis church	7.5	150		Easy	39
56	Nicosia	34 NE	Pentadactylos peak	4.5	190	YES	Easy	39

LIST OF WETLANDS IN CYPRUS						
No.	Nearest town / resort	Distance (km) + Direction	Name	Capacity (Mil.cubic meters)	Kind	Map No.
1	Agia Napa	20 NW	Achna dam	6.8	Dam	3
2	Larnaca	5 E	Voroklini lake		Swamp	4
3	Larnaca	1 SW	Larnaca salt lakes		Salt lakes	5
4	Larnaca	12 S	Larnaca sewage works	1	Man made pools	5
5	Larnaca	8 SW	Kiti dam	1.6	Dam	6
6	Larnaca	30 W	Dipotamos	15.5	Dam	6
7	Nicosia	2 S	Athalassa	0.8	Dam	8
8	Nicosia	15 SW	Tamassos	2.8	Dam	9
9	Nicosia	24 SW	Klirou	2	Dam	9
10	Nicosia	20 SW	Mitsero red lake		Man made	9
11	Nicosia	32 SW	Lefkara	13.9	Dam	7
12	Nicosia	40 SW	Vyzakia	1.7	Dam	9
13	Nicosia	45 SW	Xyliatos	1.43	Dam	9
14	Limassol	25 NE	Kalavasos	17.1	Dam	12
15	Limassol	4 N	Germasogeia	13.5	Dam	14
16	Limassol	6 N	Polemidia	3.4	Dam	14
17	Limassol	2 SW	Akrotiri salt lake		Salt lake	16
18	Limassol	11 SW	Bishop's Pool		Manmade	16
19	Limassol	10 NW	Kouris	115	Dam	15
20	Platres	15 SW	Arminou	4.3	Dam	21
21	Platres	29 N	Kalopanagiotis	0.4	Dam	23
22	Paphos	16 E	Asprokremmos	53	Dam	26
23	Paphos	25 NE	Kannaviou	18	Dam	30
24	Paphos	11 N	Mavrokolympos	2.2	Dam	29
25	Polis	8 SE	Evretou	24	Dam	32
26	Polis	12.5 E	Argaka	0.99	Dam	34
27	Polis	20 SE	Pomos	0.86	Dam	34
28	Protaras	70 N	Galateia/Mehmetçik wetland		Wetland	37
29	Protaras	64 N	Ovgoros/Ergazi	6.8	Dam	37
30	Protaras	32 NW	Karaolos/Gülseren		Salt lake	38
31	Protaras	29 NW	Ais loukas	4.5	Dam	38
32	Nicosia	40 NW	Panagra/Geçitköy	1.8	Dam	42
33	Nicosia	48 NW	Agia Eirini/Akdeniz		Dam	42
34	Nicosia	56 NW	Kalo Chorio (Kapouti)/Kalkanlı		Dam	42

Note: Fishing is allowed in the vast majority of dams in the south part of Cyprus, and their list may change (slightly) each year. A fishing permit is required for which you need to contact the Department of Fisheries at 22807830 or 22807803. It is not allowed in the north part of Cyprus.

LIST OF ANCIENT TREES (DECLARED MONUMENTS OF NATURE) IN CYPRUS – 1 - 34								
No.	Nearest town / resort	Distance (km) + Direction	Kind	Nearest community	Age (years)	Trunk Perim. (m)	Height (m)	Map No.
1	Agia Napa	5 E	Juniper	Agia Napa	150	2	5	2
2	Agia Napa	0	Sycamore	Agia Napa	600	7	26	2
3	Agia Napa	0	Sycamore	Agia Napa	350	4,5	18	2
4	Agia Napa	0	Sycamore	Agia Napa	250	3,5	18	2
5	Larnaca	5 SW	Mastic trees	Kiti				6
6	Larnaca	16 SW	Olive	Anglisides	700	10,5	6	6
7	Nicosia	18 S	Cypress	Nisou	500	4,5	28	8
8	Nicosia	43 SW	Olive	Xyliatos	700	13	6	9
9	Nicosia	43 SW	Five Olives	Xyliatos				9
10	Limassol	25 NE	Olive	Eptagoneia	600	7	5	12
11	Limassol	17 N	Mastic	Apesia	1500	7	10	15
12	Limassol	20 N	Mastic	Limnatis	600	5	16	15
13	Limassol	9 W	Rose tree	Kolossi	200	4,5	26	16
14	Limassol	30 W	Olive	Avdimou	700	8,7	5	17
15	Platres	8 S	Oak	Pera Pedi	200	3	22	22
16	Platres	9 N	Black pine	Troodos - Olympus	500	4,7	20	24
17	Platres	9N	Black pine	Troodos - Olympus	450	4,2	18	24
18	Platres	9 S	Oak	Kouka	400	4,5	16	22
19	Platres	10 S	Plane	(Agia Mavri) Koilani	800	5,5	36	22
20	Platres	11 SW	Laurel	Omodos	1000	8	10	25
21	Platres	13 SE	Oak	Agios Mamas	500	5,7	22	22
22	Platres	13 SW	Olive	Potamiou	700	7,3	8	25
23	Platres	13 SW	Mastic	Potamiou	400	4,2	16	25
24	Platres	15 SE	Oak	Laneia	800	8,5	26	22
25	Platres	15 SW	Oak	Agios Nikolaos	400	4,5	10	21
26	Platres	15 SW	Mastic	Kissousa	600	5	16	25
27	Platres	25 N	Oak	Moutoullas	350	4	26	23
28	Platres	19 SW	Oak	Pachna	300	3,5	16	25
29	Platres	19 SW	Kermes oak	Pachna	350	3	14	25
30	Platres	27 N	Kermes oak	Kalopanagiotis	700	4	17	23
31	Platres	25 NE	Pine	Chandria	350	4,5	16	19
32	Platres	26 S	Mastic	Agios Therapon	350	3	10	25
33	Platres	30 E	Pine	Agios Theodoros Agrou	120	2,5	18	19
34	Platres	30 E	Oak	Agios Theodoros Agrou	300	3,5	16	19

LIST OF ANCIENT TREES (DECLARED MONUMENTS OF NATURE) IN CYPRUS – 35 - 61								
No.	Nearest town / resort	Distance (km) + Direction	Kind	Nearest community	Age (years)	Trunk Perim. (m)	Height (m)	Map No.
35	Platres	30 E	Terebinth	Agios Theodoros Agrou	200	2	6	19
36	Platres	30 SW	Three cypresses	Salamiou				25
37	Platres	30 SW	Storax	Salamiou	150	2	8	25
38	Platres	33 NE	Oak	Lagoudera	700	4,6	16	19
39	Platres	31 NE	1 Cypress, 2 oaks	Kannavia				11
40	Platres	30 NE	Cypress	Agia Eirini	200	3,10	12	11
41	Platres	33 NE	Oak	Fterikoudi	200	3	16	18
42	Platres	33 NE	Golden oak	Apliki	250	2,5	12	18
43	Platres	33 SW	White mulberry	Trachypedoula	140	2,5	8	25
44	Platres	35 SW	Olive trees	Anogyra				25
45	Platres	36 NW	Oak	Kampos	350	5	22	20
46	Platres	45 W	Golden Oak	Tsakkistra (Kremmos tis Pellis)	200	3,5	10	20
47	Paphos	17 E	Two olives	Nikokleia				26
48	Paphos	23 NE	Oak	Choulou	400	5	18	27
49	Polis	21 SE	Oak	Fyti	800	9,6	20	32
50	Polis	15 SE	Mastic	Simou	1000	6,2	16	32
51	Polis	13 SE	Olive	Filousa	600	7,3	7	32
52	Polis	7 SE	White mulberry	Steni	150	3,10	9	32
53	Polis	6 SE	Carob	Steni	210	5	16	32
54	Polis	6 SE	Olive	Steni	200	4,8	4	32
55	Polis	13 NW	Oak	Neo Chorio (Pyrgos tis Rigenas)	500	5,4	18	31
56	Polis	1 W	Oak	Prodromi	150	4	26	31
57	Polis	39 E	Pine	Pomos (Marotis)	250	3,8	36	34
58	Polis	49 NE	Oak	Kato Pyrgos	105	4	20	35
59	Protaras	30 NW	Sycamore	Famagusta (walled - in Saint Nicolas yard)	600	5	12	38
60	Nicosia	26 NW	Plane tree	Krini - Pınarbaşı				41
61	Nicosia	48 NW	Olives	Kalo Chorio Morphou (Kapouti) - Kalkanlı				42

Note: An ancient olive can be seen in the center of the roundabout next to the Presidental Palace in Nicosia. This was brought here from its original home.

LIST OF OTHER NATURAL ATTRACTIONS IN CYPRUS						
No.	Nearest town / resort	Distance (km) + Direction	Name	Type	Nearest community	Map No.
1	Agia Napa	6 E	Cape Greko	Park	Agia Napa	2
2	Agia Napa	5 E	Cape Greko Sea Caves	Sea caves	Agia Napa	2
3	Agia Napa	0	Agia Napa Sea Caves	Sea caves	Agia Napa	2
4	Agia Napa	9 W	Potamos tou Liopetriou	Very narrow Fishing port	Liopetri	2
5	Agia Napa	12 SW	Xylofagou	Sea caves	Xylofagou	3
6	Platres	2 N	Kalidonia	Waterfall	Platres	24
7	Platres	4 S	Myllomeris	Waterfall	Platres	24
8	Platres	3 NW	Chantara	Waterfall	Foini	24
9	Platres	6 E	Mesa Potamos	Waterfall	Saittas	24
10	Paphos	19 NW	Pegeia Sea Caves B	Sea caves	Pegeia	29
11	Paphos	16 NW	Pegeia Sea Caves (Kontarkastoi)	Sea caves	Pegeia	29
12	Polis	10 NW	Akamas	Peninsula	Neo Chorio	31
13	Polis	10 NW	Aphrodite's Baths	Cave	Neo Chorio	31
14	Protaras	120 NE	Karpasia/Karpaz	Park	Rizokarpaso/ Dipkarpaz	36

LIST OF MEDIEVAL BRIDGES IN CYPRUS					
No.	Nearest town / resort	Distance (km) + Direction	Name	Nearest community	Map No.
1	Larnaca	37 W	Kato Drys	Choirokoitia	6
2	Nicosia	48 SW	Xyliatos	Xyliatos	9
3	Limassol	25 NE	Akapnou	Akapnou	12
4	Limassol	0	Aristos	Limassol	14
5	Platres	1 S	Milia	Pano Platres	24
6	Platres	3 W	Stavros	Foini	24
7	Platres	8 W	Piskopos	Foini	24
8	Platres	9 SE	Trimiklini	Trimiklini	22
9	Platres	10 S	Agia Mavri	Koilani	22
10	Platres	11 S	Koilani	Koilani	22
11	Platres	13 E	Kardaki	Kato Amiantos	24
12	Platres	13 SW	Potamiou	Potamiou	25
13	Platres	16 SE	Pelendri	Agios Mamas	22
14	Platres	17 NW	Mylos	Treis Elies	21
15	Platres	17 NW	Treis Elies	Treis Elies	21
16	Platres	20 W	Elia	Kaminaria	21
17	Platres	20 W	Kelefos	Agios Nikolaos	21
18	Platres	22 E	Potamitissa	Potamitissa	19
19	Platres	25 W	Roudias	Vretsia	25
20	Platres	26 N	Kalopanagiotis	Kalopanagiotis	23
21	Platres	31 N	Orkontas	Kalopanagiotis	23
22	Polis	16 SE	Skarfos	Simou	32
23	Nicosia	7 NW	Ortakioi/Ortaköy	Ortakioi	40

LIST OF WATERMILLS IN CYPRUS - 1 - 27				
No.	Nearest town / resort	Distance (km) + Direction	Nearest community	Map No.
1	Larnaca	26 SW	Alaminos	6
2	Larnaca	29 SW	Agios Theodoros	6
3	Nicosia	22 S	Dali	8
4	Nicosia	19 SW	Pera	9
5	Nicosia	19 SW	Pera	9
6	Nicosia	25 SW	Agios Ioannis Malountas	9
7	Nicosia	22 SW	Agios Ioannis Malountas	9
8	Nicosia	22 SW	Agios Ioannis Malountas	9
9	Nicosia	39 SW	Kato Moni	9
10	Nicosia	40 SW	Kato Moni	9
11	Nicosia	53 SW	Platanistasa	9
12	Nicosia	26 W	Akaki	10
13	Nicosia	27 W	Akaki	10
14	Nicosia	34 SW	Orounta	10
15	Nicosia	47 SW	Pano Koutrafas	11
16	Limassol	20 NE	Kalavasos	12
17	Limassol	21 NE	Kalavasos	12
18	Limassol	12 NE	Pyrgos Lemesou	14
19	Limassol	14 W	Kantou	17
20	Limassol	15 W	Kantou	17
21	Platres	8 S	Pera Pedi	22
22	Platres	15 E	Kato Amiantos	24
23	Platres	15 SW	Kissousa	25
24	Platres	26 N	Kalopanagiotis	23
25	Platres	19 NW	Palaiomylos	24
26	Platres	22 E	Potamitissa	19
27	Platres	25 SW	Kidasi	25

LIST OF WATERMILLS IN CYPRUS - 28 - 54				
No.	Nearest town / resort	Distance (km) + Direction	Nearest community	Map No.
28	Platres	26 W	Vretsia	25
29	Platres	27 N	Kakopetria	11
30	Platres	28 N	Galata	11
31	Platres	28 N	Galata	11
32	Platres	28 SW	Agios Ioannis	25
33	Platres	29 SW	Agios Mamas	25
34	Platres	29 SW	Archangelos Michail	25
35	Platres	30 SW	Galataria	25
36	Platres	33 N	Evrychou	11
37	Platres	34 SW	Pentalia	25
38	Platres	34 SW	Salamiou	25
39	Platres	35 N	Flasou	11
40	Platres	36 N	Flasou	11
41	Platres	38 N	Katydata	11
42	Paphos	25 E	Mamonia	25
43	Paphos	17 E	Nikokleia	26
44	Paphos	19 E	Souskiou	26
45	Paphos	18 NE	Moronero	27
46	Paphos	18 NE	Moronero	27
47	Paphos	20 NE	Moronero	27
48	Paphos	23 NE	Choulou	27
49	Polis	13 S	Kato Akourdaleia	32
50	Polis	10 SE	Kouyoukas - Miliou	32
51	Polis	17 SE	Skarfos	32
52	Polis	4 S	Chrysochou	32
53	Polis	17 NE	Gialia	34
54	Nicosia	22 NW	Krini/Pınarbaşı	41

LIST OF CASTLES AND WATCHTOWERS IN CYPRUS

No.	Nearest town / resort	Distance (km) + Direction	Name	Nearest community	Map No.
1	Agia Napa	18 SW	Xylofagou tower	Xylofagou	3
2	Larnaca	15 NE	Pyla tower	Pyla	4
3	Larnaca	0	Larnaca castle	Larnaca	5
4	Larnaca	13 SW	Pyrgos tis Rigenas	Pervolia	5
5	Larnaca	26 SW	Koulas	Alaminos	6
6	Limassol	0	Limassol Castle	Limassol	14
7	Limassol	9W	Kolossi Castle	Kolossi	16
8	Paphos	0	Paphos fort	Paphos	28
9	Protaras	72 NE	Kantara	Davlos/Kaplıca	37
10	Protaras	30 NW	Walls and bastions of Famagusta	Famagusta	38
11	Nicosia	41 NE	Voufavento	Klepini /Arapköy	39
12	Nicosia	0	Walls and bastions of Nicosia	Nicosia	40
13	Nicosia	28 N	Keryneia	Keryneia/Girne	41
14	Nicosia	25 NW	Saint. Ilarion	Bogazi/Boğazköy	41

LIST OF AQUEDUCTS

No.	Nearest town / resort	Distance (km) + Direction	Name	Nearest community	Map No.
1	Agia Napa	0	Agia Napa	Agia Napa	2
2	Larnaca	0	Kamares/Bekir Pasha	Larnaca	5
3	Nicosia	0	Nicosia/Silihtar	Nicosia	40
4	Protaras	41 NW	Kythrea-Salamis	Agios Sergios/ Yeniboğaziçi	38

LIST OF UNESCO WORLD HERITAGE TROODOS PAINTED CHURCHES

No.	Nearest town / resort	Distance (km) + Direction	Name	Wheel Chair access	Nearest community	Opening Hours	Contact info	Map No.
1	Nicosia	45 SW	Church of Timios Stavros (Holy Cross) tou Agiasmati	Yes	Platanistasa	To arrange a visit please contact Mr Aristofanis (at the coffee shop)	99514179	9
2	Nicosia	50 SW	Church of Panagia (Our Lady) tis Asinou	Yes	Nikitari	Weekdays and Sat 9:30-16:00. Sun and public holidays 10:00-16:00	99830329	11
3	Platres	17 E	Church of Timios Stavros (Holy Cross)	Yes	Pelendri	Daily after 11:00	25552369	19
4	Platres	20 N	Church of Archangelos Michail	Yes	Pedoulas	Daily 9:00 -17:00 The church is open to visitors in summer until 19:00	22953636	23
5	Platres	25 N	Church of Agios Nikolaos tis Stegis (St. Nicholas of the Roof)	Yes	Kakopetria	Closed on Mon and public holidays. Weekdays and Sat 9:00-16:00 Sunday 11:00-16:00	22922583	11
6	Platres	26 N	Monastery of Agios Ioannis (St John) Lampadistis	Yes (ramp)	Kalopanagiotis	Daily: May - Oct: 09:00 - 13:00, 16:00 - 18:00, Nov - Apr: 09:00 - 13:00, 15:00 - 17:00	97781982, 22953460	23
7	Platres	26 N	Church of Panagia (Our Lady) tou Mout-oulla	Yes	Moutoullas	Please ask for the custodian at the village coffee-shop	22953385, 22952345	23
8	Platres	27 N	Panagia (Our Lady) tis Podithou	Yes (ramp)	Galata	To arrange a visit please contact Father Kyriakos	99720918	11
9	Platres	30 NE	The church of the Transfiguration of the Saviour		Palaichori	Tue and Wed 10:00-13:00. The church can be visited in the afternoon and over the weekend following prearrangement with the custodian	99974230, 99793362 - Dora and Kyriakos	18
10	Platres	33 NE	Panagia tou Araka church	Yes	Lagoudera	Daily: 09:00 - 17:00	99557369, 96301508	9

LIST OF OTHER CHAPELS AND MONASTERIES - 1 - 25						
No.	Nearest town / resort	Distance (km) + Direction	Name	Functioning monastery	Nearest community	Map No.
1	Protaras	3 W	Agioi Saranta		Paralimni	1
2	Protaras	6 SE	Agioi Anargyroi		Agia Napa	2
3	Agia Napa	0	Agia Napa		Agia Napa	2
4	Agia Napa	6 W	Agia Thekla		Agia Napa	2
5	Larnaca	11 NE	Profitis Elias		Voroklini	4
6	Larnaca	6 NE	Agios Antonios		Kellia	4
7	Larnaca	0	Saint Lazarus		Larnaca	5
8	Larnaca	5 SW	Panagia Aggeloktisti		Kiti	6
9	Larnaca	34 N	Stavrovouni	Yes	Kornos	6
10	Larnaca	40 W	Panagia Leivadiotissa		Pano Lefkara	6
11	Nicosia	31 S	Royal Chapel		Pyrga	7
12	Nicosia	38 SW	Profitis Elias		Lythrodontas	7
13	Nicosia	28 SW	Panagia Machaira		Lazanias	7
14	Nicosia	22 S	Agios Demetrianos		Potamia	8
15	Nicosia	20 S	Agioi Apostoloi		Pera Chorio	8
16	Nicosia	20 SW	Agios Irakleidios		Politiko	9
17	Nicosia	31 W	Apostles Varnavas and Ilarionas		Peristerona	10
18	Nicosia	34 SW	Agios Nicolaos	Yes	Orounta	10
19	Limassol	16 E	Agios Georgios Alamanos	Yes	Pentakomo	13
20	Limassol	23 NW	Panagia tis Amasgou	Yes	Monagri	15
21	Limassol	16 W	Agia Napa		Kantou	17
22	Platres	6 E	Timios Stavros (of Mesa Potamos)	Yes	Platres	24
23	Platres	8 NW	Trooditissa	Yes	Platres	24
24	Platres	10 S	Agia Mavri		Koilani	22
25	Platres	10 SW	Timiou Stavrou		Omodos	25

LIST OF OTHER CHAPELS AND MONASTERIES - 26 - 50						
No.	Nearest town / resort	Distance (km) + Direction	Name	Functioning monastery	Nearest community	Map No.
26	Platres	11 SW	Apostolos Philippos		Omodos	25
27	Platres	27 N	Panagia Theoskepasti		Kalopanagiotis	23
28	Platres	29 SW	Archangelos Michael		Prastio	25
29	Platres	29 SW	Agios Mamas		Prastio	25
30	Platres	30 SW	Panagia Salamiotissa	Yes	Salamiou	25
31	Platres	31 NW	Kykkos	Yes	Tsakkistra	20
32	Platres	34 SW	Timiou Stavrou		Anogyra	25
33	Platres	34 SW	Panagia tou Sinti		Pentalia	25
34	Paphos	22 NE	Agios Georgios		Choulou	27
35	Paphos	3 E	Agia Paraskevi		Geroskipou	28
36	Paphos	9 N	Agios Neophytos	Yes	Tala	29
37	Paphos	34 NE	Agia Moni	Yes	Statos Agios Fotios	30
38	Paphos	35 NE	Chrysorrogiatissa	Yes	Pano Panagia	30
39	Polis	11 SW	Agios Minas		Neo Chorio	31
40	Polis	13 S	Agia Paraskevi		Kato Akourdaleia	32
41	Polis	10 S	Agia Ekaterini		Kritou Terra	32
42	Polis	0	Agios Andronicos		Polis	32
43	Polis	21 SE	Panagia Chrysopateritissa		Pomos	34
44	Polis	51 NE	Panagia Galoktisti		Kato Pyrgos	35
45	Protaras	136 NE	Apostle Antreas		Rizokarpaso/ Dipkarpaz	36
46	Protaras	39 NW	Apostle Varnavas		Agios Sergios/ Yeniboğaziçi	38
47	Protaras	30 NW	Walled Famagusta churches		Famagusta	38
48	Nicosia	49 NE	Antiphonotis		Kalograia/Bahçeli	39
49	Nicosia	0	Walled Nicosia churches		Nicosia	40
50	Nicosia	32 N	BellaPais abbey		Belapais/Beylerbeyi	41

LIST OF OTHER CULTURAL ATTRACTIONS - MOSTLY RUINS – 1 - 22							
No.	Nearest town / resort	Distance (km) + Direction	Name	Type	Nearest community	Map No.	UNESCO World Heritage
1	Agia Napa	2 W	Makronissos ancient tombs	Hellenistic/Roman period tombs	Agia Napa	2	
2	Larnaca	4 SW	Hala Sultan Tekke	18th century mosque	Larnaca	5	
3	Larnaca	31 SW	Choirokitia	Neolithic -	Choirokitia	6	Yes
4	Nicosia	21 S	Agios Sozomenos	Deserted medieval village	Potamia	8	
5	Nicosia	21 S	Idalion	Ancient kingdom	Dali	8	
6	Nicosia	20 SW	Tamassos	Ancient kigdom	Politiko	9	
7	Limassol	17 NE	Tenta	Neolithic village	Kalavasos	12	
8	Limassol	0	Amathus	Ancient kingdom	Agios Tychonas	14	
9	Limassol	21 W	Curium/Kourion	Ancient kingdom	Episkopi	16	
10	Platres	13 SW	Agios Mnasonas	Church ruins	Potamiou	25	
11	Paphos	17 SE	Palaipaphos	Ancient kingdom - Aphrodite sanctuary	Kouklia	26	Yes
12	Paphos	23 NE	Agios Theodoros	Ruins of 12th century chapel	Choulou	27	
13	Paphos	14 E	Agios Ilarionas	Ruins of chapel	Episkopi	27	
14	Paphos	0	Nea Paphos	Ancient kingdom - St Paul events - Amazing mosaics – Tombs of the Kings, etc	Paphos	28	Yes
15	Polis	13 NW	Pyrgos tis Rigenas	Ruins of medieval monastery	Neo Chorio	31	
16	Polis	21 NE	Panagia Chrysogialotissa	Ruins of Georgian Ortho-dox monastery	Gialia	34	
17	Polis	50 NE	Troulli watchtower	Remains of medieval watchtower	Kato Pyrgos	35	
18	Protaras	123 NE	Panagia Afentrika	A collection of medieval churches (and city)	Rizokarpaso/ Dipkarpaz	36	
19	Protaras	116 NE	Agios Filon	Ruins of 4th-5th century church	Rizokarpaso/ Dipkarpaz	36	
20	Protaras	36 NW	Salamis	Ancient kingdom	Agios Sergios/ Yeniboğaziçi	38	
21	Nicosia	38 NE	Saint. Magar Armenian monastery	Medieval Armenian monastery in ruin	Charkeia/ Karaagaç	39	
22	Nicosia	25 N	Agios Ioannis Chrysostomos monastery	Restricted access medieval monastery	Koutsoventis/ Güngör	39	

INDEX

INDEX

INDEX

INDEX

INDEX

INDEX

PAGE SIDE BAR COLOR INDEX

(Natural and Cultural Attractions grouped by Nearest town/resort)

Page Side bar color	*Town/resort name*
	Protaras
	Agia Napa
	Larnaca
	Nicosia
	Limassol
	Platres
	Paphos
	Polis
	North part of Cyprus

USEFUL TELEPHONE NUMBERS IN CYPRUS

Service	Telephone Numbers
EMERGENCY	112/199
HOSPITALS	1400
POLICE	1499
POLICE – CITIZENS COMMUNICATION LINE	1460
REPORT FOREST FIRE	1407
DEPARTMENT OF FISHERIES – PERMIT FOR FISHING IN DAMS	22807818
BIRDLIFE CYPRUS	22455072
REPORT ILLEGAL HUNTING	1414
REPORT INJURED WILD BIRDS	22662428
BAT HELPLINE	99499580
REPORT INJURED WILD ANIMALS (EXCEPT FOR WILD BIRDS)	22805532
INFORMATION	11800/11888/11892
NICOSIA	Telephone Numbers
EMERGENCY ROOM	22604011
GENERAL HOSPITAL	22603000
FIRE BRIGADE	22802150
POLICE	22802020
LIMASSOL	Telephone Numbers
EMERGENCY ROOM	25801195
HOSPITAL	25801100
FIRE BRIGADE	25805400
POLICE	25805050
FAMAGUSTA (PARALIMNI)	Telephone Numbers
EMERGENCY ROOM	23200200
HOSPITAL	23200000
FIRE BRIGADE	23803232
POLICE	23803030
LARNACA	Telephone Numbers
EMERGENCY ROOM	24800369
HOSPITAL	24800500
FIRE BRIGADE	24802480
POLICE	24804040
PAPHOS	Telephone Numbers
EMERGENCY ROOM	26803145
HOSPITAL	26803100
FIRE BRIGADE	26806272
POLICE	26806060
RURAL HOSPITALS & HEALTH CENTERS	Telephone Numbers
POLIS	26821800
PLATRES	25422224
KYPEROUNTA	25806700

NOTES